JOHN HEARTFIELD

AIZ/VI 1930–38

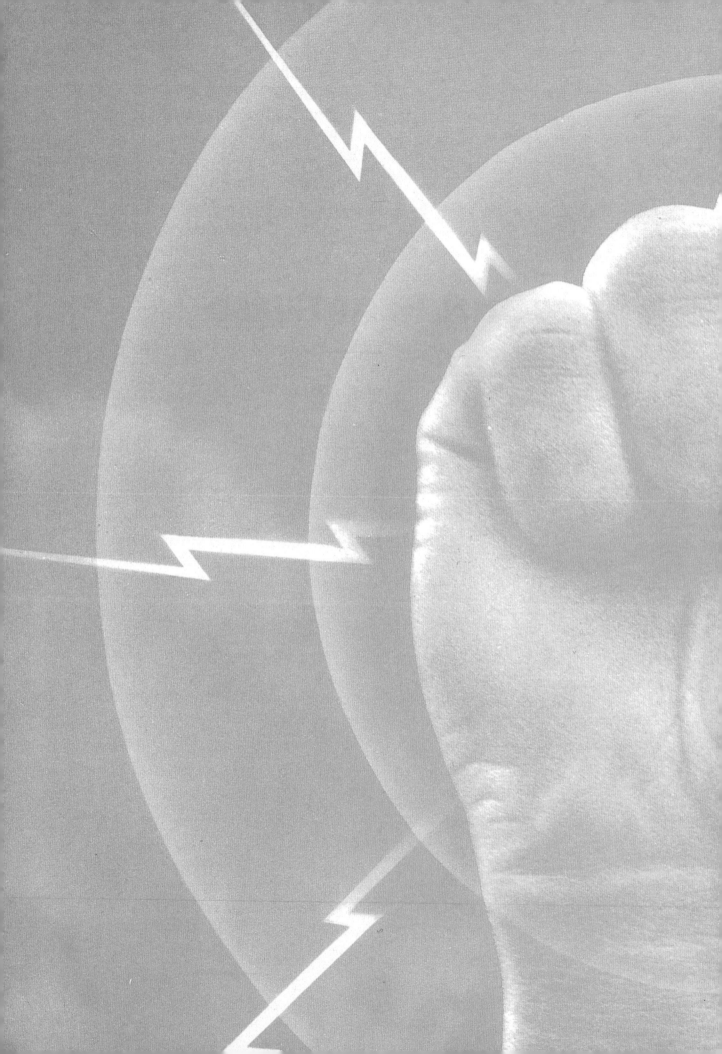

AIZ
JOHN HEARTFIELD

ARBEITER-ILLUSTRIERTE ZEITUNG

VOLKS ILLUSTRIERTE

1930–38

DAVID EVANS

EDITED BY ANNA LUNDGREN

KENT

Copyright © 1992 Kent Fine Art, Inc., Kent Gallery, Inc.
47 East 63rd Street, New York, NY 10021, U.S.A.
Telephone 212 980-9696, Telefax 212 421-5368

ISBN 1-878607-28-6
Library of Congress Catalog Card Number: 91-77792

Designed by Tony Morgan, Step Graphics Inc., New York
Typeset in Futura, Grotesk, Helvetica, and Kabel by Step Graphics
Printed by Toppan Printing Company, Ltd., Singapore
First printing 5,000

On the endpapers: John Heartfield (standing) instructing Red Army soldiers, Moscow, 1932. From *VI*, no. 13 (30 March 1938); photograph courtesy of The Marco Pinkus Collection, Instituto Valenciano de Arte Moderno/Centre Julio Gonzalez, Valencia. The image on the front endpaper has been printed in reverse.

Photograph Credits

John Heartfield Archiv, Akademie der Künste zu Berlin: Figs. 3–11, 28/36

Elefanten Press, Berlin: 11/30

Collection Kent Fine Art, Inc.: Figs. 2, 12; 3/31, 1/32, 2/32, 4/32, 6/32, 7/32, 13/32, 15/32, 16/32, 10/33, 18/33, 20/33, 28/33, 29/33, 1/34, 3/34–53/34, 1/35, 6/35, 9/35, 12/35, 19/35, 26/35, 2/36–4/36, 8/36, 9/36, 20/36, 21/36, 31/36, 35/36, 40/36, 12/37, 15/37

The Museum of Fine Arts, Houston, Museum purchase with funds provided by Max and Isabell Herzstein: image on dustjacket and page 9, 9/30

Heartfield-Sammlung des Werkbund-Archivs, Berlin: Fig. 1, 16/33

The Marco Pinkus Collection, Instituto Valenciano de Arte Moderno/Centre Julio Gonzalez, Valencia: image on endpapers, 1/30–8/30, 10/30, 3/32, 5/32, 8/32–12/32, 14/32, 17/32, 18/32, 1/33–9/33, 11/33–15/33, 17/33, 19/33, 21/33–27/33, 30/33–33/33, 2/34, 2/35–4/35, 5/35, 7/35, 8/35, 10/35, 11/35, 14/35–18/35, 20/35–25/35, 27/35, 1/36, 5/36–7/36, 10/36–19/36, 22/36–27/36, 29/36, 30/36, 32/36–34/36, 37/36–39/36, 41/36–44/36, 1/37–11/37, 13/37, 14/37, 16/37–32/37, 1/38–15/38

Photographers:
Egon Beyer, Berlin
Ali Elai, New York
Peter Schälchli, Zurich
Werner Zellien, Berlin

TABLE OF CONTENTS

In the late seventies I was associated with a London-based group of photographers and writers called Photography Workshop. We had a particular interest in John Heartfield because he seemed to confirm the possibility of making an art that was both politically emphatic and visually innovative. We were in correspondence with Eckhard Siepmann, director of the Werkbund Archivs in West Berlin and author of a major study of Heartfield, who informed us of the existence of a John Heartfield Archiv in East Berlin, run since 1968 by the artist's widow, Gertrud Heartfield. In 1979 I had the first opportunity to meet Gertrud Heartfield and to examine archive materials. Subsequently, my interest in Heartfield became a passion.

I saw Gertrud Heartfield on a number of occasions in Berlin and London between 1979 and 1983, the year of her death. She had met Heartfield in London in 1939, when they were both refugees from Nazi Germany, and they were there throughout the forties, leaving together in 1950 to settle in the newly founded German Democratic Republic. Particularly memorable about our meetings in London were our visits to antiquarian bookshops, looking for rare English books from the forties that had Heartfield dustjackets. In Berlin, "Tutti" – as everyone called her – introduced me to the full range of her husband's work, convincing me that Heartfield was a major figure – the German equivalent of El Lissitzky or Alexander Rodchenko – who redefined the role and activity of the artist in the twentieth century.

Between 1930 and 1938, John Heartfield published 237 photomontages in the German magazine *Arbeiter-Illustrierte Zeitung* (Workers' illustrated paper, abbreviated *A-I-Z* or *AIZ*), which was renamed *Volks Illustrierte* (People's illustrated, abbreviated *VI*) in 1936. Those photomontages – most of them satirical commentaries on contemporary politics – are the subject of this study.

All 237 of the photomontages Heartfield contributed to *AIZ* and *VI* are illustrated here, accompanied by translations of the German text and, where necessary, explanatory notes. My introductory essay outlines Heartfield's early career and the early history of *AIZ* and its publisher, Willi Münzenberg. I go on to show how Heartfield's montages were integrally related to the magazine's politics and design logic. I analyze Heartfield's principal satirical devices and describe his techniques, based on an examination of preparatory artwork that has survived. Finally, I have attempted to situate his work in the context of the debates about cultural politics that occupied Communist artists and intellectuals before and after the Second World War.

Heartfield's photomontages were always a combination of image and text, demanding a spectator and a reader. My translations are literal rather than literary. The notes to the plates offer explanations of German wordplays or allusions, as well as historical background, that might not be obvious to English-speaking readers with no specialized knowledge of German or of Germany in the thirties. My aim has been simply to offer points of entry into one product of the distinctively German Communist culture that evolved in the Weimar period and was forced underground when Hitler took power in 1933.

Heartfield's work resurfaced after the Second World War, for with the defeat of Fascism, the leftist culture that had been banned by the Third Reich became officially enshrined in the German Democratic Republic. The GDR existed from 1949 to 1990. From 1950 until his death in 1968, Heartfield lived there, mainly in East Berlin. After initial difficulties, he was officially honored as an exemplary Communist and anti-Fascist artist. The state gave him medals and prizes. Officially sanctioned Heartfield exhibitions toured the world. His work was used to illustrate school history textbooks. How Heartfield became part of a state ideology is not, however, the main focus of this book. His life and work were far more than a footnote in the cultural politics of the Cold War.

For their comments and suggestions during the preparation of this volume I am grateful to Martin Evans, Hilmar Frank, Wolf Grosskopf, Werner Hecht, Ian Jeffrey, Peter Kennard, Michael Krejsa, Anna Lundgren, David Mellor, Stanley Mitchell, Frédérique Poinat, John Roberts, Andreas Ruby, Irmtraud Thierse, Douglas Walla, Barbara Wallburg, Sarah Wilson, and Ursula Wulfekamp. The staffs of the John Heartfield Archiv in Berlin and the Wiener Library in London were especially helpful.

I also wish to acknowledge aid from the British Council; Goldsmiths' College, London; the former Inner London Education Authority; and Kent Gallery, Inc., New York. A British Council scholarship allowed me to research the bulk of this book in East Berlin between September 1989 and January 1990. My stay coincided with a political revolution. Now, East Berlin, and the state of which it was the capital – the German Democratic Republic – have no independent political status.

David Evans
London, December 1991

The completion of this project is the result of a four-year program that began with our desire to organize a comprehensive exhibition of the photomontages John Heartfield made for *Arbeiter-Illustrierte Zeitung*. Anna Lundgren and I traveled to several institutions in the United States to study public holdings of Heartfield's work and then to Zurich to view the extensive private collection assembled by Marco Pinkus. In the first year we made repeated efforts to contact the John Heartfield Archiv at the Akademie der Künste zu Berlin, culminating in a trip to East Berlin by Dennis Adams and myself that proved futile. Finally, Sarah Wilson of the Courtauld Institute in London told us of David Evans's ten-year research project on Heartfield. Coincidentally, we contacted Evans on the very day he was leaving for a four-month residency in East Berlin. Our collaboration with him has resulted in the most comprehensive text on Heartfield's magazine work to date.

Anna Lundgren and I traveled to East Berlin for a rendezvous with Evans ten months before the collapse of the wall between East and West. We were told only the night of our arrival that we would be able to meet the next day with the officials of the Akademie der Künste. It was due to Evans's persistence that we were able to view the entire John Heartfield Archiv, and during that meeting we learned of the Akademie's plans for a centennial Heartfield retrospective. We took notes of the scope and content of their exhibition, and for a period of several months we acted as liaison between the Akademie and several U.S. institutions. The result was a U.S. tour of the Heartfield retrospective. Ultimately our interest in Heartfield was met by warmth and generosity by the Akademie and especially by Dr. Beate Reisch, who allowed us to photograph works from the Heartfield Archiv for the purpose of reproducing them in this publication. Dr. Reisch traveled to New York to view our Heartfield exhibition in May 1991.

I would like especially to acknowledge the perseverance and dedication that Anna Lundgren has given this project, as well as her efforts in cataloging the Marco Pinkus Collection, which have led to its acquisition by the Instituto Valenciano de Arte Moderno/Centre Julio Gonzalez in Valencia. I would also like to thank Vicente Todolí and Carmen Alborch Bataller of IVAM for assisting us in the production of this book and for organizing a Spanish edition.

Douglas Walla
New York, December 1991

When Douglas Walla asked me to research Heartfield at the Museum of Modern Art library four years ago, neither of us could have possibly imagined that our interest in Heartfield would result in the publication of a catalogue raisonné of Heartfield's magazine work. I am deeply grateful to him for the privilege of overseeing this project and the invaluable experiences it has brought me.

Marco Pinkus, whose father was on the staff of *AIZ*, has spent the last thirty-five years collecting Heartfield material. Without his extraordinary knowledge, assistance, encouragement, and patience during the past four years, this book would have never been realized. We will always remember his kindness.

Many others have also helped bring this project to completion. The following deserve special mention: Carmen Alborch Bataller, Daniel Berlin, Robert Brand, Eileen Costello, Karyn Galetka, Michele Gani, Tony Morgan, Maggie Olvey, Dr. Peter Pachnicke, Dr. Elisabeth Patzwall, Dr. Beate Reisch, Vanessa Ryan, Mary Anne Staniszewski, Vicente Todolí, Anne Tucker, Jeanne Marie Wasilik, Werner Zellien, and Ingeborg Von Zitzewitz.

Anna Lundgren
New York, December 1991

In Memory of Tom Heartfield

JOHN HEARTFIELD

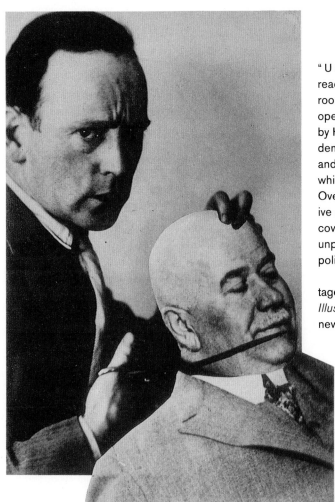

John Heartfield mit Polizeipräsident Zörgiebel (John Heartfield with Chief of Police Zörgiebel). From *AIZ* 8, no. 37 (1929); photograph courtesy of The Museum of Fine Arts, Houston, Museum purchase with funds provided by Isabell and Max Herzstein

"USE PHOTOGRAPHY AS A WEAPON!" read the slogan over the entrance to the John Heartfield room at the prestigious *Film und Foto* exhibition that opened in Stuttgart in 1929.[1] The room was dominated by Heartfield's designs for book dustjackets, a practical demonstration of how to use photography as a weapon and the main reason for his inclusion in the exhibition, which showcased the New Photography of the 1920s. Over the next decade he was to continue with a combative art, but with a major shift of emphasis – from the book cover to the magazine page, on which he was to make an unprecedented exploration of photomontage as a tool of political protest.

In 1930 Heartfield began to publish his photomontages regularly in the Berlin-based magazine *AIZ* (*Arbeiter-Illustrierte Zeitung,* or Workers' illustrated paper). His new direction coincided with the Great Depression in capitalist countries and with the turmoil over the attempt to create "Socialism in One Country" in the Soviet Union.

Heartfield's use of photomontage for political satire distinguished him from all other avant-garde artists who worked with the technique in the 1920s and 1930s. This becomes clear if one compares his work with that of the other forty-five contributors to the first exhibition devoted to photomontage, held in Berlin in 1931.[2] *Fotomontage* was curated by the Dutch painter and graphic artist Cesar Domela-Nieuwenhuis (1900–). Most of the forty-six artists who participated were from Germany and the Soviet Union. Domela's survey clearly showed how a technique that had initially interested Berlin dadaists, including Heartfield, as a way of attacking the civilization held responsible for the First World War had become widely used in graphic design for commercial and political publicity.

Domela was a member of the Ring neuer Werbegestalter (Circle of New Advertising Designers), which had been founded in 1927 by Kurt Schwitters (1887–1948) to facilitate exchanges between avant-garde artists and advertisers. Photomontage was a favored technique.[3] In the *Fotomontage* exhibition in 1931, Domela included examples of his own and Schwitters's commercial work, as well as that of other members of the circle, such as the Dutch artists Paul Schuitema (1897–1973) and Piet Zwart (1885–1977) and the Germans Jan Tschichold (1902–1974) and Friedrich Vordemberge-Gildewart (1899–1962). He also showed work by the ex-Bauhaus masters Herbert Bayer (1900–) and László Moholy-Nagy (1895–1946), who ran commercial studios in Berlin and were informally associated with Schwitters's group.[4] What linked them all was a background in abstract painting and sculpture and an interest in photomontage as an amalgam of the figurative (mainly photography) and the nonfigurative (typography or blocks of color). By using photomontage in the design of advertisements, these artists hoped to present advanced visual ideas in a form that would be accessible to a general public with no particular interest in new art.

Most of the fifteen Soviet artists represented at the *Fotomontage* exhibition, among them Gustav Klucis (1895–1944), El Lissitzky (1890–1941), and Alexander Rodchenko (1891–1956), were prominent members of the October group, which existed between 1928 and 1932.[5] They, too, had been important abstract artists, but they had moved on to *polygraphy* – a term they used to refer to graphic design that combined photography and typography – as the most effective way of serving the Russian Revolution.

Domela devoted a special section of the exhibition to the political photomontages of members of the October group's sister organization in Germany, the Assoziation Revolutionärer Bildender Künstler Deutschlands (German Association of Revolutionary Artists), frequently referred to as the ARBKD or RBKD or simply ASSO,[6] which was formed in 1928 and disbanded after Hitler's takeover in 1933. Apart from Heartfield, the two ASSO artists who were known outside party circles were Oscar Nerlinger (1893–1969), who also went by the anagram R. Nilgreen, and his wife, Alice Lex-Nerlinger (1893–1975).[7] Like many of the contributors to Domela's show, the Nerlingers were abstract painters who became interested in photography and photomontage for their didactic possibilities.

Of all the ASSO artists represented in Domela's exhibition, Heartfield had built for himself the greatest international reputation. Heartfield was born Helmut Herzfeld in Berlin in 1891, the son of the socialist writer Franz Herzfeld (1862–1908), who wrote under the pseudonym Franz Held. His younger brother Wieland, who was to become a lifelong collaborator, was born in 1896. From 1908 to 1911, Helmut Herzfeld studied at the Kunstgewerbeschule (School of Applied Arts) in Munich. His first job as a commercial artist was in Mannheim in 1912. The following year he moved to Berlin and enrolled at the Kunst- und Handwerkschule (Arts and Crafts School). During the early 1910s both he and Wieland were interested in expressionist art and literature, and the painter Franz Marc was a major inspiration.[8]

After the outbreak of the First World War in 1914, Wieland went to serve on the Western Front. Helmut was also called up in 1914. He was a guard in Berlin for most of 1915, but by the end of the year he had been discharged on account of ill health. That same year he met the illustrator, painter, and caricaturist Georg Groß (1893–1959). In 1916, according to legend as a protest against the war and German anglophobia, they both changed their names: Groß became first Georg Grosz, then anglicized his Christian name to George, and Helmut Herzfeld became John Heartfield. Wieland Herzfeld had already made a less dramatic change in his surname in 1914, when he began calling himself Herzfelde.

In 1916 and 1917 Heartfield, Herzfelde, and Grosz published the magazine *Neue Jugend* (New youth), which served as a vehicle for their antiwar and pacifist views. The following year the brothers set up the publishing house Malik Verlag in Berlin.[9] Heartfield's design for the prospectus of one of the firm's first ventures, the *Kleine Grosz-Mappe* (Little Grosz folio), a collection of twenty lithographs published in 1917, was later hailed by Jan Tschichold as "one of the earliest and most important documents of the New Typography."[10] Heartfield, Herzfelde, and Grosz all played key roles in the founding of the Berlin wing of dada, which had begun in Zurich in 1915 with artists like Jean Arp and the Romanian poet Tristan Tzara and spread to New York, Paris, Hanover, Cologne, and Barcelona.[11] Malik Verlag brought out many of the Berlin dada group's key publications, including the catalogue for the *Dada-Messe* (Dada Fair), which took place just before the group dissolved in 1920.

The Berlin dadaists first coined the term photomontage to describe their collages of printed ephemera and photographic fragments. They liked the word because of its mechanical connotations – *montieren* means to fit or assemble, and Heartfield was known among the dadaists as "Monteur-Dada" (Engineer Dada) because of the boilersuit he often wore. Grosz has suggested that his first photomontage experiments with Heartfield date to 1915 or 1916, although none of this work has survived. Those collaborations that have survived, like *Sonniges Land* and *Dada-merika,* were produced later, in 1919.

Inspired by the Bolshevik Revolution of October 1917, Grosz, Heartfield, and Herzfelde joined the newly founded German Communist Party on the last day of 1918. A commitment to Communism was to frame their art and publishing ventures in the twenties. Speaking to the art historian Francis Klingender in 1944, Heartfield recalled that transition from dadaism to Communism as a change from "protest against everything" to "a systematic and consciously guided art propaganda in the service of the working class movement." As important examples of this new type of work, he cited Grosz's collection *Das Gesicht der herrschenden Klasse* (The face of the ruling class), published by Malik Verlag in 1921, his dustjackets for other Malik Verlag books, and his *AIZ* work.[12]

Pioneering the use of photography and photomontage for the covers of Malik Verlag publications – turning "the bookjacket into a political instrument," as Walter Benjamin has put it[13] – was only one of the ways Heartfield used graphic art officially or unofficially to serve the Communist movement. Between 1923 and 1927 he and Grosz edited and contributed to the first Communist satirical magazine, *Der Knüppel* (The cudgel). He made innovative use of photography for Communist election posters. In collaboration with the theater director Erwin Piscator, he was one of the first to use photography in theater sets. He and the writer Kurt Tucholsky (1890–1935), who in 1933 would be deprived of German citizenship for his antinationalist and antimilitarist views (see 22/33), coproduced the satirical book *Deutschland, Deutschland über alles* in 1929; Tucholsky wrote the texts and Heartfield added a selection of documentary photographs and photomontages. As secretary of the Rote Gruppe (Red Group), which was founded in 1924 and replaced by ASSO in 1928, Heartfield also took part in attempts to formalize Communist visual propaganda. The formal inventiveness of all this work, despite its revolutionary message, won him the honor of a room devoted to his work at *Film und Foto* in Stuttgart in 1929.

The year after his success at the *Film und Foto* exhibition Heartfield began concentrating on his regular contributions to *AIZ*. Other artists in Domela's 1931 *Fotomontage* show shared this interest in the press. Bayer and Moholy-Nagy used photomontage for the covers and pages of the German fashion magazine *Neue Linie*,[14] and in the Soviet Union both Lissitzky and Rodchenko were experimenting with photography and photomontage in the illustrated *Soviet Union in Construction*,[15] to which Heartfield contributed when he visited the Soviet Union in 1931–32. Heartfield, however, was interested in using the press as a platform for *satirical* photomontage, aiming to politically inform and mobilize the *AIZ* readers during a period of crisis. In effect, he invented a new hybrid that combined a technique associated with the twentieth-century avant-garde with the much older tradition of caricature.

Between 1930 and 1938 Heartfield published 237 photomontages in *AIZ,* usually as full pages or double-page spreads, often as a front or back covers. He did not contribute during his extended visits to the Soviet Union (1931–32) and France (1935).

Arbeiter-Illustrierte Zeitung

In 1931, in a note congratulating *Arbeiter-Illustrierte Zeitung* on its tenth anniversary of publication, Bertolt Brecht wrote that "the camera can lie just like the typesetting machine. The task of A-I-Z to serve truth and reproduce the real facts is of immense importance, and, it seems to me, has been achieved splendidly."[16]

An extension of *Sowjet Russland im Bild* (Soviet Russia in pictures), which began publication in 1921 and became *Hammer und Sichel* in 1922, *AIZ* was founded in 1925 by the German Communist organizer and politician Willi Münzenberg (1889–1940).[17] Münzenberg intended *AIZ* to be a progressive alternative to magazines like the *Münchner Illustrierte Presse* and *Berliner Illustrierte Zeitung,* which flourished in the twenties. He was convinced that such publications were successful because "an illustrated magazine is more entertaining than a lead article in a political daily."[18] The point was not lost on the Nazi Party, which created its own version, the *Illustrierte Beobachter,* in 1926.

Sowjet Russland im Bild, Hammer und Sichel, and their foreign-language editions were all part of the activities of the charity organization Internationale Arbeiter Hilfe (Workers International Relief). Münzenberg was head of the Communist Youth International when he set up the IAH in 1921 in response to Lenin's request for a charity that could raise funds to alleviate famine in the Volga basin. Although based in Berlin, the charity was not accountable to the German Communist Party but rather answered directly to the Communist International in Moscow. This arrangement gave Münzenberg considerable leeway. IAH did not necessarily promote Communism as such, but it always presented the Soviet Union in a positive light. On its committees and in its publicity, the charity usually gave prominence to famous non-Communist sympathizers, such as Albert Einstein, Käthe Kollwitz, and George Bernard Shaw. When the famine in the Soviet Union ended, the organization continued to raise funds, and it expanded into many areas – books, films, magazines, and even a cigarette factory.

Münzenberg's charity work anticipated the United Front policies that were encouraged by the Soviet Union in the mid-twenties.[19] Those policies urged the various national Communist parties to cooperate with other organizations that had previously been considered deadly rivals. In China, for instance, the party tried to work with the Nationalist Kuomintang against the warlords; in Germany, Communists and Social Democrats pursued a joint campaign that led to a referendum on the expropriation of the former ruling princes. "Fronts" such as the League Against Imperialism were usually funded by Moscow and sought to win Communists and non-Communists over to causes supported by the Communist International. The friendship societies created in several countries to foster sympathetic interest in the Soviet Union were part of the same approach. All these initiatives were indicative of Moscow's isolation in a capitalist world that did not seem to be on the verge of collapse.

When Hitler became chancellor on 30 January 1933, Münzenberg moved most of his operations to Paris, the "city of émigrés," as he called it.[20] In Paris he established Editions du Carrefour, which published forty-five books and eleven pamphlets between 1933 and 1937. The most famous of the Carrefour publications was *Le livre brun* (The brown book), about the

Reichstag Fire trial, for which Heartfield designed the dustjacket and provided illustrations.[21] In 1933 Heartfield and Herzfelde escaped from Berlin to Prague, which like Paris was a haven for German exiles in the mid-thirties. Malik Verlag resumed operations, and Heartfield continued to design many of its dustjackets. *AIZ* published its last issue in Berlin on 5 March 1933 and began publication in Prague later that month. Heartfield's first photomontage from Prague, *Durch Licht zur Nacht* (Through light to night; 5/33), a comment on Nazi book burning, appeared on 10 May 1933.

The weekly print run of *AIZ,* which probably reached 500,000 (with a greater number for special election issues) in the early thirties, fell to a low of 12,000 in Prague.[22] Attempts to smuggle miniature versions into Nazi Germany had limited success. In 1936, three years after the move to Prague, the magazine was renamed *Volks Illustrierte* (*VI*). In October 1938, when the situation in Prague became impossible, publication was shifted to France. Heartfield did not contribute to the last seven issues of *VI,* which were published in France between 15 January and 26 February 1939.

AIZ *and Photography*

A scarcity of suitable photographs was a problem for *AIZ* from the beginning. Mainstream photographic agencies generally lacked images of the magazine's core theme, working class life. In an attempt to lessen *AIZ*'s dependence on such agencies, Münzenberg devised a plan to educate amateur photographers and create a corps of informed photocorrespondents who could send publishable material to *AIZ.* The first Worker Photographer group was set up in Hamburg in 1926, and by the early thirties there was an international network that flourished especially in the Soviet Union. In 1926 Münzenberg also started a magazine, *Der Arbeiter-Fotograf* (The worker photographer), that offered technical and ideological advice.[23] As *AF* and *AIZ* were edited from the same building in Berlin, the advice often came from *AIZ*'s own personnel.

Franz Höllering, editor of *AIZ* from 1925 to 1927, wrote an article for *AF* in 1928 in which he urged readers to steer clear of "this horrible epidemic called photomontage," which was useful only for publicity. He praised Heartfield's dustjackets but warned worker photographers that "what will always remain trivial is whimsy, hobby-work, shop talk. Photomontage seduces with these…. Simple, clear, beautiful pictures of your world – that is your goal. No dilettantish artiness."[24] By 1932, however, after several of Heartfield's photomontages had appeared in *AIZ,* the critic Alfred Kemény, who wrote under the name Durus, was encouraging *AF* readers to follow the lead of Heartfield and the ASSO artists he had influenced. Although Durus shared Höllering's distaste for photomontage in commercial contexts, he was enthusiastic about its revolutionary potential.[25]

The supply of usable material generated by the Worker Photographer movement, whether in the form of documentary photographs or photomontages, was always limited. The movement's concrete achievements failed to live up to its promise. It was as unsuccessful as comparable attempts to politicize radio, literature, film, and other leisure activities of German workers, and the establishment of the Third Reich in 1933 meant the end of the Worker Photographer movement in Germany.

Though it continued to use pictures by worker photographers in countries unaffected by Nazism, particularly the Soviet Union, *AIZ* was therefore even more dependent on commercial picture agencies when it moved to Prague in 1933. How to extract socialist meanings from the imagery of mainstream agencies became an even more urgent problem. Out of necessity, then, *AIZ*'s editors and designers evolved a montage technique that allowed them to use straightforward photographs to present the visual messages they wanted to convey. By the tendentious juxtaposition of image and image or image and text, *AIZ* could make its readers instantly aware of the sharp contrasts between, say, bourgeois and proletarian, war profiteer and war victim, or capitalism and the Soviet Union.

After 1933 *AIZ* also began using more of Heartfield's phomontages, often as an integral part of the overall mosaic of the magazine's design. Eleven of his photomontages appeared in 1930, 4 in 1931, 18 in 1932, 33 in 1933, 53 in 1934, 27 in 1935, 44 in 1936, 32 in 1937, and 15 in 1938, the last year of the magazine's existence.

War and Peace: Heartfield and *AIZ*

AIZ began as a United Front experiment, seeking to attract a wider audience than had previous publications by covering subjects that would interest a working-class readership that was not necessarily Communist. It registered changes in Moscow's revolutionary strategy: the order in 1928 that national Communist parties were to re-adopt positions similar to the classic Bolshevik stance, with a novel emphasis on Social Democratic parties as the main enemy; the introduction in 1935, primarily in response to Hitler's triumphs, of the Popular Front policy, urging the creation of the broadest possible alliance of parties and social forces to isolate and defeat Fascism.[26] Above all, however, *AIZ* always presented the Soviet Union through a rose-tinted window. The Soviet Union was, to quote Münzenberg, "our own world to defend," and capitalism was "the world to conquer."[27]

Heartfield's photomontages, particularly those dealing with German domestic politics, often contain complex allusions that demanded a culturally and politically literate readership. But they were all informed by a straightforward dialectic of war and peace. (When he was discussing with his brother the possibility of a book of his magazine work after the Second World War, Heartfield suggested the title *Krieg im Frieden* [War in peacetime], a deliberate allusion to Tolstoy.)[28] The First World War, the desperate solution of capitalism in crisis, was a constant frame of reference for Heartfield. He argued that capitalism was once again in difficulties and that a new world war, initiated by Fascists, would be its chosen way out. The best hope for peace came from the Soviet Union. And because of its promise of a different, peaceful civilization, the Soviet Union was under constant threat from Fascism.

The link between the capitalist system and the First World War is made explicit in *Krieg und Leichen – die letzte Hoffnung der Reichen* (War and corpses – the last hope of the rich; 1/32), which shows a monumental hyena crossing a field of corpses. Historical specificity is conveyed through the medal around the hyena's neck – the "Blue Max" flying medal from World War I, with the original motto "Pour le Mérite" changed to "Pour le Profit." (There were unsuccessful attempts to ban the *AIZ* issue containing this image in parts of Germany.) Heartfield returned to the same theme later in 1932 with a montage made for a special issue on the Communist-sponsored antiwar conference in Amsterdam. Called *Wollt ihr wieder fallen, damit die Aktien steigen?!* (Do you want to fall again, so that shares rise?! 7/32), it shows a soldier from the 1914–18 war collapsing against a backdrop of share certificates.

S.M. Adolf: Ich führe Euch herrlichen Pleiten entgegen! (His Majesty Adolf: I lead you toward splendid bankruptcies! 6/32) blends portraits of Kaiser Wilhelm and Adolf Hitler, and the text alters the Kaiser's boast from World War I: "I lead you toward splendid times!" In *Nach zwanzig Jahren!* (Twenty years later! 38/34), made specifically in 1934 to commemorate the twentieth anniversary of the outbreak of World War I, uniformed German children march in front of adult skeletons. To the right is General Karl Litzmann (1850–1936), a veteran of World War I who in 1929 had become an active member of the Nazi Party. His presence suggests that the militaristic attitudes that sacrificed a generation still survived in the Third Reich. Accompanying the image is a quotation encouraging warlike attitudes in young children that was taken from a contemporary newspaper from Harbin (or Kharbin), the Manchurian city that had been occupied by the Japanese since 1932. The montage was therefore not only commemorating the start of the First World War but also warning of the imminence of another world war started by Germany or Japan. (The same image, with different text, was displayed in the window of Herzfelde's Berlin bookshop in 1924 to mark the tenth anniversary of the war's beginning. Herzfelde later considered this the first example of Heartfield's distinctive use of photomontage to comment on contemporary history.)[29]

Heartfield was aware that the Nazi Party, by stressing "the shame of Versailles," or the betrayal of frontline soldiers by the politicians at the peace conference, was exploiting the trauma of World War I for its own ends. Hence the image *Antwort auf ein Nazi-Plakat* (Reply to a Nazi poster; 20/36), which reproduces a 1918 poster the Nazis reused in the thirties. "We died for you! And you want to betray us?" asks the poster. Heartfield added the reply: "No! And that is why Hitler must not be allowed to repeat the crime of 1914!"

For Heartfield, the "crime" of World War I was committed by the capitalist system, and he feared a repetition of this crime in the thirties. The link between Fascism and big business is the subject of some of his most famous images: *Adolf, der Übermensch: Schluckt Gold und redet Blech* (Adolf, the Superman: Swallows gold and spouts rubbish; 4/32); *Der Sinn des Hitlergrusses* (The meaning of the Hitler salute; 11/32); and *Werkzeug in Gottes Hand? Spielzeug in Thyssens Hand!* (Instrument in God's hand? Toy in Thyssen's hand! 18/33), depicting Hitler as a puppet manipulated by steel magnate Fritz Thyssen, a Nazi who mediated between Hitler and other Rhineland industrialists. The relationship between capital, Hitler, and the drive to a new world war is made explicit in *Faschismus sein letzter Retter – Krieg sein letzter Ausweg!* (Fascism his final savior – war his final resort! 30/34), which shows Hitler as an armed skeleton urged forward by a stereotypical businessman in a top hat and frock coat.

Heartfield's photomontages touch on all the armed conflicts instigated by the Fascist powers in the thirties, most notably Mussolini's invasion of Abyssinia (Ethiopia) in 1935, Hitler's and Mussolini's support of Franco's uprising in Spain in 1936, and Hirohito's conquest of Manchuria in 1931 and his invasion of China in 1937. They illustrate the magazine's basic assumption: Fascism meant war.

Like all orthodox Communists in the interwar period, Heartfield believed that the only hope came from the Soviet Union. He assumed that Stalin had successfully eliminated the class struggle that was the basis of capitalism. Here for the first time in human history was a society ruled by workers and peasants. "A new man" was literally "master of a new world." (*Ein neuer Mensch – Herr einer neuen Welt* is the title of 45/34, Heartfield's front cover for *AIZ*'s special 1934 issue celebrating seventeen years of the Soviet Union.) In a world without exploitation, the main task of industrial and agricultural workers was to increase production in order to overtake their capitalist enemies. Stalin had made this dream a possibility with the launching of his first Five Year Plan in 1928, and by the mid-thirties he was achieving results. *Lenins Vision ward Wirklichkeit* (Lenin's vision became reality; 21/34) commemorates the production of the 100,000th tractor in a Stalingrad factory. In *Sowjetaufbau und Naziaufbau* (Soviet construction and Nazi construction; 12/34) a photograph of a new silo in Tashkent is juxtaposed with images of collecting boxes for various Nazi charities.

Like other supporters of the Soviet Union, Heartfield saw it as threatened by the capitalist powers. His montage *15 Jahre Sowjet-Union* (15 years of the Soviet Union; 12/32), part of an *AIZ* commemorative issue, shows a saluting Soviet worker in front of a photograph of an industrial scene and is captioned: "We swear: 'In the hour of danger we do not abandon our Socialist Fatherland.'" Other montages specify the danger. *Sein Kampf mit seinem "Kampf"* (His struggle with his "Struggle"; 35/34) suggests that Hitler was abandoning all the promises he made in *Mein Kampf* in 1925 except the threat to invade the Soviet Union. *Fantasie zweier Ostpaktjäger* (Fantasy of two Eastern Pact hunters; 6/35) shows Hermann Göring and the Polish foreign minister discussing how to carve up the constellation the Great Bear (the Soviet Union).

Whereas in class-ridden societies the army was an important limb of the repressive state, in the Soviet Union, where class conflict had allegedly been eliminated, the Red Army's role was purely defensive. The threat of foreign invasion, especially by Germany from the west and Japan from the east, necessitated the Red Army's continued existence. *Klumpfüsschens Wunschtraum* (Little Clubfoot's wishful thinking; 16/35) was the back cover of a special issue on the Red Army that began by quoting Stalin: "We are for peace and we defend the cause of peace but we fear no threats." In the montage Nazi Propaganda Minister Josef Goebbels, dwarfed by monumental Soviet soldiers, cries: "Away with these degenerate subhumans," a quote from his anti-Soviet speech at the Nürnberg party rally in 1935.

Im Westen wie im Osten, Steht sie auf Posten, Die stärkste Armee der Welt! (In the West as in the East, It stands on guard, The strongest army in the world! 10/38) emphasizes the Red Army's role as "one of the greatest weapons of peace." Heartfield created the photomontage to tie in with an article about a border incident that was interpreted as a Japanese provocation aimed at luring the Soviet Union into war. By 1935 Communists had come to see the Red Army not only as the defender of the Soviet Union but also as the key force in the creation of a global Popular Front to defeat Fascism, east and west. *Nur die geeinte Front der Schaffenden sichert den Frieden!* (Only the united front of the productive classes secures the peace! 13/35) is dominated by a Red Army soldier clasping the hands of two unidentified allies. Barking ineffectually at his feet are the dogs of Japanese and German Fascism.

Heartfield and Meaning: The Impact of AIZ as Context

Heartfield's designs were regularly part of a special issue or section of *AIZ,* or, later, *VI.* Often, however, the links with neighboring items extended beyond overlapping themes. On occasion a planned interaction with other pages created meanings in Heartfield's montages that remain invisible if they are viewed outside the context of the magazine. Take the well-known *In diesem Zeichen will man euch verraten und verkaufen!* (In this sign shall ye be betrayed and sold! 2/32). The title is an adaption of "In hoc signo vinces" (In this sign shalt thou conquer), the words beneath the cross that is said to have appeared in a vision to the emperor Constantine as he marched on Rome in 312. In Heartfield's vision, the "crooked cross" of Nazism – here a swastika made from coins – would lead Germany not to victory but to disaster. Viewed in isolation, the montage seems to be a reminder of the potentially catastrophic alliance of Nazism and capital, one of Heartfield's favorite themes. But it appeared in a special issue that aimed to show that white-collar workers and blue-collar workers were natural allies against a common capitalist enemy. Immediately following the Heartfield montage was a two-page article that used contrasting photographs and captions to highlight the irreconcilable class interests of the general director of the Deutsche Bank (a regular breakfast guest of Adolf Hitler, according to the piece) and one of his employees. Viewed within this issue and next to this article – itself a clear example of the synthetic montage favored by *AIZ* – the meaning of Heartfield's montage shifts. Not only is it an attack on the collusion of Hitler and finance capital, but it is also an appeal to those employed by organizations like the Deutsche Bank to recognize their wage slavery and draw the appropriate political conclusions.

Der Krieg (The war; 16/33), an updating of Franz von Stuck's 1894 painting with the same title (which was at the time on exhibit in Munich), shows a Teutonic horseman crossing a battlefield littered with corpses. Heartfield added a lightning flash shaped like a swastika and a photograph of Hitler, who sits awkwardly behind the warrior. Detached from the pages of *AIZ,* the montage is a parody of one of Hitler's favorite painters and a general statement about Nazi militarism. Seen as a scripto-visual epigraph to the article that followed it, "Against the East we want to ride! The Third Reich arms for war," however, the montage becomes more specifically a comment on Hitler's aim, elaborated in *Mein Kampf* in 1925, to revive the Drive to the East in emulation of the Teutonic knights of the thirteenth and fourteenth centuries.

Another device pioneered by Heartfield and *AIZ* was the creation of a dynamic interaction between the front page and the photomontage on the third page of the issue. The cover of the 1933 Christmas issue, for example, was a photo-text synthesis showing an American battleship on maneuvers. The reader saw the headline "And peace on earth!" and then opened the magazine and was confronted with Heartfield's response: *Friede auf Erden? Kein Friede auf Erden, solange die Armen ärmer werden!* (Peace on earth? No peace on earth, as long as the poor become poorer! 32/33). The image shows poor people peering into a shop window stocked with Christmas goods they cannot afford.

The next issue used the same sequential technique to create an argument across pages. The front cover showed a group of people waiting for the sentencing at the end of the Reichstag Fire trial in Leipzig. The reader turned the page and was faced with Heartfield's *Das Urteil der Welt!* (The judgment of the world! 33/33). The image is a portrait of Göring, the Nazis' chief prosecutor at the trial, surrounded by flames. The implication is that the real arsonist is Göring, whose "features reveal what the court remained silent about."

Heartfield regularly designed either the front or back cover of *AIZ,* but on one occasion he used both to make a photomontage diptych for a special issue on the twentieth anniversary of the outbreak of the First World War. Heartfield's front cover – *Faschismus sein letzter Retter – Krieg sein letzter Ausweg!* (Fascism his final savior – war his final resort! 30/34) – shows a capitalist advising an armed Hitler, who has been reduced to a skeleton and is recognizable only by his mustache. The back cover – *Schluss damit!* (Stop it! 31/34) – offers a solution, showing a worker attacking the profit system that generates Fascism, economic crisis, and war.

At the *Fotomontage* exhibition in Berlin in 1931, the ex-dadaist Raoul Hausmann gave a speech in which he described the new technique of photomontage as "static film."[30] His characterization emphasizes a major distinction between film montage and photomontage in the twenties and thirties: the former played with time, the latter with space. What distinguishes Heartfield's work is that it explodes that distinction. He began his experiments with sequentiality in his Malik Verlag dustjackets, which frequently created an argument between front and back, spine and flaps, and continued them in *AIZ,* where he made montages not only *on* pages but *between* them.

Heartfield's Weapons: "Those Furious Lampoons"

"Which of our readers does not know him?" asked an article on Heartfield in an April 1934 issue of *AIZ* that was prompted by the scandal over the removal of Heartfield's photomontages, at the insistence of the German and Austrian envoys, from an exhibition of caricatures in Prague. "Everyone knows him, if not by his appearance, then from his photomontages, those furious lampoons that inspire the friend and wound the foe, and that make laughter into a devastating weapon."[31]

Just how Heartfield's "furious lampoons" made "laughter into a devastating weapon" can perhaps best be shown by comparing one of his photomontages with an anonymous synthetic montage that uses some of the same raw material to convey a similar message (Fig.1). The anonymous montage, published in *AIZ* in 1932, brings into one frame four separate photographs: a portrait of Adolf Hitler and one of Nazi steel magnate Fritz Thyssen; a menu from the luxurious Park Hotel in Düsseldorf; and a view of the exterior of the hotel, with anti-Hitler demonstrators in the foreground.[32] A brief caption

Fig. 1. "Hitler mit seinem Freund, dem Scharfmacher Thyssen..." (Hitler with his friend the agitator Thyssen). Anonymous photomontage. *AIZ* 11, no. 7 (1932), p. 147

fleshes out the images, noting that Thyssen introduced Hitler, the "workers' leader," to the *Industrieklub* during a dinner at the hotel, while on the street outside protesters made their presence felt.

Heartfield used the same photograph of Thyssen for his own comment on the relationship between Hitler and big business in *Werkzeug in Gottes Hand*?

Fig. 2. *Werkzeug in Gottes Hand? Spielzeug in Thyssens Hand!* (Instrument in God's hand? Toy in Thyssen's hand! 18/33). Photomontage by John Heartfield. *AIZ* 12, no. 31 (10 August 1933), p. 529

Spielzeug in Thyssens Hand! (Instrument in God's hand? Toy in Thyssen's hand! 18/33). The image (Fig. 2) shows Thyssen – Heartfield added a cigar to signal his economic position and a swastika tie pin to convey his politics – pulling the strings of a Hitler jumping jack. Two texts add to the image and title: one cites a leading Nazi on Hitler's perception of himself as God's instrument; another provides factual information on Thyssen's economic wealth and importance.

Both montages deal with that key moment when Hitler consolidated his power by securing the backing of big business, in the process abandoning the *socialist* aspects of his National Socialism. In the first montage, Thyssen is behind Hitler, "backing" him, but the portraits are the same size, suggesting a collusion of equals. There is no such ambiguity in the Heartfield photomontage, where a giant Thyssen is clearly the puppet master pulling the strings of the politician. The photomontage is an elaborate combination of photographs, but the attention to scale, lighting, and the relationship between the figures hints at a single documentary image, an image that deflates the lofty Nazi rhetoric in the caption. In contrast, the synthetic montage is more a mosaic of information, inviting the viewer to construct a narrative from the four related photographs, and the caption underneath merely clarifies the images. In Heartfield's hands, then, the images of Thyssen and Hitler are manipulated with a greater tendentiousness to produce a comment on both economic and ideological aspects of Nazism.

In this instance, Heartfield used four satirical devices to convey his message: metamorphosis; hybridization; contrasts of large and small, high and low; and unmasking, through the mismatch of image and quotation. He used these same devices, endlessly reworked and recombined, in many of his montages to transform reportage into comic art.

Metamorphosis

In *Deutsche Naturgeschichte* (German natural history; 34/34), Heartfield made his own additions to a dictionary definition of metamorphosis: "1. In mythology: the transformation of humans into trees, animals, stones and so on. 2. In zoology: the development of some animals through forms of larvae and chrysalis, for example, caterpillar, chrysalis, butterfly. 3. In the history of the Weimar Republic: the succession in a straight line EBERT–HINDENBURG–HITLER." His photomontage is an allegory of the Weimar Republic's inevitable evolution into the Third Reich. Friedrich Ebert, Social Democratic president from 1919 to 1925, is a caterpillar. Paul von Hindenburg, his successor from 1925 to 1934, is a chrysalis. Hitler, who combined the posts of chancellor and president to become Führer in 1934, is the result – a German death's-head moth. The site for this "natural history

lesson" is Germany, represented by a withered branch of an oak tree.

The montage makes use of both metamorphosis, or the transformation of one thing into another (Ebert–Hindenburg–Hitler), and hybridization, or the merging of elements usually considered incompatible (Ebert as a caterpillar, Hindenburg as a chrysalis, and Hitler as a death's-head moth). Heartfield's satires frequently emphasized one or the other of these two devices.

Heartfield often "metamorphosed" well-known figures, showing them in lowly, commonplace roles at odds with the presumptions of their public positions. Just as he made Fritz Thyssen a puppeteer, he presented Saarland industrialist Hermann Röchling as a schoolteacher demonstrating dubious logic to an imaginary class in *Die Röchling-Rechnung* (The Röchling calculation; 52/34). And in *Ein Millionär möchte den Ersatz-"Sozialismus" retten* (A millionaire would like to save the ersatz "Socialism"; 2/37), Dutch oil tycoon Henry Deterding is an allotment gardener coming to the aid of the Third Reich with a wheelbarrow full of produce. Nazi leaders were similarly ridiculed: Göring as a butcher in *Goering, Der Henker des Dritten Reichs* (Göring, the executioner of the Third Reich; 23/33); Ley, Goebbels, and Hitler as troubled fathers having problems administering a laxative to a difficult child, the working class, in *Die Väter des Arbeitsgesetzes in Nöten* (The fathers of the labor law in difficulty; 19/34); Goebbels as a faith healer trying to revive the ideas of the French pharmacist and therapist Emile Coué in *Dr. Goebbels, Der Gesundbeter* (Dr. Goebbels, the faith healer; 20/34).

Others of Heartfield's metamorphoses called on circus or fairground imagery. Reichsbank President Hjalmar Schacht attempts a tricky balancing act with the German mark in *Hjalmar oder Das wachsende Defizit* (Hjalmar or The growing deficit; 14/34). Schacht and others try to hoist a gigantic mark in *Neudeutscher Kraft-Akt* (New German strong-man act; 50/34). Goebbels, Göring, and Hitler are clowns overambitiously attempting to walk the highwire in *Die drei Weisen aus dem Sorgenland* (The three magi from the Land of Sorrow; 1/35). Goebbels blows up hot-air balloons in *Großer internationaler Lügenwettbewerb* (Great international lies competition; 23/37). To paraphrase Walter Benjamin's comment on Brecht, Heartfield equipped prominent figures with new clothes to display them in a single posture – naked.[33]

Hybridization

Hybridization, which has been defined as the "inmixing of binary opposites, particularly of high and low, such that there is a heterodox merging of elements usually perceived as incompatible,"[34] is the theme of *Brauner Künstlertraum* (Brown artist's dream; 9/38). The brown artist is the German sculptor Georg Kolbe, whom the Nazis had commissioned to make monuments to both Beethoven and General Franco. The montage shows him in his studio, asking himself, "Franco and Beethoven, just how do I do it? The best thing, I suppose, would be to make a centaur, half beast, half human." In the background is a sculpture that is indeed half beast (Franco) and half human (Beethoven). Kaiser Wilhelm and Hitler have been combined to make a another human hybrid in *S.M. Adolf: Ich führe Euch herrlichen Pleiten entgegen!* (His Majesty Adolf: I lead you toward splendid bankruptcies! 6/32).

Some of Heartfield's hybrids merge the human and the inanimate: for example, the "cabbagehead" in *Wer Bürgerblätter liest wird blind und taub* (Whoever reads bourgeois newspapers becomes blind and deaf; 1/30) and Hitler with a spine of coins in *Adolf, der Übermensch: Schluckt Gold und redet Blech* (Adolf, the Superman: Swallows gold and spouts rubbish; 4/32). Most often, however, he combined humans with animals or insects, as in *Deutsche Naturgeschichte* (German natural history; 34/34). Capitalism has a human body and a tiger's head in *Zum Krisen-Parteitag der SPD* (On the occasion of the crisis party conference of the SPD; 2/31). Reich Minister of the Interior Wilhelm Frick is a human bug in *Die Wanze als Kammerjäger* (The bug as vermin exterminator; 22/33). The Nazis arrest a human beefsteak in *Beefsteaks raus! Nieder mit den Schnitzeln!* (Beefsteaks out! Down with cutlets! 37/36). The dogfish in *Der friedfertige Raubfisch* (The peaceful fish of prey; 15/37) has Göring's obese body. And the head of Sudeten German Nazi leader Konrad Henlein sits on the body of a cock in *Heimgefunden!* (Back home! 14/38).

Anthropomorphism

Heartfield also anthropomorphized animals, in the tradition of fables and medieval bestiaries.[35] On occasion he made the link to fables quite explicit: in *Illustration zu Grimms Märchen von der Katze und der Maus* (Illustration to Grimm's fairy tale about the cat and the mouse; 2/38), the cat is Germany, the threatened mouse, Austria; in *Der Fuchs und der Igel. Eine Tierfabel nach Lafontaine* (The fox and the hedgehog. An animal fable after La Fontaine; 7/38), the sly fox is Germany, the prudent hedgehog, Czechoslovakia. In other instances he linked animal symbolism to the names of politicians. *Hitlers Friedenstaube* (Hitler's dove of peace; 5/35) works through the contradiction of the title and the picture of a hawk, but it is also playing with the word *Habicht* (hawk), the surname of the leader of the illegal Nazi Party in Austria. And in *Kein Fraß für Krebse!* (No food for crabs! 11/38) the Sudeten German Nazi Hans Krebs is depicted as a crab.

Metaphors of Scale

Contrast, of large and small or of high and low, was another of Heartfield's satirical devices.[36] In his montages scale often became a metaphor for relations of power. Contrast of large and small was also a visually simple way of contradicting the Nazi claims to independently represent the interests of the German community. The most famous example of this is *Der Sinn des Hitlergrusses. Motto: Millionen stehen hinter Mir!* (The meaning of the Hitler salute. Motto: Millions stand behind me! 11/32). But Heartfield used the same device in different contexts. In *6 Millionen Naziwähler: Futter für ein großes Maul* (6 million Nazi voters: fodder for a big mouth; 7/30) the big fish is capital and the litttle fish is Nazism, preying on 6 million voters. *Der friedfertige Raubfisch* (The peaceful fish of prey; 15/37) evokes the same proverb, with its depiction of small fish threatened by a bloated dogfish, an unambiguous allusion to Göring. (The Nazis objected to this montage, but *VI*, in mock innocence, responded that it contained no specific reference to any country or individual.)

Heartfield also used the contrast of large and small to signal the strength of resistance to oppression. *China, der Riese, erwacht – wehe dem Eindringling!* (China, the giant, awakes – woe to the invader! 5/38) alludes to Jonathan Swift, the master of the metaphor of scale, by depicting China as Gulliver and the Japanese invaders as Lilliputians only temporarily holding down the sleeping giant.

Mikhail Bakhtin has said that "the essential principle of grotesque realism is degradation, that is, the lowering of all that is high, spiritual, ideal, abstract; it is a transfer to the material level, to the sphere of earth and body in their indissoluble unity."[37] Heartfield's metaphors of scale were often interlocked with metaphors of space, especially the contrast of high and low. This allowed him to represent visually, and mischievously invert, the hierarchy of power implicit in, say, the courtroom relationship between state accuser and accused, or the Nazi racial distinction between *Übermensch* (superman) and *Untermensch* (subhuman).

Through hierarchy inversion Heartfield pronounced *his* unequivocal judgment on the Reichstag Fire trial in Leipzig. *Der Richter, Der Gerichtete* (The Judge, The Judged; 30/33) was directly related to the issue's cover, which showed Göring, the chief prosecutor, before the Leipzig court with an accompanying text headed "Just you wait, you swindler!" The threat was aimed at the defendant, the well-known Bulgarian Communist activist Georgi Dimitrov, who also sought to exploit the show quality of the trial by using it as a platform from which to attack Nazism. When readers opened the magazine they immediately saw Heartfield's montage. Heartfield used the same photograph of Göring, but he extracted Göring from the courtroom and reverse printed the image. Göring's courtroom speech is reduced to a stream of abuse aimed at Dimitrov: "Red tramp – criminal – scum – swindler – to the gallows!" Most importantly, Heartfield visually reversed the courtroom relationship, putting Göring in his place, a minuscule figure before a monumental Dimitrov.

The same device activates *Klumpfüsschens Wunschtraum* (Little Clubfoot's wishful thinking; 16/35), the back cover of a special issue honoring the Red Army. Heartfield's starting point was Goebbels's anti-Soviet speech at a Nürnberg Party rally in 1935. A minute Goebbels (whose own small size and deformed foot belied Nazi myths about Nordic ideal types) stands atop an unstable pile of books, gesticulating wildly as he calls for the eradication of "diesen degenerierten Untermenschen" (these degenerate subhumans). Among the books are Hitler's *Mein Kampf* and Alfred Rosenberg's *Mythus des zwanzigsten Jahrhunderts* (Myth of the twentieth century), another source of Nazi racist rhetoric. The large size of the books relative to Goebbel's is a comment on the propaganda minister's lack of intellectual originality. And the Red Army – a large, healthy, collective body – towers above the diminutive, deformed, and isolated figure of "Little Clubfoot," the spokesman for the Germanic *Übermensch* (superman) brought down to earth.

Word and Image: Heartfield's Use of Language

Language plays a vital role in Heartfield's photomontages. Nearly always, his message is conveyed through an inseparable melding of word and image. When he did publish an image without text, *Bild ohne Worte...* (Picture without words...; 7/37), he invited readers to send a title, poem, or fable to complete the unfinished montage, a picture of a dove of peace being attacked by a bird of prey. And only once did he use words without photographs: *Ernst Moritz Arndt* (3/35), which adapts an anti-Napoleonic poem by Arndt, presented in lapidary style, to the contemporary struggle against Hitler's attempt to influence the outcome of the League of Nations plebiscite in the Saar.

Heartfield's choice and arrangement of type for his *AIZ* work was in general unadventurous. It was not that he had no interest in typography. On the contrary, in 1928, in his survey *Die neue Typographie,* Tschichold had hailed Heartfield's innovative use of typography for his Malik Verlag dustjackets. A dustjacket and a magazine page call for two very different kinds of designs, however. The text on a magazine page functions like the subtitles on silent films: the clarity of the message counts for more than striking or experimental typography.

Most of the text in Heartfield's *AIZ* montages was set in Kabel. Capitals, italics, and different sizes and weights of the same typeface were often combined to give variety to a page. Gothic script was occasionally introduced, usually to connote Nazism, as in *S.M. Adolf: Ich führe Euch herrlichen Pleiten entgegen!* (His Majesty Adolf: I lead you toward splendid bankruptcies! 6/32), *Deutsche Eicheln 1933* (German acorns 1933; 24/33), and *Das tausendjährige Reich* (The Thousand Year Reich; 39/34). A script typeface that emulated handwriting was sometimes used for exclamations and exhortations, as in *Ein*

neues Jahr! (A new year! 11/30), *In diesem Zeichen will man euch verraten und verkaufen!* (In this sign shall ye be betrayed and sold! 2/32), and *Wollt ihr wieder fallen, damit die Aktien steigen?!* (Do you want to fall again, so that shares rise?! 7/32). Quotations were usually set in Kabel, but sometimes, to confirm their authenticity, Heartfield reproduced statements torn directly from newspapers, as in *Vandervelde* (4/30), *Man muß eine besondere Veranlagung zum Selbstmord haben...* (One must have a special disposition toward suicide...; 1/31), *Alles in schönster Ordnung!* (Everything's fine! 12/33), and *Ruhe herrscht wieder in Barcelona* (Quiet rules again in Barcelona; 43/34).

Heartfield's love of puns, both visual and verbal, and his penchant for illustrating figures of speech underscore the impossibility of erecting any clear-cut boundary between word and image in his montages. Making sense of the image often depends on the viewer's recognizing the visual presentation of a colloquial expression: the Third Reich as a "house of cards" in *Das tausendjährige Reich* (The Thousand Year Reich; 39/34); Göring "playing with fire" in *Das Spiel der Nazis mit dem Feuer* (The Nazis playing with fire; 8/35); power politics summed up as "big fish eat little fish" in *Der friedfertige Raubfisch* (The peaceful fish of prey; 15/37).

In other montages text is integrated into the visual component. In *Der wahre Torpedo gegen den Frieden* (The real torpedo against peace; 20/37) a list of Nazi provocations against other countries is engraved on a German torpedo. In *So ward aus Hugenberg der Hugenzwerg* (Thus Hugenberg the mountain became Hugenberg the dwarf; 13/33) balloons inscribed with episodes from Hugenberg's political career float off into space, and in *Großer internationaler Lügenwettbewerb* (Great international lies competition; 23/37) Goebbels is blowing up hot-air balloons inscribed with Nazi propaganda. Information written on a blackboard features prominently in both *Völkische Tiefenschau* (The profound view of the people; 21/33) and *Die Röchling-Rechnung* (The Röchling calculation; 52/34). Heartfield also delighted in inserting text in places the casual observer might miss. For instance, "Nürnberger Trichter" (Nürnberg funnel) is written on the funnel on the laboratory shelves of the "brown alchemist" in *Wieder einmal in der Welt voran...* (Once again first in the world...; 35/36). The inscription condenses references to the Nürnberg rallies, the anti-Jewish Nürnberg laws of 1935, and the popular saying "jemandem etwas mit dem Nürnberger Trichter beibringen" (literally, to teach someone with the Nürnberg funnel), which means to drum something into somebody.

Heartfield regularly incorporated printed matter into his photomontages. He used postage stamps in *Ab 1. Januar, neue Briefmarken im Dritten Reich* (From 1 January, new postage stamps in the Third Reich; 1/34) and *Briefmarken sprechen* (Postage stamps speak;

19/37), in which stamps that "speak" about Fascism, war, and peace are arranged in columns according to national groupings. (Wieland Herzfelde survived in New York during the Second World War as a stamp dealer.) Posters are key elements in *Noch ist Deutschland nicht verloren* (Germany is not yet lost; 8/30) and *Antwort auf ein Nazi-Plakat* (Reply to a Nazi poster; 20/36). Hitler's books appear in *Sein Kampf mit seinem "Kampf"* (His struggle with his "Struggle"; 35/34) and *Neueste Muster der Nazi-Lebensmittelindustrie 1936* (Latest samples of the Nazi food industry 1936; 2/36), in which an edition of his speeches – "Garantiert arisches Führerschmalz" (Guaranteed Aryan Führer lard) – is offered to sustain the German population. Literature of a different kind, including Malik Verlag titles with Heartfield dustjackets, is featured in Heartfield's attack on Nazi book burning, *Durch Licht zur Nacht* (Through light to night; 5/33).

Appropriately enough, Heartfield frequently used newspapers in his designs. Sometimes a figure holds a significant title: Marx with the Communist daily *Die Rote Fahne* in *Die letzte Weisheit der SPD: "Nieder mit dem Marxismus!"* (The latest idea of the SPD: "Down with Marxism!" 4/31); a monkey reading the anti-Semitic *Der Stürmer* in *Gespräch im berliner Zoo* (Talk in the Berlin zoo; 23/34); newspaper editors carrying their pro-Franco front pages like banners in *Fremdenlegionäre fern vom Schuß* (Foreign legionnaires far from the shooting; 41/36). Sometimes the papers serve a more elaborate purpose: for *Wer Bürgerblätter liest wird blind und taub* (Whoever reads bourgeois newspapers becomes blind and deaf; 1/30) Heartfield made a cabbagehead from Social Democratic newspapers, and in *Man muß eine besondere Veranlagung zum Selbstmord haben...* (One must have a special disposition toward suicide...; 1/31) the corpse of the Communist martyr Karl Liebknecht appears to be smothered by Social Democratic press cuttings hostile to Communism.

For other montages he created "calligrams": the swastika made of anti-Semitic headlines from *Der Stürmer* in a montage about the newspaper's editor Julius Streicher, *Hitlers bester Freund* (Hitler's best friend; 11/35), or the Christian cross made from a list of Fascist atrocities in the Spanish Civil War in *Den katholischen Opfern des Faschismus zum Gedenken!* (In memory of the Catholic victims of Fascism! 18/37).

In some montages the image merely offers a visual summary of text: a group of singing Nazis next to Herzfelde's *Lied der Heil-Armee* (Song of the Heil-Army; 21/35); an Italian, a Moroccan, and a German soldier as a backdrop to Herzfelde's poem *Die Mütter an ihre Söhne in Francos Diensten* (The mothers to their sons in the service of Franco; 43/36); four flags corresponding to the four martyrs of the Spanish Civil War who are the subject of Herzfelde's elegy *Durch Einheit zum Sieg* (Through unity to victory; 6/37); or a literal visual interpretation of the story in *Illustration zu Grimms Märchen*

von der Katze und der Maus (Illustration to Grimm's fairy tale about the cat and the mouse; 2/38).

In other montages the visual component plays a less subordinate role. In *Hitler und Hummel: der gleiche Rummel* (Hitler and Hummel: the same racket; 13/32) the five-versed saga compares the careers of Hitler and Hummel, a con man who became a nationalist hero, and Heartfield underscores the ridicule through the simple device of shortening both figures' legs, a visualization of the German proverb "Lies have short legs." *Die Nachtleuchter tagen in Brüssel* (The dimwits meet in Brussels; 24/34) includes a nonsense poem by Christian Morgenstern called "Die Tagnachtlampe" (The day and night lamp) about a lamp that could change day into night and vice versa. Rather than literally illustrating the poem, Heartfield adapts its theme to satirize major leaders of European Social Democratic parties, whose lamps can only change day into night. This montage also shows Heartfield's delight in the sly detail: one leader, the German Otto Wels, has only a *Nachtleuchter*, a candlestick, but in colloquial German also a dimwit. In both these examples, title, verse, and montage play off each other.

In still other montages more laconic texts are ironically juxtaposed with images. *Zum Krisen-Parteitag der SPD* (On the occasion of the crisis party conference of the SPD; 2/31) depicts capitalism as a human tiger (with a swastika tie pin) and quotes delegate Fritz Tarnow, a trade unionist who was well known for his revisionist views, assuring the conference that "Social Democracy does not want the breakdown of capitalism. Like a doctor, it wants to try to heal and improve it." In *6 Millionen kommunistische Stimmen* (6 million Communist votes; 15/32) Von Papen's message, "No means can be too severe to exterminate Bolshevism in Germany root and branch!" is visually deflated by the image, showing him trying to drain a wild sea with a ladle. Heartfield particularly liked to recontextualize the statements of Fascist leaders, as in *Das tausendjährige Reich* (The Thousand Year Reich; 39/34), where an extract from a speech by Hitler about the survival of his revolution for a millennium is contradicted by the image of the Third Reich as a collapsing house of skat cards.

Two comparisons help to clarify how Heartfield used text in different ways. Take *Der Platz an der Sonne* (The place in the sun; 18/35), a comment on the Italian invasion of Abyssinia. The montage shows a jackal roaming the desert amid the corpses of dead soldiers, while the subtitle quotes Mussolini's boast, "I want to provide my people with a place in the sun!" *An einen sterbenden italienischen Soldaten* (To a dying Italian soldier; 6/36) uses a similar image of Italian bodies in the Abyssinian desert, but as a backdrop for an elegy addressed to the dying soldiers. In the first example, the ironic effect is created through a visual undermining of Mussolini's rhetoric; in the second, the poem is enhanced by, but is not dependent on, the accompanying image.

Or take *Zu Schillers 175. Geburtstag* (On the occasion of Schiller's 175th birthday; 47/34). The image shows Reich Minister of the Interior Dr. Wilhelm Frick staring at Kügelgen's portrait of Schiller, whose birthday was celebrated in the Third Reich in 1934, and asking, "What did the guy write? 'Tyranny has bounds!' For that I would have stripped him of citizenship." The quotation about the limits of tyranny was taken from Schiller's verse drama *Wilhelm Tell* (1803–4). Heartfield used the quote again in *So würde Tell in unseren Tagen handeln* (This is how Tell would act in our day; 31/37), which presents the heroic subject of the Swiss painter Ferdinand Hodler's *Woodcutter* as a modern day William Tell cutting down the tyrannies of German and Italian Fascism. The image is accompanied by two verses from Schiller that include the key line about tyrants. The first montage depends on the contrast between the image and the text: the Nazi public reverence for Germany's classical heritage is merely a front for cultural ignorance and brutality. In the second montage, however, the Schiller quotation contributes to the overall message but is not essential to it.

Special note should be made of Heartfield's signature. Sometimes inked onto the preparatory artwork by hand, it was usually stripped in at the negative stage along with the rest of the text. The presence of his name confirmed Heartfield's status as an artist, for conventional photographs in *AIZ* were often uncredited. The fact that his name was usually typeset rather than personally signed lent the montages an air of objectivity.

Heartfield sometimes encouraged reflection on the form of his work by adding ironic asides, often as part of the credit line. In the top right corner of *Adolf, der Übermensch: Schluckt Gold und redet Blech* (Adolf, the superman: Swallows gold and spouts rubbish; 4/32) is the note "X ray by John Heartfield." At the bottom of *Völkische Tiefenschau* (The profound view of the people; 21/33), the artist added "Original photograph from the Teutonic backwoods by John Heartfield." On *Goering, Der Henker des Dritten Reichs* (Göring, the executioner of the Third Reich; 23/33) he commented, "Göring's face is taken from an original photograph and has not been retouched," and he inserted a similar remark – "For the portraits of Hitler and Göring original photographs were used unchanged" into the corner of *Zum Fall Hamsun–Ossietzky* (On the occasion of the Hamsun–Ossietzky case; 5/36). *Krisenfestes Rindvieh* (Crisis-free cattle; 48/34), showing a cow implausibly carving herself up with a knife and fork, has an additional credit line: "Picture report by our correspondent John Heartfield."

These playful comments are a reminder that the content of Heartfield's art cannot be divorced from his technique: a combination of traditional caricature and photography. This inherently comic hybrid form, suggesting both editorial cartoon and photojournalism, drew on, but also undermined, photography's claims to represent the truth.

From Idea to Page: The Making of Heartfield's Photomontages

"New political problems demand new means of propaganda. For this task, photography has the greatest persuasive power," Heartfield wrote in the catalogue of the exhibition *Gefesselter Blick* (Fettered gaze), held in Stuttgart in 1930.[38] That same year, his affiliation with *AIZ* gave him a chance to test the "persuasive power" of photography as a "new means of propaganda" before an even larger audience.

The way Heartfield manipulated written and visual source material to produce his photomontages had little in common with conventional notions of creativity and how artists work: the making of the photomontages and their integration into the overall layout of *AIZ* was a collaborative effort, akin to the making of a film in a studio or the production of an advertisement in an agency. Many times the process began with the *AIZ* editors suggesting a theme, but whether the idea was the editor's or his own, Heartfield often discussed it with his brother, Wieland Herzfelde, with whom he had worked closely ever since they had founded *Neue Jugend* together in 1916. Sometimes Herzfelde's written contributions were credited in the published montage (see 27/34, 21/35, 43/36, 6/37), but more often his involvement was not acknowledged. One can assume, however, that the two brothers continuously exchanged ideas. A letter Heartfield sent from London to his brother in New York in 1939 clearly reveals the intimate partnership that had been interrupted when Hitler's threat to Czechoslovakia forced them to leave Prague in 1938: "Please do carry on sending me montage ideas when they occur to you. Don't forget. I am in the process of producing them and hope that I can soon inform you of new publications of my work."[39] (After Heartfield's death in 1968 the collaborative nature of the brothers' work gave rise to a bitter legal wrangle between Herzfelde and Heartfield's widow, Gertrud, over the rights to the prewar work.)[40]

Typically, Heartfield first made a pencil sketch of an idea, often after discussions with his brother. He undertook the picture research, but a photographer did any original image making as well as the copying and printing to size, following his instructions. The combination of photographs was Heartfield's work, but someone else often did the retouching. The Hungarian photographer Wolf Reiss (János Reismann; 1905–1976), who worked for Heartfield from 1928 to 1931, has described the rigorous process of collaboration:

> The photographs which I made for Heartfield, in accordance with an exact pencil sketch and always under his personal supervision, often took hours, many hours. He struggled for nuances which I could no longer perceive. At the developing stage, he would also stand by the enlarger until the prints were ready. I was generally so tired that I could no longer

Fig. 3. Preparatory artwork for 46/34: *Ein gefährliches Eintopfgericht* (A dangerous hot pot). 34 x 36 cm. John Heartfield Archiv, Copyright Akademie der Künste zu Berlin

Fig. 4. Preparatory artwork for 6/33: *Hitlers Programm* (Hitler's program). 32 x 44 cm. John Heartfield Archiv, Copyright Akademie der Künste zu Berlin

stand or think; all I wanted was sleep – but he hurried home with the photos still damp, dried them, cut them out, and assembled them under a heavy sheet of glass. He would sleep for one or two hours, and early at eight in the morning he would already be sitting with the retoucher. There he would stay for two, three, four, or five hours, his nerves stretched to the limit, always fearing that the retouching could spoil it. Then the photomontage is finished, but there is not much relaxation: new tasks, new ideas. He burrows in the photo-libraries for hours, for days, looking for a suitable photo of Hermann Müller, Hugenberg, Röhm, whoever is needed – or at least a suitable head, for the rest can be managed. Then he turns again to the photographers, all of whom he hates, me included, because of the nuances which we are unable to perceive.[41]

Once the preparatory artwork was complete, it went through four further stages of production. From the "original" artwork a large-scale film negative (usually 13 x 18 cm) was made. This was retouched and strips of text were attached. The negative was then made into a positive. Finally, from the film positive the printers made the plate they would use to mechanically reproduce the photomontage. The magazine was printed with the copperplate photogravure process, which achieved a clarity of detail no other printing process could match.[42]

The end products – the printed montages from AIZ and VI – are rare but still exist. Unfortunately none of the pencil sketches have survived, and most of the preparatory artwork was also lost or destroyed, either when Heartfield fled Berlin in 1933 or when he left Prague in 1938. Some examples of artwork and film – work that was exhibited in Moscow in 1931 and in New York in 1938 and not returned to the artist until the fifties – have been preserved, however. After Heartfield's death in 1968, this work became the core of the John Heartfield Archiv, which was set up in Berlin by Gertrud Heartfield under the auspices of the Akademie der Künste of the former German Democratic Republic.[43]

Every Heartfield montage followed the sequence of artwork, film negative, film positive, magazine reproduction. At the artwork stage, however, there was considerable variation. The artwork in the Heartfield Archiv is divided into three categories: geklebt (pasted) or positiv, montages made by pasting photographic prints or positives together; negativ, images made by sandwiching negatives together in the enlarger and producing a single print from the resulting composite exposure; and inszeniert, staged montages made with a single photograph of a studio construction. One of these three terms has been penciled onto the back of each piece of preparatory artwork, probably by the artist's widow.

Most of the artwork in the Heartfield Archiv is for positiv montages like Ein gefährliches Eintopfgericht (A

dangerous hot pot; 46/34). Heartfield's original artwork is on cardboard (Fig. 3).[44] The main visual element is a photograph of an upturned Nazi helmet. About a dozen fragments of photographs showing the legs and feet of different social types, a cross section of German society under the Third Reich, were fitted with scalpel and gum into the helmet. Flames were painted in gray and black around the montaged photographs, which were retouched with the same colors. The artwork was then photographed. On the resulting film negative (29 x 39 cm), which is also preserved in the archives, all the main sections of the design – helmet, figures, and flames – were retouched with red paint to accentuate areas that would print white in the final magazine version. Light gray lettering (which would eventually print black) on thin, transparent plastic strips was lightly stuck onto the film negative. The Heartfield Archiv also has the film positive made from the negative. The artist made no further additions at this stage; both image and text correspond to the slightly reduced sepia page in AIZ.

Hitlers Programm (Hitler's program; 6/33) is another of the positiv montages for which the artwork has survived (Fig. 4).[45] Onto a piece of cardboard the artist mounted a lightly printed photograph of tenements (29.5 x 38.5 cm). In the middle he pasted a photograph of a house-painting brush (29 cm long) that was then lightly retouched with gray paint on the handle and bristles. More complicated procedures were involved in making Aufrüstung tut not! (Armament is necessary! 14/32).[46] Heartfield combined four photographs on a piece of card (Fig. 5). Three of the photographs make up the terrain that surrounds the image of two skeletons wearing boots in a mud pit, the sort of grim evidence from World War I that was suppressed during the hostilities and that Ernst Friedrich later collected and published in Krieg dem Kriege! (War against war!) in 1924. Heartfield (or one of his collaborators working under his instructions) retouched the two skeletons with white paint, and, to create the illusion of a single documentary photograph, he disguised the edges of the four fragments by, for example, adding black and gray stippling around the edge of the mud pit and painting the exposed roots of the weeds.

For Das Kreuz war noch nicht schwer genug (The cross was not yet heavy enough; 10/33), another positiv montage, the starting point was a black-and-white photographic reproduction of a painting of Christ by the Danish artist Bertel Thorwaldsen.[47] The artwork (Fig. 6) is on a card measuring 44 by 46 centimeters, which was reduced to 23.5 by 30.5 centimeters in AIZ. Heartfield painted blocks of wood and screws at each end of the cross to convert it into a swastika. He also made painted additions to Christ's gown. The Nazi figure tightening the screws is made from three photographs, but the right side of his shirt was painted. Christ's halo is painted with a luminosity that makes it the focal point of the montage.

Fig. 5. Preparatory artwork for 14/32: *Aufrüstung tut not!* (Armament is necessary!). 31 x 38.5 cm. John Heartfield Archiv, Copyright Akademie der Künste zu Berlin

Fig. 6. Preparatory artwork for 10/33: *Das Kreuz war noch nicht schwer genug* (The cross was not yet heavy enough). 44 x 46 cm.
John Heartfield Archiv, Copyright Akademie der Künste zu Berlin

Fig. 7. Preparatory artwork for 21/34: *Lenins Vision ward Wirklichkeit* (Lenin's vision became reality). John Heartfield Archiv, Copyright Akademie der Künste zu Berlin

Fig. 8. Preparatory artwork for 10/30: *Hurra, Hurra! Der Brüning-Weihnachtsmann ıst da!* (Hurrah, hurrah! Here's the Brüning Father Christmas!). John Heartfield Archiv, Copyright Akademie der Künste zu Berlin

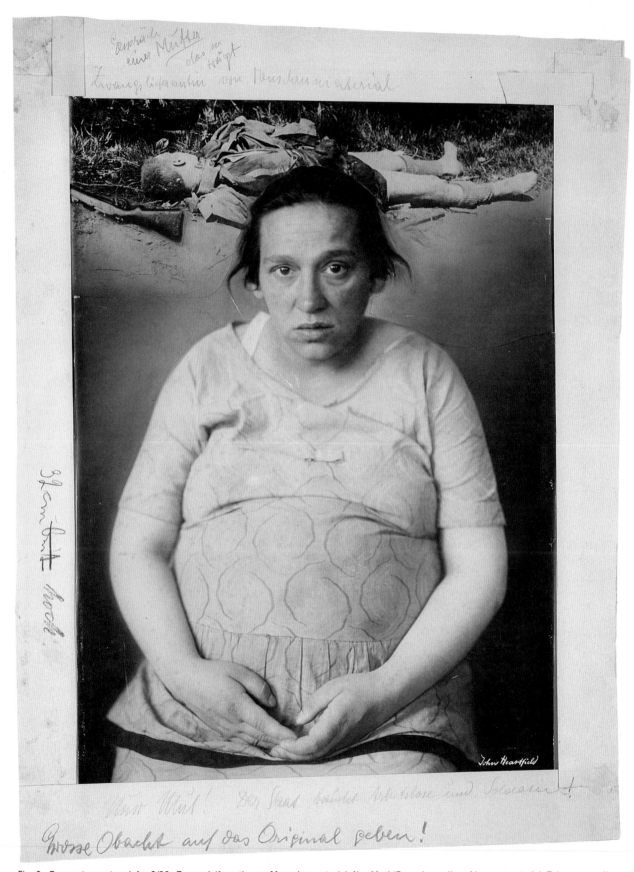

Fig. 9. Preparatory artwork for 2/30: *Zwangsleiferantin von Menschenmaterial, Nur Mut!* (Forced supplier of human material, Take courage!).
John Heartfield Archiv, Copyright Akademie der Künste zu Berlin

Heartfield rarely used the *negativ* technique to produce his montages, even though joining the images in the enlarger eliminated their edges and made the resulting montage look even more like a single photograph. Perhaps he wanted to control what he considered the most important aspect of his work — the fitting together of the images he had chosen — rather than delegating it to a photographer in the darkroom. The *negativ* technique was used for *Lenins Vision ward Wirklichkeit* (Lenin's vision became reality; 21/34) to make Lenin's giant head appear to float like a secular icon above the crowd of peasants admiring the 100,000th tractor from a factory in Stalingrad (Fig. 7). In *Alle Fäuste zu einer geballt* (All fists clenched into one; 41/34) a crowd scene of demonstrators with clenched fists was blended into a single, monumental clenched fist, a visual synecdoche for mass resistance.

Hurra, Hurra! Der Brüning-Weihnachtsmann ist da! (Hurrah, hurrah! Here's the Brüning Father Christmas! 10/30) is a staged montage. The Heartfield Archiv has a print of a photograph of a studio arrangement of a Christmas tree and presents.[48] To the traditional decorations Heartfield added ornaments adorned with swastikas and a hanging bell inscribed "Heil Hitler," and one of the presents is a policeman's truncheon.

The archive also has a later version of the artwork that corresponds more closely to what appeared in the magazine (Fig. 8).[49] The print has been cropped so that the image is framed by the trunk of the Christmas tree at the right and the truncheon along the bottom. Heartfield has painted the cap of a German Michel, who usually symbolizes stupidity, onto the head of the toy donkey and added a speech balloon with the words "Hepp Hepp" (Gee up!). The owl is hooting "Hu Hu," and a puppet hanging on the tree is saying "Juden raus" (Jews out). The truncheon and several other objects were highlighted with ink or paint. A triangle roughly covering the area between the left and top right corners was sprayed grayish white to provide a backdrop for the Herzfelde poem that was typeset and stripped in at the negative stage. In addition to these hand changes, a photograph of an advertisement for a portrait of Hitler — "the most beautiful of Christmas presents" — was pasted into the bottom left corner.

Next to the advertisement is a note in Heartfield's handwriting: "Ecke stehen lassen" (Let the edge stay), indicating that he wanted it to break out of the frame. Along the bottom he wrote, "Ecke zoll mitkommen" (The edge should come along), which meant that he wanted the strap of the truncheon to hang out of the frame. On the tracing paper that protects the artwork he wrote further instructions: "Sehr sauber halten" (Leave very clean) — referring to the grayish white area onto which the poem was to be laid. The large-format film negative for this montage has not survived, but from the finished image we can assume that the negative was retouched with red paint and that printed text was added at that stage. The image includes not only the title, the poem, and Heartfield's name but also various extra notes like the one in the right corner: "Der Hitler-Christbaumschmuck ist keine böswillige Erfindung. Die Nationalsozialisten handeln tatsächlich damit" (The Hitler Christmas-tree decoration is no malicious invention. The National Socialists actually deal in such things). From the worked-over film negative a film positive was finally made and used by the printers without further additions.

Other examples of staged montages are *Der Henker und die Gerechtigkeit* (The executioner and justice; 31/33), for which Heartfield used a plaster-of-Paris model of Justice; and *O Tannenbaum im deutschen Raum, wie krumm sind deine Äste!* (O Christmas tree in German soil, how bent are thy branches! 53/34), for which he bent the branches of an artificial Christmas tree into swastikas.

Many of Heartfield's montages do not fit so neatly into one of the three categories. In *Zwangslieferantin von Menschenmaterial, Nur Mut!* (Forced supplier of human material, Take courage! 2/30), for example, he combined a studio photograph of a pregnant working-class woman with an archival photograph from World War I of a dead young soldier (Fig. 9).[50] A similar hybrid was the basis of *Wie im Mittelalter... So im Dritten Reich* (As in the Middle Ages... So in the Third Reich; 22/34). The top panel is a photograph from a medieval church in Tübingen of a bas-relief of a man broken on the wheel; the formally similar bottom panel is a studio shot of the German actor Erwin Geschonnek posing as a man broken on the swastika. *Der Sinn von Genf* (The meaning of Geneva; 16/32) is also a combination of staged and *positiv* images: a studio shot of a dove impaled on a bayonet pasted onto an agency photograph of the League of Nations in Geneva, with the Swiss flag changed to a swastika (Fig. 10).[51]

And *Das tausendjährige Reich* (The Thousand Year Reich; 39/34) is far more than staged. The artwork has survived (Fig. 11) and shows the modifications that were made to the studio photograph.[52] Small photographs of Göring, Hitler, and steel magnate Thyssen were stuck onto individual cards. The card suits were changed or modified: money bags were painted onto the Thyssen card (to symbolize big business's support of Hitler), for example, and drops of blood were added to the hearts suit of the SA card (an allusion to the purge of SA leaders on 30 June 1934, "the Night of the Long Knives"). The swastika flag on top of the house of cards is a painted addition. The Gothic script that imitates the style of traditional skat cards was also hand painted.

Heartfield as a Party Artist

"I am for realism," Heartfield wrote in 1958. "And as a Party artist (I cannot see myself as anything else) I am for socialist realism."[53] If Heartfield saw himself as a Party artist, how his fellow Party artists and critics saw him changed over time. In the late 1920s and early 1930s the

Fig. 10. Preparatory artwork for 16/32: *Der Sinn von Genf* (The meaning of Geneva). John Heartfield Archiv, Copyright Akademie der Künste zu Berlin

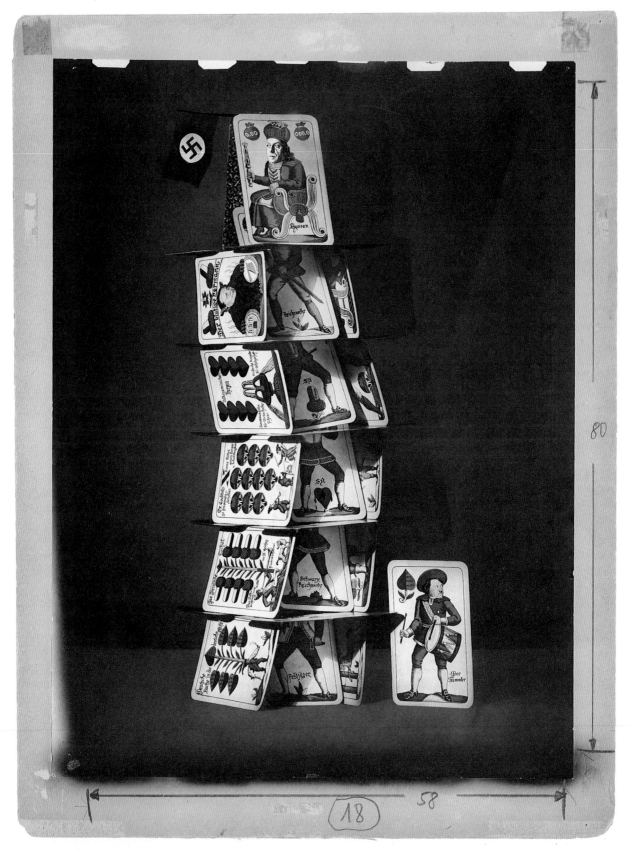

Fig. 11. Preparatory artwork for 39/34: *Das tausendjährige Reich* (The Thousand Year Reich). John Heartfield Archiv, Copyright Akademie der Künste zu Berlin

German Communist Party hailed his work as an exemplary revolutionary alternative to the increasingly widespread use of photomontage in advertising. In 1931–32 he was sympathetically received in the Soviet Union, although in the midst of increasing attacks on the artists of the October group, whose members had developed Soviet photomontage, there was some debate about the significance of his work. When he exhibited his work in Paris in 1935, it was appreciated within the novel context of the French Popular Front. Later in the thirties, especially in Moscow, some critics denounced all forms of montage, including photomontage, and those views became officially codified and enforced in the Soviet Union and its satellites during the early years of the Cold War. When Heartfield settled in East Germany in 1950, the reception was cool. Canonization came after 1956, however, and from then on his work, once again legitimized with selected, sympathetic arguments from the prewar period, was an important cultural export of the German Democratic Republic.

Weimar Germany

The Hungarian-born critic Alfred Kemény (1895–1945) was an early admirer of Heartfield's contributions to *AIZ.* As a student in Budapest Kemény had met László Moholy-Nagy, and both he and Moholy left Hungary in 1920, the year after the fall of the revolutionary government. Kemény lived first in Vienna, then in Berlin. He joined the German Communist Party in 1923, and under the pseudonym Durus he wrote art, theater, and literary reviews for the Party daily *Die Rote Fahne.* A supporter of constructivist art since the early 1920s, Kemény worked with Heartfield to found ASSO (German Association of Revolutionary Artists) in 1928. His writings on photography and photomontage appeared mainly in *Die Rote Fahne* and in the organ of the Worker Photographer movement, *Der Arbeiter-Fotograf.*[54]

"There is no question," Durus wrote in *Der Arbeiter-Fotograf* in 1931, "that as a means of agitation and propaganda, photography and film reach greater numbers of the working masses than can paintings, or even etchings and woodcuts…. The photomontage has already conquered the book jacket, the book's outer skin. Revolutionary pamphlets using photographs, and the photographic design of Heartfield's book, *Deutschland, Deutschland über alles,* have shown that books and pamphlets can be made much more lively and attractive by the inclusion of photographs in their design." He went on to warn, however, that the "technically up-to-date medium of photomontage" was "already in danger of becoming a mere vogue," and that the "seemingly apolitical appeal" of the photomontages "being turned out by the hundreds for advertising purposes" could turn "only too easily into outright propaganda for the capitalist system." He explained that

the concept "photomontage" signifies a "purely" technical procedure, the superficial coupling of details from different photographs. The recombined and newly related details are, in bourgeois photomontage as much as in proletarian-revolutionary photomontage, *parts of reality.* But while bourgeois photomontage uses photographed parts of reality to *falsify* social reality as a whole, disguising this falsification of the whole reality with the seeming *factualness* of the photographed details and thus giving the impression of true reality,… revolutionary photomontage by an "artist" (technician) of Marxist orientation brings photographic details (part of reality) into a dialectical relationship, both formally and thematically: therefore it contains the actual relationships and contradictions of social reality. Revolutionary photomontage, whose goal is ruthlessly to expose social reality, has paved the way for a completely new, previously unknown *Marxist method of artistic creation;* a method that does not start out from the pretense of the world's painterly or graphic "beauty," but from the need for political enlightenment based on the principles of historical materialism, founded on the revolutionary worldview of our age.[55]

By 1932, having seen several of Heartfield's photomontages published in *AIZ,* Durus was even more convinced of photomontage's potential as "a truly revolutionary weapon in the class struggle," as a "work of art that offers completely new opportunities – with regard to content, not just form – for uncovering *relationships, oppositions, transitions, and intersections of social reality.*" He noted, with satisfaction, that while in response to the economic crisis the "bourgeois advertising industry" was laying off photomonteurs, revolutionary publishing houses and magazines were requiring an ever greater number of them.[56]

The course for the development of "a *consciously political* proletarian photomontage," Durus continued, was set by "the very first *dadaist* works using paste and photographs (by *Heartfield, George Grosz, Hausmann, and Baader),…* despite the anarchist-individualist philosophy of their creators." The rise of German proletarian-revolutionary photomontage was, however,

> most intimately associated with the epoch-making work of the brilliant *"monteur"* John Heartfield. His works can already be considered "classic." He pioneered the use of photomontage for book jackets and in the design of political picture books. *He always focused the aesthetically effective elements of photography's "gray-scale structures," of planar division, of combinations of script and photography, on maximizing the political content….* In place of a bourgeois aesthetic we have the sharpest, strongest, most penetrating political militancy of a no longer "neutral" art…. *As a creator of satirical photomon-*

tages, [Heartfield] is unsurpassed. His satirical contributions to the *AIZ* – the "Tiger," the "Cabbage Head," "Solar Eclipse on the 'Liberated' Rhine," "6 Million Nazi Voters: Fodder for a Big Mouth" [2/31, 1/30, 6/30, 7/30], to mention just a few – are among the *most significant satirical creations of our time*.[57]

Durus noted the "high artistic and political quality" of the works of other ASSO artists who had been inspired by Heartfield. (The ten ASSO artists whom Domela had given their own section at the *Fotomontage* exhibition in Berlin in 1931 criticized him for allotting so little space to someone of Heartfield's importance.)[58] That such quality had not yet been achieved by more than a minority of the German worker photographers, Durus asserted, was merely one of the "occasional setbacks" experienced by proletarian photomontage, as was the case with "many other problems awaiting our solution."[59]

The framework for Durus's views in the late twenties and early thirties was the Comintern's strident "Class Against Class" strategy. Durus argued for a corresponding class-based art. And he assumed that photography and photomontage – capable of signaling the real more persuasively than any other form of visual representation – were particularly valuable components of an emerging militant proletarian visual culture.

The Soviet Union

Heartfield was in the Soviet Union from the summer of 1931 until the spring of 1932.[60] His visit coincided with the end of Stalin's first Five Year Plan, a socioeconomic revolution aimed at developing heavy industry and collective agriculture. Heartfield enthusiastically supported the construction of "Socialism in One Country" and viewed his own art as an attempt to defend the Soviet Union and extend its influence. He was therefore keenly interested in meeting the members of the October group, avant-garde artists who were committed to new kinds of applied or productivist art.

In the "Declaration" that marked its founding in 1928, coinciding with the start of the first Five Year Plan, the October group insisted that all the arts had to define themselves at the front of the socialist cultural revolution. For visual artists, this meant abandoning easel painting and experimenting with "polygraphic" approaches (comparable to Heartfield's work) to create an art of mass mobilization. Easel painting informed by nineteenth-century figurative ideas, and thus also the position of the rival organization, the ACHR (Association of Revolutionary Artists), had become irrelevant. By 1931 October's 500 members – from a range of fields that included applied arts, graphic design, photography, and film – amounted to a roll call of the Soviet avant-garde.[61]

In 1930 Heartfield had worked with the group's secretary, the artist A. I. Gutnov (1906–), to organize October's first exhibition in Berlin, which included architecture and photography and was designed to be a provocative alternative to the exhibition of Soviet easel painting that had just opened there. Gutnov in turn helped Heartfield with his campaign work for the German Communist Party in the parliamentary elections of 1930. (One of the plans they devised together was tying two sheep labeled "We vote National Socialist" to the Brandenburg Gate for a week.)[62] Heartfield also knew one of the most important writers in the October group, Sergei Tretjakov (1892–1939), who had visited Germany in early 1931 to lecture on productivist writing. Herzfelde's firm, Malik Verlag, became Tretjakov's German publisher, and Heartfield designed the dustjackets for *Feld-Herren* (Field commanders; 1931) and *Den Schi-Chua* (Tan Shih-hua; 1932).[63]

When Heartfield came to the Soviet Union in mid-1931, it was Tretjakov who served as his guide. Often with Tretjakov along as interpreter, he met some of the key October artists, among them Gustav Klucis, El Lissitzky, and Alexander Rodchenko. (The portrait of Heartfield by Rodchenko that *AIZ* published in 1934 [see Fig. 12] was taken during this trip.)[64] While in the Soviet Union Heartfield mounted solo exhibitions and participated in group shows. He also worked on the illustrated *USSR in Construction* – visiting the Baku oilfields with the editors and photographers for a special issue on oil to gain the first-hand experience productivists encouraged – and he contributed to the productivist campaign for the "deprofessionalization" of art by running photomontage workshops for diverse groups, including Red Army officers.

Nothing in the lecture Heartfield delivered at the Polygraphic Institute in Moscow in 1931 would have been unacceptable to the October group members and sympathizers in his audience. They would have found his political rhetoric conventional and his generalizations about photomontage uncontroversial: the camera was objective and therefore its products had greater credibility than any other form of visual representation. The art of photomontage involved the combination of these products to create targeted messages. Because of the photograph's reputation as objective visual data, photomontage had great agit-prop potential.

In his lecture, which remains the most complete statement of his aims and objectives while he was working for *AIZ*, Heartfield explained that for him, as for Durus, Germany was a site of class war between bourgeois and proletarian, with artists in one camp or the other. Capitalism was in an extreme state of decay (a reference to the "World Slump" of 1929), and this was reflected in its art. While capitalism was in decay, a new society, and a new, uniquely powerful art, was being built in the Soviet Union. In such a state of emergency, the tasks of the revolutionary artist were threefold: to win over intelligent artists from the enemy camp; to reveal to the masses the true nature of the class enemy; and to

Fig. 12. John Heartfield, 1931 or 1932. Photograph by Alexander Rodchenko. From *AIZ* 13, no. 17 (26 April 1934), p. 272

encourage the masses in schools, factories, and social institutions to use photomontage as a weapon. Heartfield suggested that many bourgeois artists were frightened by the development of photography. Expressionism, he claimed, could be understood as a flight from the mechanical reproduction of photography. But it was the duty of the proletarian artist to courageously confront photography's "technical eye." Photography was a mechanical medium and photomontage involved working with its products to create a unified whole. The idea of "shooting a film" was inappropriate. Instead one had to talk about "montaging a film"; in other words, it had to be designed or constructed. That the bourgeoisie was hostile to proletarian photomontage was proof of its power. It had tried to use photomontage for its own ends with only colorless results, for photomontage was most effective as a weapon of revolutionary artists.[65]

Heartfield made no specific reference in his speech to either his own work or that of particular Soviet artists, and he diplomatically refrained from taking a position in the debate then being waged among the October artists over the history of photomontage and his own role in that history.[66] For although most of those who heard him speak in Moscow may have agreed with what he said, not all of the October group members shared Durus's and Tretjakov's enthusiasm for his work.

Heartfield's main defender in the debate was the eminent art historian Alexei Fedorov-Davydov (1900–1969). For Fedorov-Davydov, as for Durus and Tretjakov, the history of political photomontage began with Berlin dada. Heartfield, he said, had emerged from that movement, informed as it was by the "ideology of the anarchistic petit bourgeoisie," with a simpler, more laconic type of photomontage that served the revolutionary proletariat. Not so, according to Heartfield's detractors, the most vociferous of whom was Gustav Klucis, a graphic artist, collagist, and photomonteur. Klucis insisted that political photomontage was an exclusively Soviet achievement, his own work *Dynamic City* of 1919 being a key landmark. According to Klucis, Berlin dadaism was merely parasitic on earlier work in American advertising, and there had been nothing original in the German developments after dada. Rather, it was Soviet artists who had influenced the artists of the German Communist Party, including Heartfield. "I personally know Heartfield's work well and value it highly," he said, "but I believe we can learn very little from him."[67]

Using arguments that paralleled those of Durus and Tretjakov, Fedorov-Davydov acknowledged Soviet successes but said that much could be learned from Heartfield, especially from the way in which he used the technique to display the reality behind appearances, often with satirical means. He asserted that Heartfield's development of the satirical potential of photomontage was an innovation that Soviet artists ought to emulate.

As evidence of Heartfield's originality, Fedorov-Davydov offered a photomontage he created for the cover of a 1928 issue of the German Communist daily *Die Rote Fahne*. The cover anticipates the sort of work Heartfield was to do for *AIZ;* it shows Social Democratic leader Hermann Müller grinning good-naturedly at the miniscule battleship he holds in his hand.

The debate was not merely academic. All photomontage was increasingly under attack in the Soviet Union for its alleged antirealism, and even a sympathetic critic like Fedorov-Davydov noticed "formalistic" and "mechanical" weaknesses in Heartfield's work. All sides in the October group dispute agreed that photography, because of its documentary credentials, surpassed all art forms as an effective agitational tool. But Klucis, who was particularly concerned with developing agitational posters, defended a type of photomontage that was dissonant and antiorganic, and in which photography was merely one element that clashed with color, text, or other graphic details according to the principle of maximum contrast. Heartfield, however, placed greater emphasis on organicism, illusionistic space, and visual narrative – in short, features associated with figurative easel painting in the Soviet Union. Heartfield's admirers perhaps saw the development of a Heartfield tradition in the Soviet Union as a way of fending off attacks from the realist camp; for Klucis, this amounted to surrender to the enemy.

After the October group's dissolution in 1932, Tretjakov continued to champion Heartfield and his accomplishments. In general, Tretjakov's ideas paralleled those of his artist colleagues in the October group. He believed that writing based on the nineteenth-century realist novel, with its emphasis on plot and the psychology of individuals, was as anachronistic as easel painting. He thought that writers should experiment with new types of literary documentation just as artists were experimenting with polygraphy. (He was also a keen photographer.) As a journalist, Tretjakov was particularly excited about the newspaper as an arena for the revolutionary writer, permitting new kinds of collaboration that would destroy traditional distinctions between creators and consumers and between so-called high and low artistic genres. He claimed that there was no need to wait for a "red Tolstoy" because a "collective Tolstoy" – the Soviet press – already existed.[68]

Tretjakov also wrote books intended to demonstrate new types of documentary writing. For *Feld-Herren* (Field commanders; 1931), on the collectivization of agriculture, he lived and worked on a commune. For *Den Schi-Chua* (Tan Shih-hua; 1932), which he described as a "bio-interview," he talked with one his students at the National University in Peking for four to six hours a day over a period of six months. He then "shaped" the raw material from the interviews, in effect using montage principles to edit and organize what would otherwise have been a mass of incoherent data.

His talks with artists when he toured Europe in the early thirties provided the source material for Tretjakov's *Menschen eines Scheiterhaufens* (The funeral pyre generation; an allusion to the Nazi book burnings of 1933), published in Moscow in 1936. The book is a collection of portraits of artists with documentary interests similar to his own, all of whom believed, as he did, that the complexities of the present required the dismantling of conventional forms of representation. Bertolt Brecht, the director Erwin Piscator, the dramatist Friedrich Wolf, the musician Hanns Eisler, the writer Theodor Plivier — all Germans — and the Dutch filmmaker Joris Ivens are represented, and there is a chapter on Heartfield, affectionately titled "Johnny."[69]

That same year, 1936, Tretjakov published the first monograph on Heartfield. Heartfield himself regarded Tretjakov's study as the best exposition of his work. Tretjakov's aim was not only to demonstrate further what he called a new literature of facts but also to present to a Soviet audience an example of the international documentary current based on montage principles that traversed the traditional arts. For his text he drew on shorthand notes he had made while serving as Heartfield's guide during his visit to the Soviet Union in 1931–32, and he also transcribed Heartfield's lecture at the Polygraphic Institute. The book was designed by Solomon Telingater (1903–1969), an October group member who had worked with El Lissitzky. In addition to Heartfield's montages, it included documentary photographs of Heartfield in the Soviet Union, running a workshop, for example. The aim was to make a new kind of collaborative art monograph, productivist in form as well as content.

"It is important to note," Tretjakov wrote, "that a photomontage need not necessarily be a montage of photos. No: it can be photo and text, photo and color, photo and drawing." And, he went on, it is far more than simply a scissors-and-paste technique.[70] He quoted Heartfield's remark that "a photograph can, by the addition of an unimportant spot of color, become a photomontage, a work of art of a special kind." He offered as an example Heartfield's dustjacket for Maxim Gorky's *Der 9. Januar* (published by Malik Verlag in 1926), on which a black-and-white photograph shows cossacks breaking up a demonstration and a spot of red color, dripping from the "9" in the title, succinctly conveys their methods. Like Durus, Tretjakov differentiated Heartfield's mature work from both dadaism and the "formalism" of Moholy or Tschichold. Unlike Durus, however, he was willing to use Heartfield's work to expose what he saw as the shortcomings of Soviet montage. The efforts of Soviet artists, he said, were in general looser, more schematic, and less concrete than the "photo epigrams" Heartfield created for *AIZ*. He especially admired *Zwangslieferantin von Menschenmaterial, Nur Mut!* (Forced supplier of

human material, Take courage! 2/30) — "the most dialectical and economical of all" — and *Krieg und Leichen – die letzte Hoffnung der Reichen* (War and corpses – the last hope of the rich; 1/32), with its distinctive use of illusionism. The dynamic interaction of images and text in *Der Sinn des Hitlergrusses. Motto: Millionen stehen hinter Mir!* (The meaning of the Hitler salute. Motto: Millions stand behind me! 11/32) summed up, for Tretjakov, everything that Soviet artists were *not* doing.

France

When the German and Austrian governments succeeded in censoring Heartfield's contribution to the exhibition of anti-Nazi caricatures in Prague in 1934 (see 18/34), they in effect created an international solidarity campaign in his defense.[71] One early expression of that support was an invitation to exhibit 150 of his photomontages in Paris in the spring of 1935. The exhibition, Heartfield's first in Paris, was organized by the Association des Ecrivains et Artistes Révolutionnaires (AEAR), the French equivalent of ASSO.[72] The venue was the Maison de la Culture in Paris, which had opened in April 1935 as part of what was to become a national network of meeting places for the AEAR and kindred pro-Communist organizations. The aim was to encourage a dialogue between leftist intellectuals and manual workers that would lead, it was hoped, to a renovated culture.

Louis Aragon (1897–1983), secretary of AEAR and one of its founders, opened the forum held in conjunction with the exhibition with an address entitled "Heartfield and Revolutionary Beauty."[73] Aragon, a leading figure in the Paris dada movement and well known for his surrealist writings in the 1920s, joined the French Communist Party in 1927 along with André Breton, Paul Eluard, Benjamin Péret, and other surrealists. The relationship between surrealism and Communism was to be long and complex, but by 1932 Aragon had found the two incompatible. He broke with the surrealist movement and became an enthusiastic advocate of Party cultural politics.[74] Aragon's speech on Heartfield paid homage to a Communist artist whom he considered "the prototype of the anti-fascist artist."[75] But it was also a continuation of his attempts to influence the controversies over the meaning of socialist realism.

In 1934 Aragon had attended the first Soviet Writers' Congress in Moscow and participated in the debate over socialist realism.[76] No one at the congress disagreed that socialist realism was the best way of fighting Fascism on the cultural front, but there was a lack of unanimity about just what socialist realism was. Aragon argued that Communism and avant-garde art and literature were not incompatible. How he elaborated his version of the new policy on returning to France is conveyed in *Pour un réalisme socialiste* (1935), a selection of interventions that includes his Heartfield speech.

The Heartfield exhibition and Aragon's speech anticipated the agenda of the International Congress for the Defense of Culture in Paris in June 1935.[77] Organized by the AEAR, the congress brought together writers from thirty-seven countries. The AEAR's purpose was to mobilize these artists against the Fascists' threat to the right of free expression and in defense of what was termed cultural humanism. Aragon viewed the Facist attempt to censor an artist of Heartfield's importance, and the AEAR's bold response, as a perfect illustration of the issues to be debated at the congress.

In 1936 Aragon helped organize and took part in another AEAR-sponsored debate about realism in art and literature, held at the Maison de la Culture. The opinions aired at the debate were published the same year as *La querelle du réalisme*.[78] In his contribution, Aragon asserted that painters "have not understood that the photographic experience is a human experience which they cannot neglect, and that the new realism which will come, whether they wish it or not, will see in photography not an enemy, but an auxiliary of painting. It is just this which men like Max Ernst and John Heartfield, in the pictorial avant-garde, sensed vaguely when they tried, in various ways, to incorporate the photograph into the picture."[79] Aragon was referring here to the dada provocations of Ernst and Heartfield. By the mid-thirties, he was dismissive of Ernst's move in a surrealist direction, but he felt that Heartfield's trajectory was of great significance for a politically relevant, realist art.

Aragon's arguments were framed politically by the French Popular Front, a coalition of left and center parties, including the Communists, that was launched in July 1935 in answer to the Fascist threat and was in power from June 1936 to October 1938. "Whether one likes it or not," Aragon told his colleagues at the Maison de la Culture in 1936,

> in art and in literature, the cardinal problem – the open wound – that which stirs the tempest on all sides; in short, the only issue over which, in these days of the Popular Front, one can bring the artists of the period ardently to grips, as this evening, is, in the case of both writers and painters, the question of realism. I want to see in this fact the symbol, the prophecy, the herald of the victory of those social forces which combined against the "two hundred families."[80]

Heartfield's political commitment and the subject matter and style of his work precisely fit Aragon's definition of realism. Heartfield's art, he said,

> is art in Lenin's sense, because it is a weapon in the revolutionary struggle of the Proletariat.... Master of a technique of his own invention – a technique which uses for its palette the whole range of impressions

from the world of actuality – never imposing a rein on his spirit, blending appearances at will, he has no guide other than dialectical materialism, none but the reality of the historical process which he translates into black and white with the rage of combat. John Heartfield *today knows how to salute beauty*. And if the visitor who goes through the show of the Maison de la Culture finds the ancient shadow of dada in these photomontages of the last few years – in this Schacht with a gigantic collar [14/34], in this cow which is cutting itself up with a knife [48/34], in this anti-Semitic dialogue of two birds [23/34?] – let him stop at this dove stuck on a bayonet in front of the Palace of the League of Nations [16/32], or at this Nazi Christmas tree whose branches are distorted to form swastikas [53/34]; he will find not only the heritage of dada but also that of centuries of painting. There are still lifes by Heartfield, such as this scale tipped by the weight of a revolver, or von Papen's wallet, and this scaffolding of Hitlerian cards [36/34, 33/34, 39/34], which inevitably make me think of Chardin. Here, with only scissors and paste, the artist has surpassed the best endeavors of modern art, with the cubists, who are on that lost pathway of quotidian mystery. Simple objects, like apples for Cézanne in earlier days, and the guitar for Picasso. But here there is also *meaning,* and meaning hasn't disfigured beauty.[81]

Photography, Aragon pronounced, had become "more revealing and more denunciatory than painting."[82] In the future the photograph would be the painter's "documentary aid in the same sense in which, in our day, files of daily newspapers are indispensable to the novelist.... The painting of tomorrow will use the photographic eye as it has used the human eye."[83] In Aragon's view, Heartfield was the potential savior of realist painting, replenishing exhausted artistic traditions with his audacious, painterly uses of press photographs. It was a view that had little influence at the time but was later reactivated in the German Democratic Republic.

The German Democratic Republic

Heartfield settled in the newly founded German Democratic Republic in 1950 and lived there until his death in 1968.[84] During the first years after his return he was professionally "marginalized." His difficulties were linked to official suspicion of those emigrés who had gone west rather than east in the thirties. Yet others with comparable interests and experiences were treated more sympathetically: Bertolt Brecht was allowed to create the Berliner Ensemble; Wieland Herzfelde was made a professor of journalism in Leipzig. Heartfield's problems were compounded, it has been suggested, by his association with the publisher of *AIZ,* Willi Münzenberg.[85] In 1939 Münzenberg had broken with Moscow over the

Nazi-Soviet Pact, and the following year he was murdered, probably by an agent of Stalin. In the German Democratic Republic Münzenberg's achievements were omitted from the history books, and his former colleagues were treated with wariness.

The neglect of Heartfield during the early fifties was also due to the influence of Andrei Zhdanov (1896–1948), the Soviet politician in charge of imposing cultural orthodoxy in the Soviet Union and its allies immediately after the Second World War. Zhdanov condemned avant-garde art as "formalism" and linked it to "cosmopolitanism" and "American cultural barbarism." This crude codification of the socialist realist positions that had evolved in the thirties in opposition to Fascism came to be called "Zhdanovism."[86] In France in the fifties Louis Aragon was the most prestigious Zhdanovist, now condemning the avant-garde art he had attempted to present within a socialist realist framework in the mid-thirties.[87] In the German Democratic Republic Georg Lukács (1885–1971) was the main authority invoked to attack "formalism."

Lukács's views had emerged in the late thirties in a debate among contributors to *Das Wort,* a Moscow-based German-language literary magazine that provided a forum for anti-Fascist emigrés.[88] Lukács insisted that avant-garde techniques in literature, such as montage, documentation, and the baring of devices, encouraged a fragmentary, subjectivist view of the world. Only Fascism could benefit from the fatalism and irrationalism that ensued. He argued for the continuing relevance of the nineteenth-century realist novel. Balzac and Tolstoy and other nineteenth-century novelists, he believed, had clearly revealed the abstract connections that underlie appearances, and adapting their methods to modern circumstances was the most responsible way in which an author could contribute to the defeat of Fascism. In short, he was making a case for a revolutionary culture that cauterized all traces of the avant-garde and drew inspiration from classic bourgeois traditions.

Lukács's references to photomontage were brief and dismissive. He conceded that photomontage could have the effect of a good joke and could even on occasion become a powerful political weapon, probably a begrudging reference to Heartfield. But he claimed that photomontage was generally incapable of making any significant statement about the world because its basic element, the photograph, was only a record of surface appearances and revealed nothing of society's hidden mechanisms. In this sense, photography and photomontage had a built-in naturalism that precluded the attainment of the cognitive insights that distinguished the greatest realism. (Lukács frequently used the term "photographic" in a pejorative sense when attacking literary naturalism.) "The details may be dazzlingly colorful in their diversity," he said of photomontage, "but the whole will never be more than unrelieved gray on gray. After all,

a puddle can never be more than dirty water, even though it may contain rainbow tints."[89]

An outcast professionally and also suffering from poor health, Heartfield kept going during those early years of the fifties through the support of his brother and friends. One of his staunchest defenders was Bertolt Brecht.[90] When Heartfield asked Brecht for a reference in support of his request for hospital treatment and a pension, Brecht wrote an eloquent statement that is now frequently invoked as an authoritative confirmation of Heartfield's "classic" status:

> John Heartfield is one of the most important European artists. He works in a field that he created himself, the field of photomontage. Through this new form of art he exercises social criticism. Steadfastly on the side of the working class, he unmasked the forces of the Weimar Republic driving toward war; driven into exile he fought against Hitler. The works of this great artist, which mainly appeared in the workers' press, are regarded as classics by many, including the author of these lines.[91]

Brecht's diplomacy is striking. He lauded Heartfield as the inventor of photomontage and emphasized his proletarian anti-Fascist credentials. Notably absent was any comment on the controversy about photomontage as an appropriate technique for revolutionary art.

Stalin died in 1953, and in 1956 Khrushchev made his famous attack on Stalin at the Twentieth Party Congress of the Soviet Communist Party. Cultural liberalization in the German Democratic Republic resulted in a more sympathetic appraisal of the revolutionary avant-garde. Heartfield was nominated by Brecht to the Akademie der Künste in 1956 and was accepted.

In 1957 Heartfield had his first official exhibition under the auspices of the Akademie der Künste. In the exhibition catalogue, the writer Bodo Uhse (1904–1963) condemned those who dismissed photomontage as "formalist." He had in mind not only contemporary critics, but also Lukács.[92] Uhse condemned the documentary current of the twenties and early thirties that had been the target of Lukács and his allies. But he did not explore Heartfield's association with that current, especially through his friendship with Tretjakov – anathema to Lukács – and other members of the October group. Instead, he emphasized Heartfield's premodern roots, linking him to artists such as Hogarth, Goya, and Daumier who had combined interests in social criticism and mechanically reproduced art. Uhse also cited with approval Aragon's claim that in the mid-thirties Heartfield was replenishing, rather than challenging, painting traditions. This kind of interpretation made Heartfield ideal for export during the continuing Cold War of the sixties: against the abstract art of the capitalist West, the German Democratic Republic pitched an artist who was avant-garde and traditional, a twentieth-century Daumier. Heartfield went on to receive an honorary professorship (1960), a peace prize (1961), and the Karl Marx Order (1967).

With Heartfield's cooperation, Wieland Herzfelde published *John Heartfield: Leben und Werk* in Dresden in 1962. New editions appeared in 1971, 1976, and 1986. The book, produced mainly for export to the West, included many revisions of Heartfield's magazine work of the thirties. In his introduction to the 1976 edition, Herzfelde explained:

> Like my brother, I am not and have never been interested in achieving lexical perfection. What we actually did was to make a *selection* according to personal and political criteria. What mattered to us, as stressed in the first edition and repeated in the conclusion to the second edition, was "to offer inspiration for what must happen today and tomorrow, so that the earth will become, and will remain, habitable."[93]

Many montages that were originally responses to the politics of the thirties were adapted to a new situation in which the United States and its ally, the Federal Republic of Germany, were viewed as the threat to world peace. The postwar revisions often retained the prewar dates of the first versions, and these same curious hybrids were frequently included in the exhibitions of Heartfield's work that toured the world in the sixties. In the adaptation of *Der Sinn von Genf* (The meaning of Geneva; 16/32), for example, which is dated 1960, the photograph of the League of Nations in Geneva with a Fascist flag flying above it was replaced by painted flames, and the subtitle "Where capital lives, peace cannot live!" became the slogan "Niemals wieder!" (Never again!).[94] A specific attack on the League had become a

more free-floating warning of the threat to peace posed by the enemies of the German Democratic Republic − the United States and its West German allies. Similarly, the prewar version of *Gleiche Brüder, gleiche Mörder* (Like brothers, like murderers; 29/33) is a comparison of atrocities in Hitler's Germany and Mussolini's Italy, while the postwar montage, still dated 1933, that appears in Herzfelde's book is designed to signal the continuing danger of a Fascist revival in the Federal Republic of Germany.[95] In the original version a quote from a news report informs the reader that the Italian Fascist Party had a prize dagger presented to Hitler's representative, Rudolf Hess. The image shows Nazi leader Julius Streicher standing on a corpse as an Italian Blackshirt presents him with a dagger and tells him, "You deserve the dagger! − You have surpassed us in assassination." In *Leben und Werk* the Blackshirt and all the original text were dropped from the montage. Streicher and the corpse remain, with a new title, *Ein Pangermane* (A Pan-German), and the warning "The womb from which that crept is still fertile."

John Heartfield died in 1968. One of his final works, cosigned with his brother, was an updating of *Mahnung* (Warning; 26/37). The original 1937 version shows a cinema audience watching a newsreel of Japanese atrocities in China and is captioned: "Today you still see the war in other countries on film. But know this: if you don't unite to defend yourselves, tomorrow it will kill you too!" In the 1967 version the image and title remain the same, but the supporting text now warns the viewer about the contemporary situation in Vietnam.[96] To the end, Heartfield remained the Party artist, determined to use his art as a political weapon, even if this often meant recycling ideas from his most creative period.

NOTES

1. On Heartfield's contribution to this exhibition, including previously unpublished photographs of his room, see Patzwall, "Zur Rekonstruktion des Heartfield-Raums." Mellor, *Germany, the New Photography, 1927–33,* is the most convenient introduction to the New Photography.

2. The catalogue, *Fotomontage,* lists the artists represented in the exhibition and includes essays by Cesar Domela and Gustav Klucis.

3. See Lemoine, "Merz, Futura, DIN et cicéro," and *Ring neuer Werbegestalter.*

4. For a good introduction to their work, see Neumann, "De l'enseignement du Bauhaus."

5. A selection of key documents relating to the October group is in Gaßner and Gillen, *Zwischen Revolutionskunst und Sozialistischem Realismus,* pp. 172–263. See also Leclanche-Boulé, *Typographies et photomontages constructivistes en U.R.S.S.*

6. The organization is the subject of the catalogue *Revolution und Realismus.*

7. See *Alice Lex-Nerlinger / Oskar Nerlinger.*

8. For John Heartfield's biography, see Töteberg, *John Heartfield;* and Michael Krejsa and Petra Albrecht, "Biografische Dokumentation," in *John Heartfield* (1991), pp. 388–415. The richest collection of documents relating to all aspects of Heartfield's life and work is März, *John Heartfield.*

9. For the history of Malik Verlag, see Herzfelde, *Der Malik-Verlag, 1916–1947.*

10. Tschichold, *Die neue Typographie,* p. 228.

11. For Heartfield and Berlin dada, see Adkins, "Der Sträfling."

12. Klingender, "Diskussion mit John Heartfield," reprinted in März, *John Heartfield,* p. 60.

13. Walter Benjamin, "The Author as Producer" (Paris, 1934), in Benjamin, *Understanding Brecht,* p. 94.

14. For an introduction to their work in *Neue Linie,* see Lusk, *Montagen ins Blaue,* pp. 174–89.

15. Sample pages are in Lissitzky-Küppers, *El Lissitzky,* pp. 170–83.

16. Brecht in *AIZ* 10, no. 41 (1931).

17. Willmann, *Geschichte der Arbeiter-Illustrierten Zeitung, 1921–1938,* reprints many pages from the magazine and provides an introductory history. Willmann underplays Willi Münzenberg's role. His history is treated sympathetically by his companion, Babette Gross, in *Willi Münzenberg: A Political Biography.*

18. Münzenberg, "Tasks and Objectives" (1931), in Mellor, *Germany, the New Photography, 1927–33,* p. 51.

19. On the United Front in Germany, see Fowkes, *Communism in Germany,* especially pp. 80–90, 130–37.

20. Quoted in Palmier, *Weimar en exil,* vol. 1, p. 291.

21. See ibid., pp. 450–73.

22. The figures involve guesswork, although the dramatic contraction after the move to Prague seems beyond dispute. The varying estimates are discussed in *Ästhetik und Kommunikation,* no. 10 (January 1973), p. 71 (a special issue on *AIZ* and Worker Photography).

23. For information on and reprints from the movement's magazine, see Büthe et al., *Der Arbeiter-Fotograf.*

24. Höllering, "Fotomontage" (1928), translated in Phillips, *Photography in the Modern Era,* pp. 130–31.

25. Durus, "Fotomontage als Waffe im Klassenkampf," translated in ibid., pp. 204–6.

26. See Beetham, *Marxists in Face of Fascism.* Particularly relevant is the section "The Communist International: From 'Social-Fascism' to Popular Front," pp. 149–86.

27. Quoted in Mellor, *Germany, the New Photography, 1927–33,* p. 51.

28. Letter from John Heartfield to Wieland Herzfelde, 5 May 1945, cited in März, *John Heartfield,* pp. 417–18.

29. Herzfelde, *John Heartfield* (1962), p. 378.

30. Hausmann, "Fotomontage," translated in Phillips, *Photography in the Modern Era,* pp. 178–81.

31. *AIZ* 13, no. 17 (26 April 1934), p. 272. For more of the quote, see 18/34.

32. "Hitler an der Festtafel der Schwerindustrie," *AIZ* 11, no. 7 (1932), p. 147.

33. Benjamin, "Brecht's *Threepenny Novel,*" in Benjamin, *Understanding Brecht,* pp. 83–84.

34. Stallybrass and White, *Politics and Poetics of Transgression,* p. 44.

35. For a discussion of the "political bestiary" in the history of cartooning, see Gombrich, "Cartoonist's Armoury," in Gombrich, *Meditations on a Hobby Horse,* pp. 127–42, especially pp. 136–38.

36. The contrast of scales is also stressed by Gombrich (ibid., pp. 141–42).

37. Bakhtin, *Rabelais and His World,* pp. 19–20.

38. Heartfield in Rasch and Rasch, *Gefesselter Blick,* p. 53.

39. Letter from John Heartfield to Wieland Herzfelde, 22 August 1939, Wieland Herzfelde Archiv, file 24/3.

40. Ibid., file 26. The widow sought legal support for the view that Heartfield was the sole creator of the *AIZ* montages signed with his name, although she was willing to concede that any work done after 1950, when the brothers were reunited in the German Democratic Republic, belonged to both of them. Herzfelde, however, claimed equal credit for the thirties work. He conceded that no legally binding documents existed to support his claim, but stressed that he and his brother were lifetime artistic and political partners who never needed contracts. Both sides in the dispute, however, seemed to be arguing from a traditional notion of creativity that does not really apply in this case.

41. See Reiss, "Als ich mit Heartfield zusammenarbeitete," pp. 188–91.

42. For a detailed discussion of the printing process, see "Johnny montiert," in Siepmann, *Montage,* pp. 270–81.

43. Materials relating to the setting up of the archive are in the Wieland Herzfelde Archiv, file 26.

44. John Heartfield Archiv, inv. no. 461. The film negative and film positive have not been given inventory numbers.

45. Ibid., inv. no. 476.

46. Ibid., inv. no. 1827.

47. Ibid., inv. no. 418.

48. Ibid., inv. no. 1878.
49. Ibid., inv. no. 491.
50. Ibid., inv. no. 514.
51. Ibid., inv. no. 421.
52. Ibid., inv. no. 2182.
53. Quoted in März, *John Heartfield*, p. 459.
54. For a list of Durus's relevant writings, see the Bibliography.
55. Durus, "Fotomontage, Fotogramm," translated in Phillips, *Photography in the Modern Era*, pp. 182–84.
56. Durus, "Fotomontage als Waffe im Klassenkampf," translated in ibid., pp. 204–5.
57. Ibid., pp. 205–6.
58. See *Die Welt am Abend* (Berlin), 19 May 1931, cited in März, *John Heartfield*, pp. 177–78.
59. Durus, "Fotomontage als Waffe im Klassenkampf," translated in Phillips, *Photography in the Modern Era*, p. 206.
60. Gaßner, "Heartfields Moskauer Lehrzeit," offers the most detailed investigation of Heartfield's Soviet trip.
61. See Gaßner and Gillen, *Zwischen Revolutionskunst und Sozialistischem Realismus*, pp. 180–83; and also Phillips, *Photography in the Modern Era*, p. 283.
62. Gaßner and Gillen, *Zwischen Revolutionskunst und Sozialistischem Realismus*, pp. 189–90; Gaßner, "Heartfields Moskauer Lehrzeit," p. 303.
63. For a German introduction to Tretjakov's writings, see Mierau, *Sergej Tretjakow: Lyrik, Dramatik, Prosa*, and Mierau, *Sergej Tretjakow: Gesichter der Avantgarde*. Little has been translated into English, but Tretjakov's *Chinese Testament: The Autobiography of Tan Shih-hua* (London: Victor Gollancz, 1934) conveys some idea of what Tretjakov meant by a "literature of facts."
64. On the article that the portrait accompanied, see 18/34.
65. The lecture, transcribed by Tretjakov, is most conveniently found in März, *John Heartfield*, pp. 274–75.
66. The debate is discussed in detail in Gaßner, "Heartfields Moskauer Lehrzeit."
67. German translations of the responses of Klucis and Fedorov-Davydov are in *Wem gehört die Welt*, pp. 248–49.
68. Tretjakov, "Der neue Lew Tolstoi" (1927), in Mierau, *Sergej Tretjakow: Lyrik, Dramatik, Prosa*, pp. 191–96.
69. For a German translation of "Johnny," see Mierau, *Sergej Tretjakow: Lyrik, Dramatik, Prosa*, pp. 302–19; and Mierau, *Sergej Tretjakow: Gesichter der Avantgarde*, pp. 137–52.
70. A German translation of Tretjakov's text is found in März, *John Heartfield*, pp. 291–315. To appreciate Telingater's contribution as a designer, it is necessary to look at the original Moscow edition of 1936.
71. Documents relating to the scandal are found in März, *John Heartfield*, pp. 331–50.
72. For further information on the AEAR, which existed from 1932 to 1936, and its house journal, see Klein, *Commune*.
73. The English translation is in Phillips, *Photography in the Modern Era*, pp. 60–67.
74. See Lewis, *Politics of Surrealism*, especially chaps. 6 and 7, which deal specifically with the controversies around Aragon and socialist realism.
75. Aragon, "Heartfield et la beauté révolutionnaire," translated in Phillips, *Photography in the Modern Era*, p. 65.
76. Robin, *Réalisme socialiste*, provides an exhaustive analysis of the Moscow congress.
77. The congress is described in detail in Palmier, *Weimar en exil*, vol. 1, pp. 484–92.
78. The complete debates are found in Fauchereau, *Querelle du réalisme*.
79. Aragon, untitled essay, in Fauchereau, *Querelle du réalisme*, translated in Phillips, *Photography in the Modern Era*, p. 75.
80. Ibid., pp. 68–69.
81. Aragon, "Heartfield et la beauté révolutionnaire," translated in ibid., pp. 65–66.
82. Aragon, untitled contribution to *Querelle du réalisme*, translated in ibid., p. 73.
83. Ibid., p. 75. See also Aragon, *Pour un réalisme socialiste*.
84. On Heartfield in the GDR, see the document collection in März, *John Heartfield*, pp. 434–75.
85. Michael Krejsa, unpublished research paper, John Heartfield Archiv.
86. See Bathrick, "Affirmative and Negative Culture."
87. See Wilson, "Beauté révolutionnaire?"
88. Bloch et al., *Aesthetics and Politics*, presents in English some of the key contributions. A clear exposition is offered by Lunn, *Marxism and Modernism*.
89. Lukács (1938), quoted in Bloch et al., *Aesthetics and Politics*, p. 43.
90. I would like to thank Werner Hecht and Barbara Wallburg of the Brecht Zentrum, Berlin, for showing me the relevant correspondence.
91. Cited in März, *John Heartfield*, p. 437.
92. Reprinted in ibid., pp. 443–52.
93. Herzfelde, *John Heartfield*, p. 6.
94. Ibid., p. 235.
95. Ibid., p. 173.
96. *John Heartfield, 1891–1968*, p. 20.

PLATES

WER BÜRGERBLÄTTER LIEST WIRD BLIND UND TAUB.
WEG MIT DEN VERDUMMUNGSBANDAGEN!

ICH BIN EIN KOHLKOPF. KENNT IHR MEINE BLÄTTER?
ICH WEISS VOR SORGEN ZWAR NICHT AUS NOCH EIN,
DOCH HALT' ICH STILL UND HOFF' AUF EINEN RETTER,
ICH WILL EIN SCHWARZ-ROT-GOLDNER KOHLKOPF SEIN!
ICH WILL NICHTS SEH'N UND HÖREN,
DAS STAATSGESCHÄFT NICHT STÖREN.
UND ZIEHT MAN MICH AUCH BIS AUF'S HEMDE AUS,
DIE ROTE PRESSE KOMMT MIR NICHT INS HAUS!

WHOEVER READS BOURGEOIS NEWSPAPERS
BECOMES BLIND AND DEAF.
AWAY WITH THE STULTIFYING BANDAGES!

I AM A CABBAGEHEAD. DO YOU KNOW MY LEAVES?
FROM WORRIES I AM AT MY WIT'S END,
BUT I KEEP QUIET AND HOPE FOR A SAVIOR,
I WANT TO BE A BLACK-RED-GOLD CABBAGEHEAD!
I DON'T WANT TO SEE AND HEAR ANYTHING,
OR TO INTERFERE WITH PUBLIC AFFAIRS.
AND YOU CAN STRIP ME RIGHT DOWN TO MY SHIRT,
BUT I'M NOT HAVING ANY RED PRESS IN MY HOUSE!

The design involves a play on the word *Blätter*, which means both
newspapers and (cabbage) leaves. The newspapers *Tempo* and
Vorwärts exemplify the Social Democratic press. The figure wears
the uniform of the Reichsbanner Schwarz-Rot-Gold (Black-Red-
Gold), a paramilitary organization of Social Democratic ex-
servicemen. According to Wieland Herzfelde (*John Heartfield*, p. 367,
n. 133), the verse is a parody of the Prussian nationalist song "Ich
bin ein Preuße, kennt ihr meine Farben?" (I am a Prussian, do you
know my colors?).

All Heartfield's montages were informed by the strategy
and tactics of the German Communist Party and the Communist
International, Moscow. This one registers Communist hostility to the
Social Democratic Party, a position that became less intransigent
after Hitler took power in 1933. See also 3/30, 4/30, 5/30, 6/30,
8/30, 1/31, 2/31, 4/31, 24/34.

ICH BIN EIN KOHLKOPF, KENNT IHR MEINE BLÄTTER?
ICH WEISS VOR SORGEN ZWAR NICHT AUS NOCH EIN,
DOCH HALT' ICH STILL UND HOFF' AUF EINEN RETTER,
ICH WILL EIN SCHWARZ-ROT-GOLDNER KOHLKOPF SEIN!
ICH WILL NICHTS SEH'N UND HÖREN,
      DAS STAATSGESCHÄFT NICHT STÖREN.
UND ZIEHT MAN MICH AUCH BIS AUF'S HEMDE AUS,
DIE ROTE PRESSE KOMMT MIR NICHT INS HAUS!

JOHN HEARTFIELD

WER BÜRGERBLÄTTER LIEST WIRD BLIND UND TAUB.
WEG MIT DEN VERDUMMUNGSBANDAGEN!

2/30. **AIZ** 9, NUMBER 10, 1930, PAGE 183

**Zwangslieferantin von Menschenmaterial
Nur Mut! Der Staat braucht Arbeitslose und
Soldaten!**

**Forced supplier of human material
Take courage! The state needs unemployed
workers and soldiers!**

The issue this montage appeared in carried a range of items commemorating International Women's Day, 8 March 1930. The issue also included, for example, "Von der Arbeitssklavin zur Kämpferin" (From slave laborer to militant), an illustrated history of the advancement of women (pp. 190–91). See also 49/34. For the original artwork for this montage, see Fig. 9.

    The montage was published in 1962 in Wieland Herzfelde's book *John Heartfield: Leben und Werk* (p. 135) with the title *Ihr Mütter, lasset eure Kinder leben…!* (Mothers, let your children live…!), which is the final line of Brecht's poem "An meine Landsleute" (To my compatriots) of 1949 (*Die Gedichte von Bertolt Brecht in einem Band* [Frankfurt: Suhrkamp, 1981], p. 965).

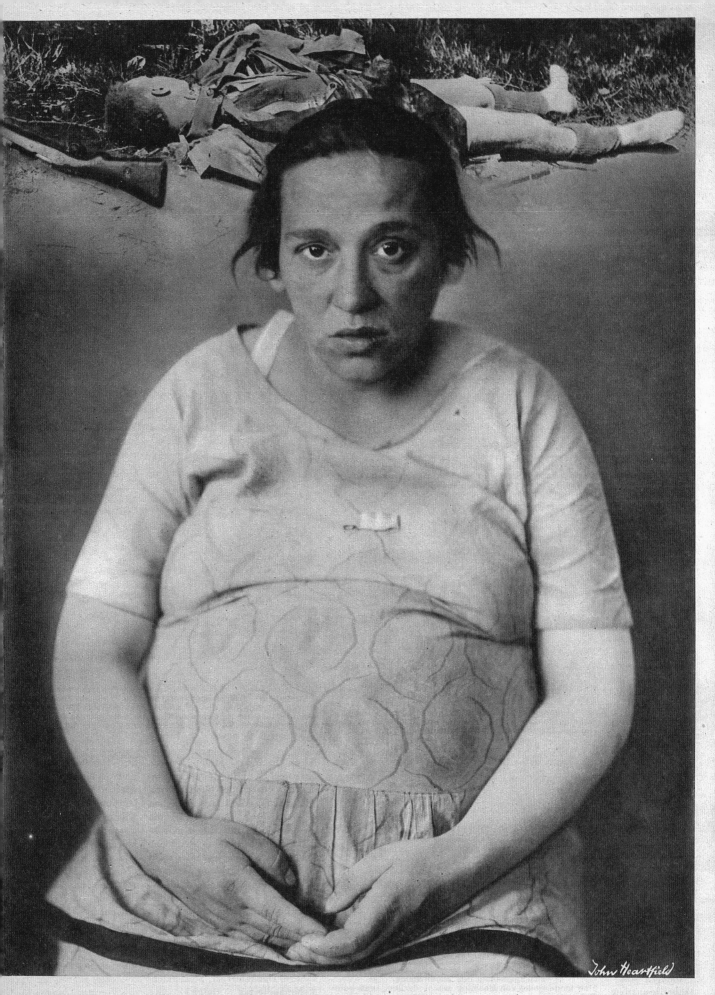

Zwangslieferantin von Menschenmaterial Nur Mut! Der Staat braucht Arbeitslose und Soldaten!

FÜR TREUE DIENSTE

Unser bewährtes Aufsichtsratsmitglied
1920   1930
Herrn Reichsinnenminister
Karl Severing
Mitglied der Deutschen Sozialdemokratischen Partei
ernennen wir hiermit
In Erinnerung an die schicksalschwangeren Tage vor zehn
Jahren, als der Kapp-Lüttwitz-Putsch das Reich in Unruhe
versetzte und die Arbeiterschaft die Flamme des Aufruhrs
schürte
In Anerkennung seiner außerordentlichen Verdienste bei der
Abwicklung des Kapp-Abenteuers sowie der Zersch-
metterung der Roten Armee durch Zustandebringen des
Bielefelder Abkommens und im Zusammenwirken mit Seiner
Excellenz General von Watter
In Dankbarkeit für das Niederhalten der Ruhrkumpels mittels
Speckzulagen und blauen Bohnen, für die geschickte
Provozierung des mitteldeutschen Aufstandes und seine
Liquidierung durch einen energisch durchgeführten, für
unsere Wirtschaft heilsamen Aderlaß am bolschewistisch
verseuchten Volkskörper
Im vollen Vertrauen darauf, daß der Mann, der vom kleinen
Metallarbeiter zu einem der bestbezahlten Diener an
unserem Staate emporgestiegen ist, wie im Laufe der letzten
10 Jahre so auch weiterhin gestützt auf das Republik-
Schutzgesetz durch Verbot von Streiks und roten
Kampforganisationen und durch zielbewußtes Ausnutzen
der Schiedsgerichtsbarkeit sich als wahrer Förderer und nur
Billiges fordernder Wahrer unserer wohl (blutig) erworbenen
aber inzwischen angestammten Rechte erweisen wird
zum Ehrendoktor (Dr. sanguinis causa)
an der Polizeifakultät am
Reichsinstitut für rationelle Ausbeutung
Die deutsche Bourgeoisie
Im Auftrage: Schacht
Berlin, den 23. März 1930
Genehmigt unter 27804 Morgan & Co.

FOR LOYAL SERVICES

Our well-tested member of the supervisory board
1920   1930
Mr. Reich Minister of the Interior
Karl Severing
Member of the Social Democratic Party
we appoint herewith
In memory of the fateful days of ten years ago, when the
Kapp-Lüttwitz Putsch created disorder in the Reich and the
work force fanned the flames of rebellion
In recognition of his extraordinary services in the resolution
of the Kapp adventure as well as the smashing of the Red
Army with the signing of the Bielefeld Treaty and in
cooperation with His Excellency General von Watter
In gratitude for the suppression of the Ruhr miners with
bacon and blue beans, for the skillful provocation of the
revolt in Middle Germany and its liquidation through the
energetic bloodletting of the Bolshevik-contaminated body of
the people, which was healthy for the recovery of the
economy
With fullest confidence that the man who climbed from a
lowly metalworker to one of the best-paid servants of our
state will continue to prove himself the true promoter and just
preserver of our (bloodily) acquired but now ancestral
rights, as he has done in the last ten years, based on the
Republic's protection law, by the prohibition of strikes and
Red militant organizations and the purposeful exploitation of
arbitral jurisdiction
to honorary Doctor (Dr. sanguinis causa)
at the Police Faculty of the
Reich Institute for Efficient Exploitation
The German bourgeoisie
By order: Schacht
Berlin, 23 March 1930
Authorization under 27804 Morgan & Co.

In 1920 Wolfgang Kapp and General von Lüttwitz attempted a right-wing putsch and for a brief time controlled Berlin. This montage was part of a special issue on the putsch and immediately preceded an article entitled "Von Kapp bis Severing" (From Kapp to Severing). Karl Severing (1875–1952), who in the early years of the Republic was responsible for containing not only the Kapp putsch but also industrial and political unrest in the Ruhr and Middle Germany, was Reich minister of the interior from 1928 to 1930 and held a similar position in Prussia from 1930 to 1932. For Schacht, see 14/34; for Morgan & Co., see 9/33. "Blue beans" (*blaue Bohnen*) is slang for bullets.

FÜR TREUE DIENSTE

Unfer bewährtes Aufsichtsratsmitglied

1920   1930

Herrn Reichsinnenminifter

Karl Severing

Mitglied der Deutschen Sozialdemokratischen Partei

ernennen wir hiermit

In Erinnerung an die schicksalschwangeren Tage vor zehn Jahren, als der Kapp-Lüttwitz-Putsch das Reich in Unruhe verfetzte und die Arbeiterschaft die Flamme des Aufruhrs schürte

In Anerkennung feiner außerordentlichen Verdienfte bei der Abwicklung des Kapp-Abenteuers fowie der Zerfchmetterung der Roten Armee durch Zuftandebringen des Bielefelder Abkommens und im Zufammenwirken mit Seiner Excellenz General von Watter

In Dankbarkeit für das Niederhalten der Ruhrkumpels mittels Speckzulagen und blauen Bohnen, für die gefchickte Provozierung des mitteldeutfchen Aufftandes und feine Liquidierung durch einen energifch durchgeführten, für unfere Wirtfchaft heilfamen Aderlaß am bolfchewiftifch verfeuchten Volkskörper

Im vollen Vertrauen darauf, daß der Mann, der vom kleinen Metallarbeiter zu einem der beftbezahlten Diener an unferem Staate emporgeftiegen ift, wie im Laufe der letzten 10 Jahre fo auch weiterhin geftützt auf das Republik-Schutzgefetz durch Verbot von Streiks und roten Kampforganifationen und durch zielbewußtes Ausnutzen der Schiedsgerichtsbarkeit fich als wahrer Förderer und nur Billiges fordernder Wahrer unferer wohl(blutig)erworbenen aber inzwifchen angeftammten Rechte erweifen wird

zum **Ehrendoktor** (Dr. sanguinis causa)

an der Polizeifakultät am
Reichsinftitut für rationelle Ausbeutung

Die deutfche Bourgeoifie
Im Auftrage:

Berlin, den 23. März 1930
Genehmigt unter 27804 Morgan & Co.

John Heartfield

Vandervelde *oder* Die vollkommene Schamlosigkeit

Vandervelde im Namen der II. Internationale:
"Arbeiter Rußlands, kehret zurück zu den geordneten Zuständen der Demokratie!"

Vandervelde *or* The Absolute Lack of Shame

Vandervelde in the name of the Second International:
"Russian workers, return to the orderly condition of democracy!"

Emile Vandervelde (1866–1938) was a Belgian Social Democratic leader active in the Second International, which was founded in 1889 and continued after the First World War as an association of Social Democratic parties. Its rival was the Third International of Communist Parties formed in 1919 and based in Moscow (see also 24/34).

Here Vandervelde is surrounded by press cuttings in English, French, and German about violent conflicts in the capitalist countries that contradicted his assumption of an orderly non-Soviet world. From his mouth, like a speech balloon, comes a press cutting that reads: "Den Völkern der Sowjetunion muß die Freiheit wieder gegeben werden" (Liberty must be given back to the peoples of the Soviet Union).

Mont. JOHN HEARTFIELD

...andervelde im Namen der II. Internationale:

...Arbeiter Rußlands, kehret zurück zu den geordneten Zuständen der Demokratie!"

Mac Donald – Socialism
Macdonald – Sozialismus

"Ich kann doch nicht untätig zusehen, daß noch ein weiteres Sechstel der Erde dem Kapitalismus verloren geht"

NACH INDIEN
TO INDIA

"Die fortschreitende Verwirklichung der Selbstverwaltung Indiens." "The progressive realization of Indian Self-government"

Peschawar vom Feind entsetzt.
Die Lage bessert sich. Die Afridis fliehen. Ihr Widerstand war nur schwer zu brechen. Erst das Eingreifen von 80 Flugzeugen, die 5000 Bomben abwarfen entschied den Sieg.
Vorwärts Nr. 265
10. Juni 1930.

Macdonald – Socialism

"I really cannot remain inactive while capitalism is being threatened with the loss of another sixth of the world"

TO INDIA

"The progressive realization of Indian Self-government"

Peshawar frightened by the enemy.
The situation improves. The Afridis flee. But their resistance was hard to break. Only the action of 80 airplanes that dropped 5,000 bombs secured victory.
Vorwärts No. 265
10 June 1930.

Heartfield's aim with this montage, his contribution to a special bilingual issue dedicated to the liberation struggle of the Indian people against the British, was to expose the contradiction between Social Democratic ideals and the treatment of colonial peoples. The report from the Social Democratic newspaper *Vorwärts* refers to a tribal revolt on India's Northwest Frontier. Labour Party Prime Minister James Ramsay MacDonald (1866–1937) directed the British response to Indian resistance, which in 1930 included Nehru's declaration of independence and Gandhi's mass campaign of civil disobedience.

Macdonald = Sozialismus

NACH IN DIEN
TO JNDIA

Peschawar vom Feind entsetzt.
Die Lage bessert sich. Die Afridis fliehen. Ihr Widerstand war nur schwer zu brechen. Erst das Eingreifen von **80 Flugzeugen, die 5000 Bomben abwarfen** entschied den Sieg.
Vorwärts Nr. 265
10. Juni 1930.

„Die fortschreitende Verwirklichung der Selbstverwaltung Indiens"
„The progressive realisation of Indian self-government"

Montage: JOHN HEARTFIELD

„Ich kann doch nicht untätig zusehen, daß noch ein weiteres Sechstel der Erde dem Kapitalismus verloren geht"
"I really cannot remain inactive while capitalism is being threatened with the loss of another sixth of the world"

SONNENFINSTERNIS AM "BEFREITEN" RHEIN

Hindenburg: "Brav pariert, lieber Braun!"

SOLAR ECLIPSE OVER THE "LIBERATED" RHINE

Hindenburg: "Well parried, dear Braun!"

The Treaty of Versailles, signed in 1919, specified that the Rhineland was to be a demilitarized zone occupied by the Allied troops for fifteen years. Parts of the zone were prematurely evacuated in 1930. Carl Otto Braun (1872–1955), a Social Democrat and Prussian prime minister for most of the period from 1921 to 1932, negotiated the evacuation. General Field Marshal Paul von Hindenburg (1847–1934) was president of the Weimar Republic from 1925 to 1934 (see also 34/34).

An updated version of the montage appeared in 1962 in Herzfelde's *John Heartfield: Leben und Werk* (p. 236). The images of the two politicians were dropped and the title became *Weg mit der Sonnenfinsternis am Rhein!* (Away with the solar eclipse over the Rhine!), referring to alleged militarization in the Federal Republic of Germany.

SONNENFINSTERNIS AM „BEFREITEN" RHEIN

Hindenburg: „Brav pariert, lieber Braun!"

6 Millionen Naziwähler: Futter für ein großes Maul

"Und *den* Fisch hab' ich gewählt!"

MIT GOTT FÜR HITLER UND KAPITAL

6 million Nazi voters: fodder for a big mouth

"And *this* is the fish I elected!"

WITH GOD FOR HITLER AND CAPITAL

In the election of 14 September 1930 the Nazis increased the number of seats they held in the Reichstag from 12 to 107, becoming the second largest party.

The Communist idea of Hitler as a tool of big business was a recurrent theme in Heartfield's montages; see, for example, 4/32, 11/32, and 18/33.

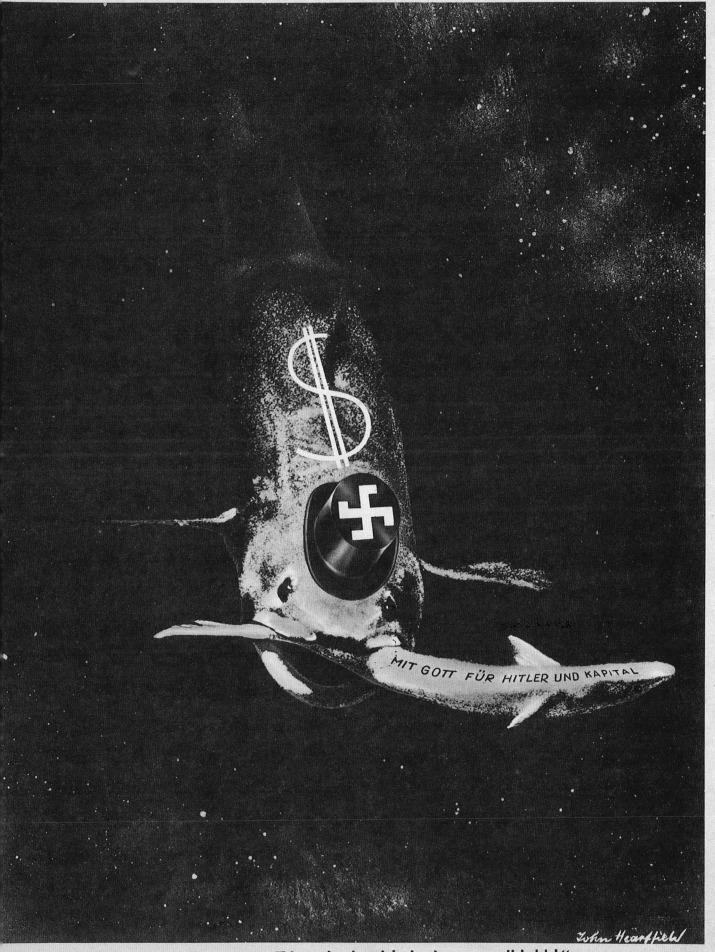

MIT GOTT FÜR HITLER UND KAPITAL

John Heartfield

„Und den Fisch hab' ich gewählt!"

Noch ist Deutschland nicht verloren!

"Die Sozialisierung marschiert!"
haben "Sozial"-Demokraten plakatiert, –
und haben zugleich beschlossen:
Sozialisten werden niedergeschossen.

Seitdem marschiert die Reaktion:
und heute schreien, wie zum Hohn,
National-"Sozialisten"
(daß ich nicht lache): "Deutschland erwache!"

Umsonst! – Ihr Parteien der Niedertracht
habt die Rechnung ohne den Wirt gemacht:
Der deutsche Arbeiter wird erwachen
und den Sozialismus zur Wirklichkeit machen!

Germany is not yet lost!

"Socialization is on the march!"
the "Social" Democrats placarded, –
and at the same time decided:
Socialists are to be shot down.

Since then reaction is on the march:
and today how mockingly scream
National "Socialists"
(I cannot help laughing): "Germany awake!"

In vain! – For you vile parties
have overlooked a vital factor:
The German worker will awake
and make Socialism a reality!

"Deutschland erwache!" (Germany awake!) was one of Hitler's
favorite slogans. The colloquialism "haben die Rechnung ohne den
Wirt gemacht" means literally to reckon without the landlord.

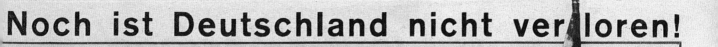

Die Sozialisierung marschiert!

Aus der Erklärung der Reichsregierung.

Größer als die politische Gefahr ist die wirtschaftliche Notlage unseres Landes.

Es lautet daher das erste Gebot: An die Arbeit! Nur sie kann uns retten. Jeder Streik bringt uns dem Untergang näher.

Wie in allen Verhandlungen mit den Vertretern der Arbeiter erklären wir auch heute: Gleich wie die politische ist uns die wirtschaftliche Demokratie. Nur sie vermag alle Kräfte zu wecken und Werke zu erhalten, die den völligen Untergang abwenden können. Wir sind gewillt, das Gesetz der wirtschaftlichen Demokratie zu schaffen, nämlich:

einheitliche sozialistische Wirtschaft auf freiheitlicher Grundlage

den die Organe der wirtschaftlichen Demokratie ausbauen wird. Wir haben daher die in den Verhandlungen mit den Bergarbeitern aus Halle und dem Ruhrgebiet über Wahlen beschlossen, dass in ihnen Vertreter aller Arbeiter sein. So werden wirtschaftlichen Demokratie

exekutive wirtschaftlich-demokratischer Grundsätze!

werden durch Anwendung von der Sozialisierung derjenigen Wirtschaftszweige, Aufnahme und Schaffung, oder in Konkurrenz der Allgemeinheit und, der politischen und wirtschaftlichen Bau und Erzeugung von Energien.

Deutschland muss ein freier sein; Niedergang und genußsüchtige Wohltentum Mitteln werden.

Drum auf zu schaffender Arbeit! Steht zu uns, wie wir zu Euch stehen.

Gehen wir einig vor, ist uns die Zukunft sicher!

Das Reichsministerium:

Scheidemann, Schiffer, Bauer, Bell, Graf Brockdorff-Rantzau, David, Erzberger, Diesberg, Giesberts, Noth, Landsberg, Noske, Preuß, Robert Schmidt, Wissel.

JOHN HEARTFIELD

„Die Sozialisierung marschiert!"
haben „Sozial"-Demokraten plakatiert, —
und haben zugleich beschlossen:
Sozialisten werden niedergeschossen.

Seitdem marschiert die Reaktion:
und heute schreien, wie zum Hohn,
National-„Sozialisten"
(daß ich nicht lache): „Deutschland erwache!"

Umsonst! — Ihr Parteien der Niedertracht
habt die Rechnung ohne den Wirt gemacht:
**Der deutsche Arbeiter wird erwachen
und den Sozialismus zur Wirklichkeit machen!**

Das tote Parlament

Das blieb vom Jahre 1848 übrig!
So sieht der Reichstag aus, der am 13. Oktober eröffnet wird.

The dead parliament

That's all that's left from 1848!
That's how the Reichstag, opened as of 13 October, looks.

The montage plays with the double connotation of "48": The first
German parliament opened in 1848, and Article 48 of the Weimar
Constitution allowed the Reich president to suspend temporarily all
fundamental rights of the citizens, permitting government by
emergency decree without the consent of the parliamentary majority.
After Hitler's success in the September election (see 7/30),
Chancellor Heinrich Brüning convinced President Hindenburg to
invoke Article 48. See also 10/30, 8/32.

Das tote Parlament

John Heartfield

Das blieb vom Jahre 1848 übrig!
So sieht der Reichstag aus, der am 13. Oktober eröffnet wird.

Hurra, Hurra! Der Brüning-Weihnachtsmann ist da!

Er hat uns Not verordnet
und Lohnabbau diktiert,
den Krankenschein besteuert,
dafür das Heer verteuert.
Er hat sich nicht geniert
Kriegsopfern, Blinden, Kindern
das Brot vom Mund zu reißen.
Um es den Großagrariern
und Schiebern nachzuschmeißen.
Auch Stillgeld ist ein Luxus,
das Trinken überhaupt.
Wir brauchen Panzerkreuzer.
Wer hungert – wird beraubt!
Ein deutscher Mann ist niemals arbeitslos:
Die 4 Millionen sind vom Feind bestochen,
sonst hätten sie sich längst verkrochen
und unsre arme Wirtschaft wär' sie los.
Das hat sogar die SPD begriffen
drum stellte sie sich Mann für Mann
zum Schutz der Notverordnung an.
(So folgt der Hund, wenn ihm sein Herr gepfiffen.)
Herr Hitler rüstet unterdes zum Wotansfeste
Sein Christbaumschmuck ist anerkannt der beste
(Man kann zum Fest der Liebe sich im Hängen üben!)
Wie jeder Papst fischt Adolf auch im Trüben.
Es schließen Brüning, Hitler, Braun
(das war den Brüdern zuzutraun)
Burgfrieden unterm Weihnachtsbaum
auf daß die Dividenden steigen.

Doch aus ist dieser schöne Traum
wenn die Proleten zeigen,
daß sie zu kämpfen lernten…
Wer Hakenkreuze sät, wird rote Fäuste ernten!

Der Hitler-Christbaumschmuck ist keine böswillige Erfindung
Die Nationalsozialisten handeln tatsächlich damit

Hurrah, Hurrah! Here's the Brüning Father Christmas!

He decreed misery for us
and dictated wage cuts,
taxed the medical insurance card,
and in return made the army more expensive.

He did not feel embarrassed
about snatching bread from the mouths of
war victims, the blind, children,
so that he could hand it out to
the big farmers and racketeers.
The benefit for nursing mothers is also a luxury,
as is drinking generally.
We need battleships.
Whoever is hungry – will be robbed!
A German man is never unemployed:
The 4 million are bribed by the enemy,
otherwise they would have hidden long ago
and our poor economy would be free of them.
Even the SPD realized that
and therefore lined up man for man
behind the protection of the emergency decree.
(Just as a dog comes when his master whistles.)
Mr. Hitler arms in the meantime for his Wotan festival
His Christmas-tree decoration is recognized as the best
(During the Festival of Love one can practice hanging!)
Like every pope, Adolf fishes in murky waters.
Brüning, Hitler, Braun
(one could have expected this from the brothers)
make a truce under the Christmas tree
so that dividends rise.

Yet the beautiful dream is over
when the proletarians show
that they have learned how to fight…
Whoever sows swastikas, shall reap red fists!

The Hitler Christmas-tree decoration is no malicious invention
The National Socialists actually deal in such things

The puppet is saying "Jews out!" The advertisement at the left is for a portrait of Hitler – "the most beautiful of Christmas presents." Heinrich Brüning (1885–1970) led the Catholic Center Party and was appointed chancellor in 1930. The montage conveys the Communists' antipathy toward his economic policies and his attempts to rule by emergency decree. He was replaced as chancellor by Franz von Papen in 1932 and left the country in 1934 (see also 14/33). For Hitler, see 4/32; for Braun, see 6/30. For the artwork for this montage, see Fig. 8.

Hurra, Hurra! Der Brüning-Weihnachtsmann ist da!

Er hat uns Not verordnet
und Lohnabbau diktiert,
den Krankenschein besteuert,
dafür das Heer verteuert.
Er hat sich nicht geniert
Kriegsopfern, Blinden, Kindern
das Brot vom Mund zu reißen.
Um es den Großagrariern
und Schiebern nachzuschmeißen.
Auch Stillgeld ist ein Luxus,
das Trinken überhaupt.
Wir brauchen Panzerkreuzer.
Wer hungert — wird beraubt!
Ein deutscher Mann ist niemals
                    arbeitslos:
Die 4 Millionen sind vom Feind
                    bestochen,
sonst hätten sie sich längst verkrochen
und unsre arme Wirtschaft wär' sie los.
Das hat sogar die SPD begriffen
drum stellte sie sich Mann für Mann
zum Schutz der Notverordnung an.
(So folgt der Hund, wenn ihm
            sein Herr gepfiffen.)
Herr Hitler rüstet unterdes zum
                    Wotansfeste
Sein Christbaumschmuck ist
            anerkannt der beste
(Man kann zum Fest der Liebe
            sich im Hängen üben!)
Wie jeder Papst fischt Adolf auch im
                    Trüben.

Es schließen Brüning, Hitler, Braun
(das war den Brüdern zuzutraun)
Burgfrieden unterm Weihnachtsbaum
auf daß die Dividenden steigen.

Doch aus ist dieser schöne Traum
wenn die Proleten zeigen,
daß sie zu kämpfen lernten . . .
Wer Hakenkreuze sät, wird
    rote Fäuste ernten!

JUDEN RAUS!

Heil Hitler

STEUERN

Hepp, hepp

GOEBBELS
WEISSE
MÄUSE

HUHU

SCHLICH

MARKE: HUNGERSTILLER
PATENT SEVERING   UNSERN LIEBEN ERWERBSLOSEN

Das schönste
Weihnachtsgeschenk
für jeden Deutschen:
Adolf Hitler

Montiert: JOHN HEARTFIELD

Der Hitler-Christbaumschmuck ist keine böswillige Erfindung
Die Nationalsozialisten handeln tatsächlich damit

Ein neues Jahr!

Ein Jahr wie jedes andre war?
Nein!!
Das darf nicht sein!
Damit aus Not und Qual
die neue Welt ensteht:
Schlag zu, Prolet!

A new year!

A year like all the others?
No!!
That must not be!
So that from misery and pain
the new world arises:
Strike, proletarian!

The image of the worker as a blacksmith alludes to the final verse of the Communist anthem, the "Internationale" (written by Eugène Pottier in 1871).

Ein neues Jahr!
Ein Jahr wie jedes
andre war?
Nein!!
Das darf nicht sein!
Damit aus Not und Qual
die neue Welt ersteht:
Schlag zu, Prolet!

John Heartfield

1023

Man muß eine besondere Veranlagung zum Selbstmord haben, wenn man vergißt, daß man die Sozialdemokratie in der Periode des Spartakismus sehr dringend gebraucht hat, und nicht bedenkt, daß man sie vielleicht eines Tages noch dringlicher brauchen wird.
Theodor Wolff
im Berliner Tageblatt
vom 15. Februar 1931

One must have a special disposition toward suicide to forget that Social Democracy was needed very urgently in the period of Spartacism and not to bear in mind that perhaps one day it will be needed even more urgently.
Theodor Wolff
in the Berliner Tageblatt
15 February 1931

The corpse is that of Karl Liebknecht (1871–1919), leader of the Spartacist uprising of 1919 and patron saint of German Communism. He and Rosa Luxemburg were captured in Berlin at the Eden Hotel (shown at the top right of the montage) by the Freikorps (shown at the bottom left), the irregular militia of ex-soldiers hired by Social Democratic Minister of Defense Noske to help suppress the Spartacists. The quotations, taken from the Social Democratic newspaper *Vorwärts* from 1919 to 1923 (another year of failed Communist insurrections), are presented as evidence of consistent Social Democratic hostility to Communism.

The celebrated liberal journalist Theodor Wolff (1868–1943) edited the *Berliner Tageblatt* from 1906 to 1933.

Man muß eine besondere Veranlagung zum Selbstmord haben, wenn man vergißt, daß man die Sozialdemokratie in der Periode des Spartakismus sehr dringend gebraucht hat, und nicht bedenkt, daß man sie vielleicht eines Tages noch dring-   licher brauchen wird.

Theodor Wolff
im Berliner Tageblatt
vom 15. Februar 1931

Karl Liebknecht nach seiner Einlieferung ins Leichenschauhaus.

Maschinengewehrnest der Noskegarden

MONTIERT: JOHN HEARTFIELD

Zum Krisen-Parteitag der SPD

Die Tierärzte von Leipzig: "Selbstverständlich werden wir dem Tiger die Zähne ausbrechen, aber zunächst einmal müssen wir ihn gesundpflegen und herausfüttern."

Die Sozialdemokratie will nicht den Zusammenbruch des Kapitalismus. Sie will wie ein Arzt zu heilen und zu bessern versuchen (Fritz Tarnow, Vorsitzender des Holzarbeiterverbandes)

On the occasion of the crisis party conference of the SPD

The veterinarians of Leipzig: "Of course we will break out the teeth of the tiger, but first of all we must nurse him back to health and feed him."

Social Democracy does not want the breakdown of capitalism. Like a doctor, it wants to try to heal and improve it (Fritz Tarnow, chairman of the Woodworkers' Federation)

Fritz Tarnow (1880–1951) was a trade unionist well known for his view that since the capitalist system was not in danger of imminent collapse, unionists needed to adapt themselves to it. The "veterinarians of Leipzig" are the delegates to the SPD (Sozialdemokratische Partei Deutschlands) conference, which was held in Leipzig (see also 4/31).

In Wieland Herzfelde's *John Heartfield: Leben und Werk* (p. 142), this montage appears with the same title but without the supporting text. In the new, more laconic version the tiger's head is less obviously a symbol of capitalism and appears instead to represent the leadership of the Social Democratic Party, past and present.

Zum Krisen-Parteitag der SPD

Die Sozialdemokratie will nicht den Zusammenbruch des Kapitalismus. Sie will wie ein Arzt zu heilen und zu bessern versuchen (Fritz Tarnow, Vorsitzender des Holzarbeiterverbandes)

FOTO-MONTAGE: JOHN HEARTFIELD

Die Tierärzte von Leipzig: „Selbstverständlich werden wir dem Tiger die Zähne ausbrechen, aber zunächst einmal müssen wir ihn gesundpflegen und herausfüttern."

**Ob schwarz, ob weiß –
im Kampf vereint!
Wir kennen
nur eine Rasse,
wir kennen alle
nur einen Feind –
die Ausbeuterklasse.**

**Whether black, or white –
in struggle united!
We know
only one race,
we all know
only one enemy –
the exploiting class.**

This was Heartfield's contribution to a special issue called "Leben und Kampf der Schwarzen Rasse" (Life and struggle of the black race).

In 1961 Heartfield and Herzfelde published a poster using the same image and new text: "Spartacus / Jeanne d'Arc / Lincoln / Karl Liebknecht / Rosa Luxemburg / Ernst Thälmann … / gleich ihren Namen / wird / durch die Jahrhunderte / leuchten / der Name / Patrice Lumumba. Brüder Heartfield Herzfelde" (…like their names the name Patrice Lumumba will shine through the centuries. Brothers Heartfield Herzfelde). Patrice Lumumba (1925–1961), who was murdered shortly after taking office in 1960 as the first prime minister of the Republic of the Congo, was regarded in the Communist world as a martyr to the cause of anticolonialism. (See Herzfelde, *John Heartfield*, p. 376, n. 242).

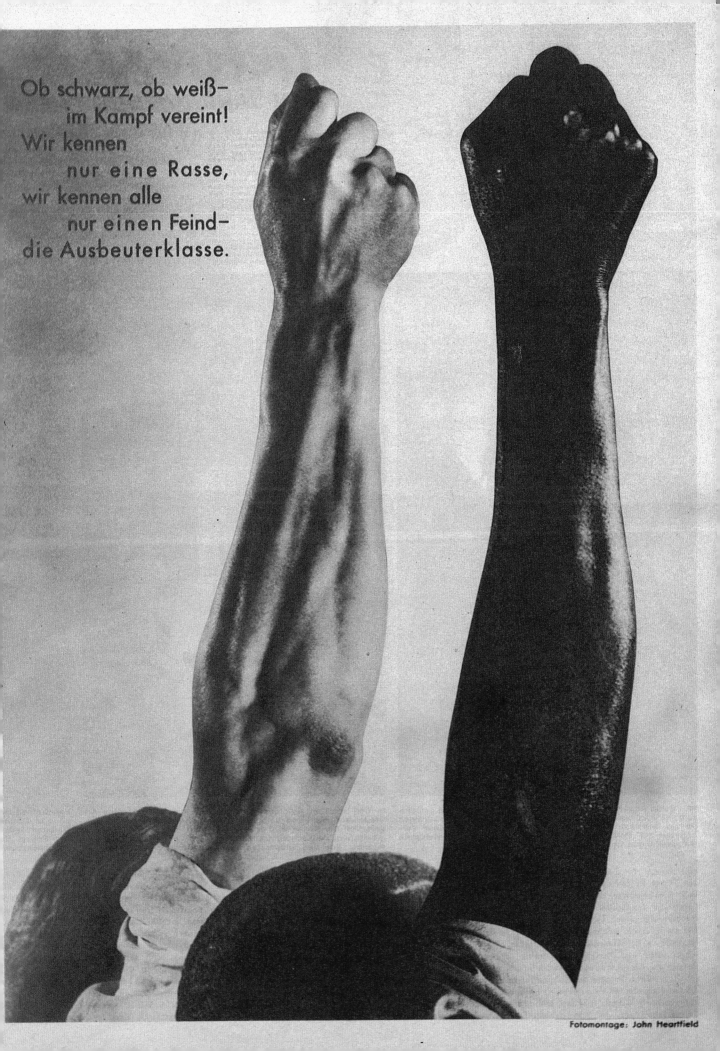

Ob schwarz, ob weiß—
    im Kampf vereint!
Wir kennen
    nur eine Rasse,
wir kennen alle
    nur einen Feind—
die Ausbeuterklasse.

Fotomontage: John Heartfield

Die letzte Weisheit der SPD: "Nieder mit dem Marxismus!"

Sie sind verhaftet als falscher Prophet, Herr Karl Marx – wir haben nicht unsere Ketten zu verlieren, sondern unsere Futterkrippen und Ministersessel

Als Karl Marx vor mehr als 80 Jahren das Wort prägte, daß die Arbeiter nichts zu verlieren hätten als ihre Ketten, war es eine revolutionäre Tat. Jetzt ist es, wenn es für die Gegenwart nachgebetet wird, eine stockreaktionäre Phrase! (Sollmann – Köln auf dem Leipziger SPD-Parteitag)

The latest idea of the SPD: "Down with Marxism!"

You are arrested as a false prophet, Mr. Karl Marx – we have not our chains to lose, but our feeding troughs and ministers' seats

When Karl Marx, more than eighty years ago, coined the phrase workers have nothing to lose but their chains, it was a revolutionary act. Now, when it is mechanically repeated in the present situation, it is an ultrareactionary phrase! (Sollmann – Köln at the Leipzig SPD party rally)

Wilhelm Sollmann (1881–1951) was a politician and journalist based in Cologne. A member of the Reichstag from 1920 to 1933, he belonged to the right wing of the Social Democratic Party, which was still in theory Marxist. Karl Marx (1818–1883) is holding a copy of the German Communist Party's newspaper *Die Rote Fahne* (The red banner).

Marx and Engels's *Manifest der Kommunistischen Partei* (The Communist Manifesto), published in 1848, concludes: "Die Proletarier haben nichts in ihr zu verlieren als ihre Ketten. Sie haben eine Welt zu gewinnen. *Proletarier aller Länder, vereinigt euch!*" (Proletarians have nothing to lose but their chains. They have a world to win. *Proletarians of the world, unite!)*

Heartfield made no further contributions to *AIZ* until spring 1932, after his return from an extended trip to the Soviet Union.

Die letzte Weisheit der SPD: „Nieder mit dem Marxismus!"

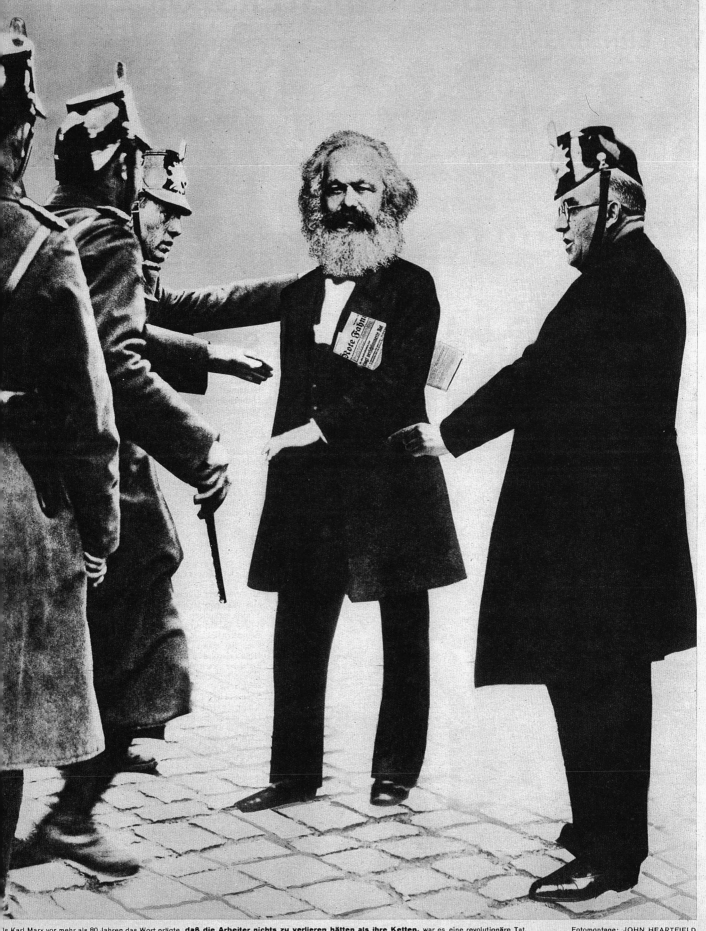

Als Karl Marx vor mehr als 80 Jahren das Wort prägte, **daß die Arbeiter nichts zu verlieren hätten als ihre Ketten**, war es eine revolutionäre Tat. **Jetzt ist es**, wenn es für die Gegenwart nachgebetet wird, **eine stockreaktionäre Phrase!** (Sollmann-Köln auf dem Leipziger SPD-Parteitag)

Fotomontage: JOHN HEARTFIELD

Sie sind verhaftet als falscher Prophet, Herr Karl Marx — wir haben nicht unsere Ketten zu verlieren, sondern unsere Futterkrippen und Ministersessel

KRIEG UND LEICHEN – DIE LE

FOTOMONTAGE: JOHN HEARTFIELD

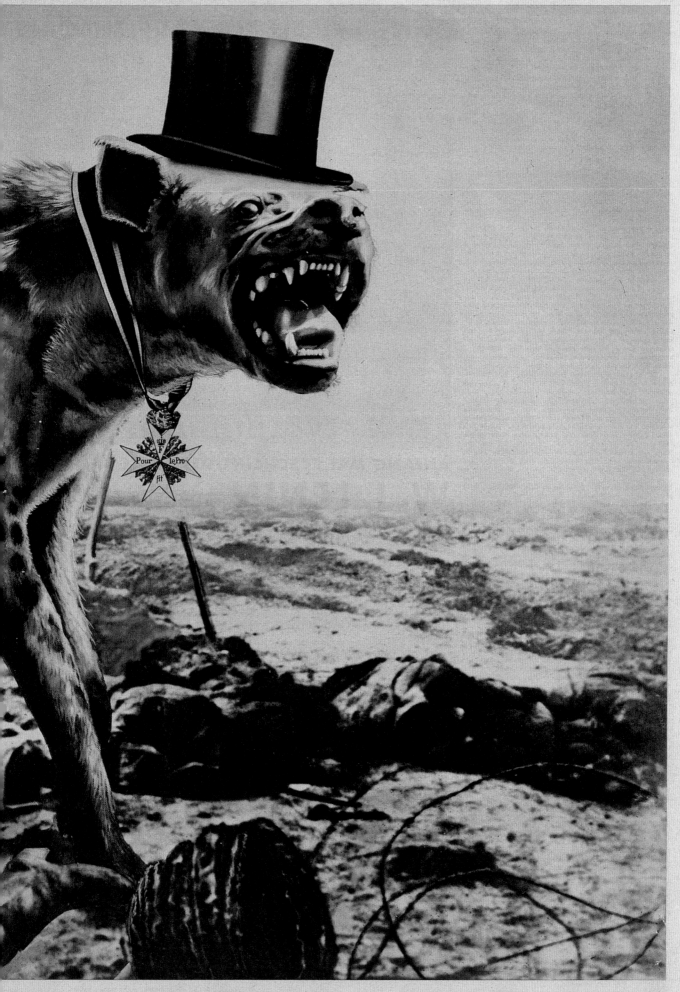

Pour le Profit

TE HOFFNUNG DER REICHEN

1/32. **AIZ** 11, NUMBER 18, 24 APRIL 1932, PAGES 420–21

2/32. **AIZ** 11, NUMBER 27, 3 JULY 1932, PAGE 627

KRIEG UND LEICHEN – DIE LETZTE HOFFNUNG DER REICHEN

WAR AND CORPSES – THE LAST HOPE OF THE RICH

In diesem Zeichen will man euch verraten und verkaufen!

In this sign shall ye be betrayed and sold!

The hyena wears a "Blue Max," a flying medal from World War I. The original motto, "Pour le Mérite," has been changed to "Pour le Profit" (see also 6/32, 23/33).

      This montage, Heartfield's first after returning from the Soviet Union, appeared in a special May Day issue entitled "Mit Lenin zum Sieg" (With Lenin to victory). The issue carried an editorial by *AIZ* publisher Willi Münzenberg that remembered Lenin's call for the withdrawal of Russia from the "imperialist war" in 1917 and stressed the threat to the Soviet Union, fifteen years later, of attack by capitalist states in crisis. There were unsuccessful attempts to ban copies of this issue of *AIZ* in Baden, provoking protests from sympathetic artists and writers (see Herzfelde, *John Heartfield,* p. 369, n. 155).

      Willi Münzenberg (1889–1940) was a German Communist who was best known in the Weimar period for his publishing ventures, which included *AIZ*. In 1933 he escaped from Berlin and based himself in Paris. (For further information, see Gross, *Willi Münzenberg).*

(pages 74–75)

According to the chronicler Eusebius, Constantine (c. 274–337) had a vision while marching on Rome against Maxentius in 312. In front of the sun he saw a cross above the words "In hoc signo vinces" (In this sign shalt thou conquer). When he reached the walls of Rome, a further vision bade him to put Christ's monogram on the shields of his soldiers. This was done and Constantine was victorious. Soon afterward, he issued an edict mandating toleration of Christians. In Heartfield's "vision," the "crooked cross" of Nazism leads to disaster rather than victory. The phrase "verraten und verkauft sein" also means to have lost all hope.

      The montage appeared in a special issue about white-collar workers that described their lives and sought to show how they and blue-collar workers were natural allies in the struggle against their common capitalist enemy. Heartfield's design was an appeal to white-collar workers to abandon Nazism and become Communists. It was immediately followed by an article called "Bankdirektor und Bankangestellter" (Bank manager and bank employee) that through contrasting portraits and captions suggested irreconcilable class interests.

In diesem Zeichen

will man euch

verraten und verkaufen!

Montage: John Heartfield

627

PRAKTISCHES CHRISTENTUM
Zum Devaheim-Prozeß

PASTOR CREMER: "Lasset die Kindlein zu mir kommen…"

PRACTICAL CHRISTIANITY
On the occasion of the Devaheim trial

PASTOR CREMER: "Suffer the little children to come
unto me…"

The reference is to a court case involving embezzlement in a
Lutheran children's home. The biblical quotation is from Mark 10:14.

PRAKTISCHES CHRISTENTUM

Zum Devaheim-Prozeß

MONTAGE: JOHN HEARTFIELD

PASTOR CREMER: „Lasset die Kindlein zu mir kommen..."

ADOLF, DER ÜBERMENSCH: Schluckt Gold und redet Blech

ADOLF, THE SUPERMAN: Swallows gold and spouts rubbish

Adolf Hitler (1889–1945) founded the Nationalsozialistische Deutsche Arbeiterpartei (National Socialist German Workers' Party, usually abbreviated NSDAP or Nazi Party) in 1920. He was Reich chancellor from 1933 to 1945. The special issue in which this montage appeared was published just six months after Hitler's important address to Rhineland industrialists in Düsseldorf on 27 January 1932. The issue, titled "Prinz und Arbeiter in einer Partei?" (Prince and worker in one party?), dealt with the contradictory class appeals of Nazism. Heartfield's montage preceded an article that examined the distinction between the anticapitalist rhetoric of the Nazis and their procapitalist practices.

 Blech is tinplate or sheet metal; *Blech reden* is to talk rubbish. Note the annotation at the top right: "Röntgenaufnahme von JOHN HEARTFIELD" (X ray by John Heartfield).

 See also 6/32, 11/32, 13/32, 1/33, 3/33, 6/33, 8/33, 14/33, 16/33, 18/33, 20/33, 24/33, 28/33, 4/34, 7/34, 16/34, 19/34, 26/34, 30/34, 31/34, 34/34, 35/34, 39/34, 1/35, 2/35, 11/35, 12/35, 17/35, 1/36, 2/36, 5/36, 9/36, 5/37, 15/38.

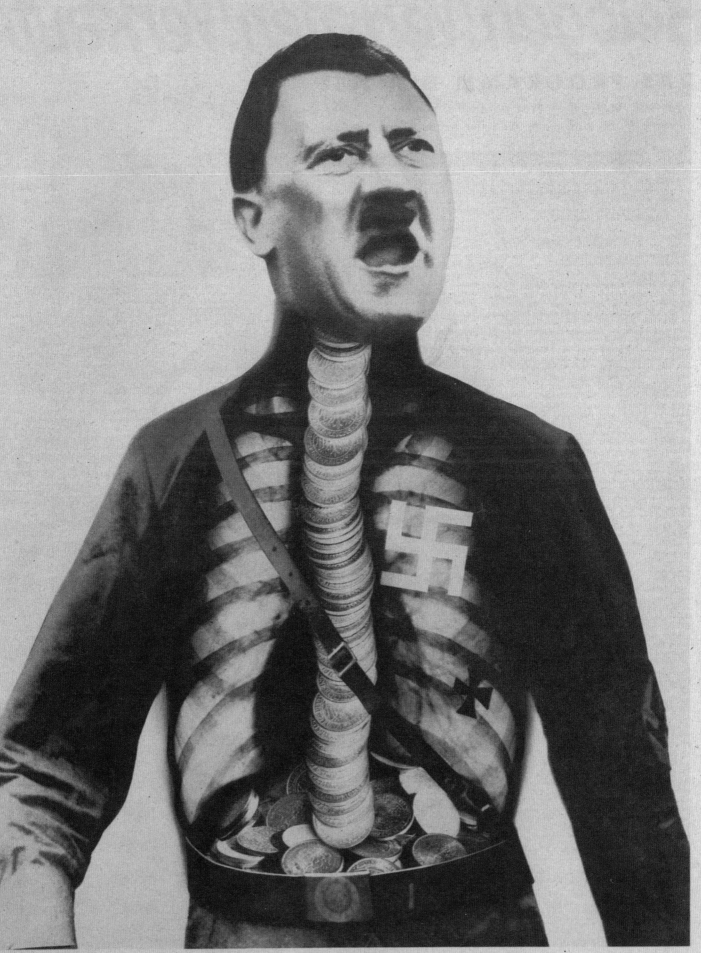

ADOLF, DER ÜBERMENSCH: **Schluckt Gold und redet Blech**

Die Rote Einheit macht euch frei!
WÄHLT LISTE 3

Red unity liberates you!
VOTE LIST 3

Reichstag elections took place on 31 July 1932. On the flag is the
Communist symbol for the United Front, which was an attempt to
bring together the rank and file of the Communist and Social
Democratic parties. The armbands bear the symbols of both parties.
This issue also included an article on the Anti-Fascist Unity Congress
in Berlin (p. 699).

ERSCHEINT WÖCHENTLICH
EINMAL / JAHRGANG XI
Nr. 30 / 1932 / 24. VII.
Preis: 20 Pfg., Kc. 1,60,
30 Gr. V. b. b. / Neuer
Deutscher Verlag / Berlin W8

Die Rote Einheit
macht euch frei!
WÄHLT LISTE 3

John Heartfield

S.M. ADOLF

Ich führe Euch herrlichen Pleiten entgegen!

HIS MAJESTY ADOLF

I lead you toward splendid bankruptcies!

The image conflates a portrait of Hitler (see 4/32) with one of Kaiser Wilhelm (1859–1941), who ruled Germany from 1888 to 1918. Heartfield has altered Kaiser Wilhelm's boast during the First World War: "Ich führe Euch herrlichen Zeiten entgegen!" (I lead you toward splendid times!). Hitler wears a "Blue Max" flying medal, with the motto changed from "Pour le Mérite" to "Pour le Profit" (see also 1/32, 23/33). On 13 August 1932 President Paul von Hindenburg had offered Hitler a cabinet post, which he refused.

      A revised version of the montage appeared on the cover of *Picture Post* (London) on 23 September 1939. Behind the human hybrid Heartfield added a map of Europe, and he changed the title to *KAISER ADOLF: The Man Against Europe.*

S.M. ADOLF

Fotomontage: John Heartfield

Ich
führe Euch herrlichen Pleiten entgegen!

Wollt ihr wieder fallen,
damit die Aktien steigen?!

Do you want to fall again,
so that shares rise?!

The montage was made for a special issue dedicated to the delegates
to the Communist-sponsored antiwar conference in Amsterdam.

Wollt ihr wieder fallen, damit die Aktien steigen?!

John Heartfield

Zum 30. August 1932

…Wenn das Parlament es wagen sollte, sich dem
Reichspräsidenten zu versagen, muß ohne Zögern und
Schwanken der Reichstag abermals aufgelöst, das
parlamentarische System endgültig liquidiert werden.
DAZ (Deutsche Allgemeine Zeitung)

On the occasion of 30 August 1932

…If Parliament should dare to oppose the Reich president,
the Reichstag must be dissolved again without delay and
vacillation, and the parliamentary system must finally be
liquidated.
DAZ (Deutsche Allgemeine Zeitung)

Another montage about rule by emergency decree, invoking Article
48 of the constitution (see 9/30, 10/30).

Montage: JOHN HEARTFIELD

...Wenn das Parlament es wagen sollte, sich dem Reichspräsidenten zu versagen, muß ohne Zögern und Schwanken der Reichstag abermals aufgelöst, das parlamentarische System endgültig liquidiert werden.

DAZ (Deutsche Allgemeine Zeitung)

Arbeitsbeschaffung:
"Von den sieben Millionen Arbeitslosen bauen zwei
Millionen neue Zuchthäuser für die anderen fünf Millionen,
die keine Arbeit bekommen können."

Job creation:
"Of the seven million unemployed, two million are building
prisons for the other five million who cannot find a job."

The montage is a mordant comment on unemployment, which
increased dramatically while Heinrich Brüning was chancellor (March
1930–May 1932). On Brüning, see also 10/30, 14/33.

A · I · Z

ERSCHEINT WÖCHENTLICH EINMAL
PREIS 20 PFG., Kc. 1,50, 30 GR.,
30 SCHWEIZER RP. — — V. b. b.

NEUER DEUTSCHER VERLAG, BERLIN
W8 | JAHRG. XI | NR. 38 | 1932 | 18. 9.

Montage: JOHN HEARTFIELD

Arbeitsbeschaffung:

*„Von den sieben Millionen Arbeitslosen bauen zwei Millionen neue Zucht-
häuser für die anderen fünf Millionen, die keine Arbeit bekommen können."*

Je höher der Brotkorb – desto strammer der Maulkorb

The higher the bread basket – the tighter the muzzle

The text plays with the changed meanings of *Korb* (basket) when different prefixes are added: *Brotkorb* is a bread basket, *Maulkorb*, literally a mouth basket. The left-hand section shows wage agreements; on the right are Communist newspapers.

Je höher der Brotkorb – desto strammer der Maulkorb

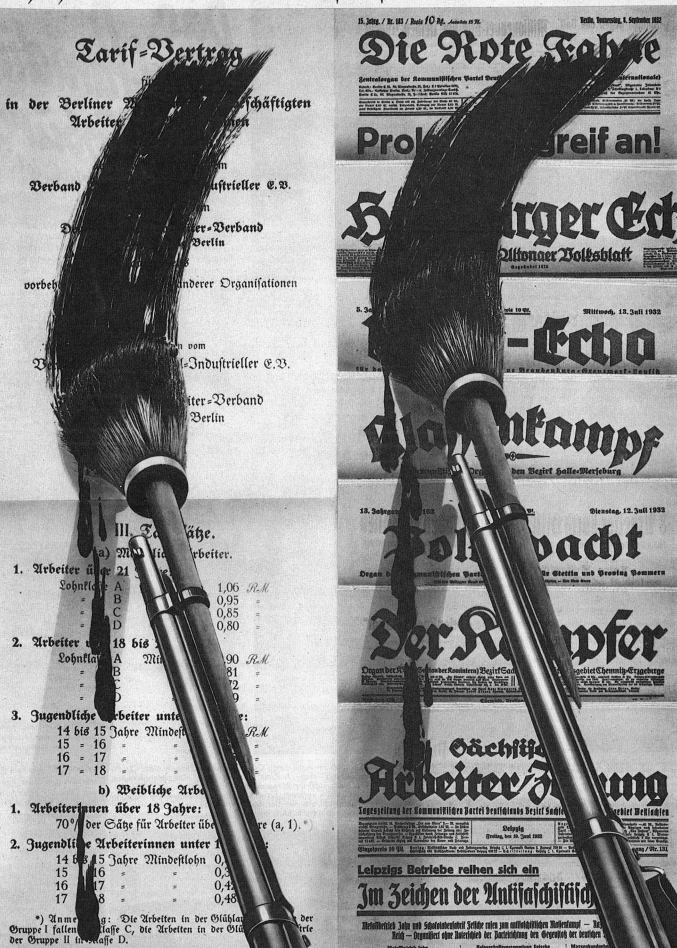

Montage: JOHN HEARTFIELD

DER SINN DES HITLERGRUSSES:

Kleiner Mann bittet um große Gaben

Motto:
MILLIONEN STEHEN HINTER MIR!

THE MEANING OF THE HITLER SALUTE:

Little man asks for big gifts

Motto:
MILLIONS STAND BEHIND ME!

The montage links Hitler's electoral successes (in the Reichstag elections of 31 July Nazis won 230 of 608 seats) and his attempts to court the Rhineland industrialists (particularly significant was his speech to a gathering of them in Düsseldorf on 27 January 1932). See also 4/32.

ERSCHEINT WÖCHENTLICH EINMAL ● PREIS 20 PFG., Kc. 1,60
30 GR., 30 SCHWEIZER RP. ● V. b. b. ● NEUER DEUTSCHER
VERLAG, BERLIN W8 ● JAHRGANG XI ● NR. 42 ● 16. 10. 1932

DER SINN DES HITLERGRUSSES:

Motto:
**MILLIONEN
STEHEN
HINTER MIR!**

Kleiner Mann bittet um große Gaben

Montage: JOHN HEARTFIELD

15 JAHRE SOWJET-UNION

Wir schwören: "In der Stunde der Gefahr lassen wir unser sozialistisches Vaterland nicht im Stich"

15 YEARS OF THE SOVIET UNION

We swear: "In the hour of danger we do not abandon our Socialist Fatherland"

The montage was part of a special issue celebrating fifteen years of the Soviet Union that had a photograph of Stalin on the cover and, on the page facing the montage, an editorial by *AIZ* publisher Willi Münzenberg (see 1/32), "Sozialismus die Lösung / Sozialismus die Rettung" (Socialism the solution / Socialism the salvation).

The idea of the Soviet Union needing to defend itself against a continuous threat from its capitalist neighbors, especially Nazi Germany after 1933, was a major, ongoing theme for Heartfield. See 1/32, 16/32, 35/34, 14/35, 16/35, 17/35, 17/36, 3/38, 10/38.

15 JAHRE SOWJET-UNION

Montage: JOHN HEARTFIELD

Wir schwören: „In der Stunde der Gefahr lassen wir unser sozialistisches Vaterland nicht im Stich"

Hitler und Hummel
der gleiche Rummel

LÜGEN HABEN KURZE BEINE

Es kam ein Mann aus Österreich
Versprach dem Volk das Dritte Reich:
"Ich führ' heraus euch aus der Not!"
"Heil Hitler!
Schlagt die Roten tot!"

Es kam ein Mann aus Afrikar,
Der niemals dort gewesen war,
Ein schwergeprüfter Patriot.
"Heil Daubmann!
Schlagt den Franzmann tot!"

Der falsche Daubmann hatte Pech
Er trieb's ein bißchen gar zu frech.
Der ruhmbedeckte deutsche Held
Hieß Hummel
Und log auch für's Geld.

Der große Adolf schwätzt noch munter
Das dümmste Zeug vom Himmel runter.
Das Kapital hält ihn noch aus
Den Retter
Aus dem Braunen Haus.

Herr Hitler ist ein zweiter Hummel.
Macht Schluß mit seinem Nazi-Rummel!
Er spielt sich auf als Sozialist
Dieweil er
Knecht der Reichen ist.

Hitler and Hummel
the same racket

LIES HAVE SHORT LEGS

A man came out of Austria
Who promised the people the Third Reich:
"I lead you out of misery!"
"Heil Hitler!
Strike the Reds dead!"

A man came out of Africa,
Who had never been there,
A sorely tested patriot.
"Heil Daubmann!
Strike the Frenchy dead!"

The impostor Daubmann was down on his luck
He got a bit too cheeky.
The German hero covered in glory
Was called Hummel
And also lied for money.

The great Adolf still prattles
The greatest load of rubbish under the sun.
Capital still keeps him going
As the savior
From the Brown House.

Mr. Hitler is a second Hummel.
Put an end to his Nazi racket!
He poses as a socialist
While he is
the servant of the rich.

The montage is a visualization of the German popular saying "Lügen haben kurze Beine" (Lies have short legs). Hummel, aka Daubmann, was a con man who became a nationalist hero. He was especially hailed by the right for his claim to be the last person released from a French jail in Africa after World War I. In December 1932 *AIZ* ran a series of articles exposing the fact and fiction about Daubmann (nos. 50–52 [11, 18, and 25 December], pp. 1177–80, 1205–7, 1234–36).

The inscription on the ribbon reads: "HEIL DAUBMANN! DIE NSDAP / HUGENBERG, SELDTE IN DANKBARKEIT" (Heil Daubmann! The NSDAP / Hugenberg, Seldte in gratitude). NSDAP stands for the Nationalsozialistische Deutsche Arbeiterpartei (National Socialist German Workers' Party, or Nazi Party), which Hitler and other nationalists created in 1920. Alfred Hugenberg was a communications tycoon and nationalist politician (see 13/33). Franz Seldte (1882–1947) founded the Stahlhelm (Steel Helmet), a nationalist veterans' organization, in 1918. He was Reich minister of labor from 1933 to 1945.

ERSCHEINT WÖCHENTLICH EINMAL
PREIS 20 PFG., Kc. 1,60, 30 GR.,
30 SCHWEIZER RP. — — V. b. b.
NEUER DEUTSCHER VERLAG, BERLIN
W8 | JAHRG. XI | NR. 45 | 1932 | 6. 11.

Hitler und Hummel
der gleiche Rummel

Montage: JOHN HEARTFIELD

Es kam ein Mann aus Österreich
Versprach dem Volk das Dritte Reich:
„Ich führ' heraus euch aus der Not!"
„Heil Hitler!
Schlagt die Roten tot!"

Der große Adolf schwätzt noch munter
Das dümmste Zeug vom Himmel runter.
Das Kapital hält ihn noch aus
Den Retter
Aus dem Braunen Haus.

Es kam ein Mann aus Afrikar,
Der niemals dort gewesen war,
Ein schwergeprüfter Patriot.
„Heil Daubmann!
Schlagt den Franzmann tot!"

Herr Hitler ist ein zweiter Hummel.
Macht Schluß mit seinem Nazi-Rummel!
Er spielt sich auf als Sozialist
Dieweil er
Knecht der Reichen ist.

Der falsche Daubmann hatte Pech
Er trieb's ein bißchen gar zu frech.
Der ruhmbedeckte deutsche Held
Hieß Hummel
Und log auch für's Geld.

Aufrüstung tut not!

JA, JA, der Profit aus unsern Knochen nimmt auch mal ein Ende.

Nur keine Bange, für Nachschub wird schon gesorgt.

Armament is necessary!

YES, YES, the profit from our bones will come to an end some day.

Don't worry, supplies are being taken care of.

Heartfield was suggesting that the slaughter of the First World War was for the benefit of the capitalist system, and that capitalists had a vested interest in creating another such conflict. For the original artwork for this montage, see Fig. 5.

Aufrüstung tut not!

Montage: JOHN HEARTFIELD

6 Millionen kommunistische Stimmen

"Aber Papen, was machen Sie denn da?"
"Ich lege den bolschewistischen Sumpf trocken."

"Kein Mittel kann scharf genug sein, den Bolschewismus in
Deutschland mit Stumpf und Stiel auszurotten!"
(Aus Papens Rundfunkrede vom 4. November)

6 million Communist votes

"But Papen, what are you doing there?"
"I am draining the Bolshevik swamp."

"No means can be too severe to exterminate Bolshevism in
Germany root and branch!"
(From Papen's radio speech of 4 November)

In the Reichstag elections of November 1932, the Communists
gained 750,000 votes and the Nazis lost two million. Franz von
Papen (1879–1969) was a diplomat and politician. He replaced
Brüning (see 10/30) as chancellor in June 1932 and served as
Hitler's vice-chancellor from January 1933 until 1934. His diplomatic
career is the subject of 33/34 and 42/34.

The montage was given a new title, *WIE FELS IM MEER*
(Like a rock in the ocean), when it was published in 1962 in Wieland
Herzfelde's book *John Heartfield: Leben und Werk* (p. 156).

ERSCHEINT WÖCHENTLICH EINMAL — PREIS 20 PFG., Kc. 1,60, 30 GR., 30 SCHWEIZER RP.
V. b. b. — NEUER DEUTSCHER VERLAG, BERLIN W 8 — JAHRGANG XI — NR. 47 — 20. 11. 1932

A-I-Z

6 Millionen kommunistische Stimmen

„Kein Mittel kann scharf genug sein, den Bolschewismus in Deutschland mit Stumpf und Stiel auszurotten!"
(Aus Papens Rundfunkrede vom 4. November)

„Aber Papen, was machen Sie denn da?"
„Ich lege den bolschewistischen Sumpf trocken."

Montage: JOHN HEARTFIELD

DER SINN VON GENF

Wo das Kapital lebt, kann der Friede nicht leben!

In Genf, der Stadt des Völkerbundes, wurde mit Maschinengewehren in die gegen den Faschismus demonstrierenden
Arbeitermassen geschossen.
15 Tote, über 60 Verwundete blieben auf dem Platze.
(Ausführliche Bildreportage unseres Sonderberichterstatters
auf den Innenseiten)

THE MEANING OF GENEVA

Where capital lives, peace cannot live!

In Geneva, city of the League of Nations, crowds of
workers demonstrating against Fascism were shot at with
machine guns.
15 dead, more than 60 wounded left on the square.
(Detailed phototext report by our special correspondent in
this issue)

Heartfield's subtitle, "Wo das Kapital lebt, kann der Friede nicht
leben" (Where captial lives, peace cannot live), was also the title of
the phototext report in the same issue (pp. 1158–59). For the
original artwork for this montage, see Fig. 10.

Wieland Herzfelde included a different version of the
montage, dated 1960, in *John Heartfield: Leben und Werk* (p. 235).
The only text was the new title *Niemals wieder!* (Never again!), and
the background photograph of the League of Nations was replaced
by painted flames. A specific attack on the League had become a
generalized antiwar statement (although in the context of the Cold
War Heartfield would have regarded the enemies of the Soviet Union
and its allies as the greatest threat to world peace).

A·I·Z

ERSCHEINT WÖCHENTLICH EINMAL — PREIS 20 PFG.,
Kc. 1,60, 30 GR., 30 SCHWEIZER RP. — V. b. b. — NEUER DEUTSCHER
VERLAG, BERLIN W8 — JAHRGANG XI — NR. 48 — 27. 11. 1932

In Genf, der Stadt des Völkerbundes, wurde mit
Maschinengewehren in die gegen den Faschismus
demonstrierenden Arbeitermassen geschossen.
15 Tote, über 60 Verwundete blieben auf dem Platze.
(Ausführliche Bildreportage unseres
Sonderberichterstatters auf den Innenseiten)

DER SINN VON GENF

Wo das Kapital lebt, kann der Friede nicht leben!

VÖLKERBUND

Montage: JOHN HEARTFIELD

....und Friede auf Erden!

....and peace on earth!

A *Stempelkarte* is a dole card. Urbin is a brand of shoe polish. The Berliner Winterhilfe (Berlin Winter Help) was a charitable organization. The books are titled *Praktischer Führer durch die Notverordnungen* (Practical guide to the emergency decrees) and *Das Goldene Giftgas Kochbuch* (The golden poison gas cookbook).

The montage was a seasonal contribution to a special issue called "Das Kind" (The child). Facing it was an editorial, "KAPITALISMUS = KINDERNOT / SOZIALISMUS = KINDERGLÜCK" (Capitalism = The misery of children / Socialism = The happiness of children).

...und Friede auf Erden!

Montage: JOHN HEARTFIELD

Kleiner SA-Mann, was nun?

Zur "Beurlaubung" Gregor Strassers durch Adolf Hitler

Armer Hitlermann,
kleiner Hitlermann,
möchtest auch auf "Urlaub" fahren,
wie die hohen Herrn,
die sich gar zu gern
liegen in den blonden Haaren.
Ach, was fällt dir ein?
du bist nur "gemein"
und du wirst es bald erfahren,
der dich führt, hat dich verführt,
und der Platz, für den, der friert,
ist bei den Kommunisten!

Little SA man, what now?

On the occasion of Gregor Strasser's "leave of absence" imposed by Adolf Hitler

Poor Hitler man,
little Hitler man,
you would also like to go on a "holiday,"
like the top people,
who so enjoy getting in each other's blond hair.
Ah, what occurs to you?
you are only "common"
and you will soon discover,
that he who leads you has led you astray,
and the place for one who is cold
is with the Communists!

The title alludes to the 1932 bestselling novel *Kleiner Mann – was nun?* (Little man – what now?) by Hans Fallada (1893–1947), which describes the lives of a shop assistant and his wife during the Depression.

The suitcase on the platform has the initials of Gregor Strasser (1892–1934), who represented the socialist current of National Socialism and was committed to the SA (the Sturmabteilung, or Storm Troopers), the plebeian wing of the Nazi Party (see 3/33, 15/33, 28/34, 29/34). In December 1932 Strasser had a serious quarrel with Hitler that caused him to resign from the party leadership. He distanced himself from the crisis by taking a vacation in Italy, hence the sticker on the case: "nach Bolzano" (to Bolzano, a town in the South Tyrol). Heartfield used quotes to emphasize the word *Beurlaubung* in the subtitle; *Beurlaubung* is a leave of absence, but it can also refer to the suspension of an official. It also contains within it the word *Urlaub* (holiday), used in the third line of the poem.

The sign reads: "Gleis 1 / Fernschnellzug (Nur I. u. II. Kl. Besonders zuschlagpflichtig) über München ins Dritte Reich / reserviert für Führer der NSDAP" (Platform 1 / Long distance express train [First and second class only: surcharge required] into the Third Reich via Munich / reserved for leaders of the NSDAP). The leader of the NSDAP was of course Adolf Hitler (see 4/32, 13/32). "Gebt für die Reisespesen unserer Führer!" means Donate to the traveling expenses of our leaders! and refers to Strasser.

Zur „Beurlaubung" Gregor Strassers durch Adolf Hitler

Kleiner SA-Mann, was nun?

Gleis
1

Fernschnellzug
(Nur I. u. II. Kl. Besonders zuschlagpflichtig)
über München ins Dritte Reich

reserviert für
Führer der NSDAP

Gebt
für die
Reisespesen
unserer
Führer!

G. St.

MITROPA

SPEISEWAGEN

**Armer Hitlermann,
kleiner Hitlermann,
möchtest auch auf „Urlaub" fahren,
wie die hohen Herrn,
die sich gar zu gern
liegen in den blonden Haaren.**

**Ach, was fällt dir ein?
du bist nur „gemein"
und du wirst es bald erfahren,
der dich führt, hat dich verführt,
und der Platz, für den, der friert,
ist bei den Kommunisten!**

Montage: JOHN HEARTFIELD

Glückliche Reise ins Neue Jahr wünscht die AIZ!

AIZ wishes you a happy journey into the new year!

The tumbling figures are Adolf Hitler (see 4/32) and Theodor Leipart (1867–1947), a Social Democrat and trade union leader in the Weimar period who was known for his anti-Communism.

TODESKONJUNKTUR

Die Rüstungs-Industrie betet:

"Je mehr Chinesen ihr Leben verhauchen,
umso kräftiger unsre Schlote rauchen:
Tausend tote Chinesen
decken schon unsre Spesen.
Hunderttausend tote Chinesen
und wir werden genesen.
Zehn Millionen tote Chinesen
könnten uns von der Krise erlösen.

Oh, Herr! Steh bei uns Herrn der Erde,
daß das Feuer im Osten größer werde!"

THE DEATH BOOM

The arms industry prays:

"The more Chinese who give up the ghost,
the more powerfully our chimneys will smoke:
A thousand dead Chinese
will soon cover our expenses.
A hundred thousand dead Chinese
and we will recover.
Ten million dead Chinese
could deliver us from the crisis.

Oh Lord! Stand by us, the lords of the earth,
so that the fire in the East will spread!"

Japan had occupied the northern province of Manchuria in 1931, and when this issue was published in 1933 the civil war in China between Communists and Nationalists was continuing.

The text accompanying the montage says: "Werktätige! Kämpft gegen die imperialistische Kriegspolitik! Wählt zur Betriebsrätewahl: Einheitsliste!" (Workers! Fight against the imperialist politics of war! Vote at the factory councils election: United list!)

When this montage was published in Wieland Herzfelde's *John Heartfield: Leben und Werk* (p. 157), the title was changed to *GOTTESLÄSTERER* (Blasphemers), and the names "Krupp" (see 2/34) and "Skoda" (both leading arms manufacturers) were removed from the gun barrels.

TODESKONJUNKTUR

Die Rüstungs-Industrie betet:

„Je mehr Chinesen ihr Leben verhauchen,
umso kräftiger unsre Schlote rauchen:
Tausend tote Chinesen
decken schon unsre Spesen.
Hunderttausend tote Chinesen
und wir werden genesen.
Zehn Millionen tote Chinesen
könnten uns von der Krise erlösen.

Oh, Herr! Steh bei uns Herrn der Erde,
daß das Feuer im Osten größer werde!"

Schneider-Creuzot

Armstrong

Vickers

Bethlehem Steel

Krupp

Skoda

Montage:
JOHN
HEARTFIELD

Kleiner SA-Heldenbilderbogen

"Lieber Onkel Schupo, führ' mich demonstrieren!"

"Liebling des Volks zu sein, Heil Hitler Dir!"

Röhm's großer Tag am Bülowplatz: "Huch nein, die süßen Schupos!"

Der Angriff
Der gestrige Tag hat es bewiesen:
Berlin gehört uns!
Ja Ja Ja Ja Ja Ja Ja Ja
Da lachen ja die Hühner!

Small picture sheet of SA heroes

"Dear Uncle Cop, take me demonstrating!"

"To be the beloved of the people, Heil Hitler to thee!"

Röhm's great day at Bülowplatz: "Oh no, the sweet cops!"

Der Angriff
It was proven yesterday:
Berlin is ours!
YesYesYesYes YesYesYesYes
The chickens laugh about that!

Schupo, on the top left-hand image, means cop, short for *Schutzpolizist* (policeman). The image at the bottom left shows SA leader Ernst Röhm (see 28/34) admiring the backsides of "süßen Schupos" (sweet cops), an allusion to his homosexuality.

Note the chants of the demonstrators in the Hitler montage: "Hitler verrecke! / Nieder! / Capitalsknecht! / Arbeitermörder! / Nieder! Nieder!" (Perish Hitler! / Down! / Slave of capital! / Murderer of workers! / Down! Down!). "Hitler verrecke!" was a Communist counterslogan to the Nazis' "Heil Hitler! Juda verrecke!" (Heil Hitler! Perish Judah!). Hitler is saying, "Heil Hitler Dir!" (Heil Hitler to thee!), which is the title of an SA marching song.

The montage is a condensation of the two-page story in this issue (pp. 132–33) that reported on an SA demonstration and Communist counterdemonstration in the Communist-controlled neighborhood in Berlin that included the Büloplatz, site of the Communist headquarters. According to the report, the SA "conquered" empty streets already under police protection. Hitler did not turn up, although Röhm put in an appearance.

Kleiner SA-Heldenbilderbogen

„Lieber Onkel Schupo, führ' mich demonstrieren!"

„Liebling des Volks zu sein, Heil Hitler Dir!"

Röhm's großer Tag am Bülowplatz: „Huch nein, die süßen Schupos!"

**Da lachen ja
die Hühner!**

Montage: JOHN HEARTFIELD

131

Vereint kämpfen!

Schließt die Reihen
gegen Faschismus und Reaktion!
WÄHLT KOMMUNISTEN LISTE 3

Fight united!

Close ranks
against fascism and reaction!
VOTE COMMUNIST LIST 3

This issue featured the Reichstag and Prussian Landtag elections
(pp. 170–75, 189). This cover was Heartfield's final contribution to
the Berlin-based magazine. Hitler had become chancellor on 30
January 1933, and after the 5 March issue the publication of *AIZ*
moved to Prague. Production resumed in Prague in late March, but
Heartfield's next montage (5/33) did not appear until 10 May.

ERSCHEINT WÖCHENTLICH EINMAL • PREIS 20 PFG., Kc. 1,60, 30 GR., 30
SCHWEIZER RP., IN NORDAMERIKA UND KANADA 10 CENTS • V.b.b. • NEUER
DEUTSCHER VERLAG, BERLIN W8 • JAHRGANG XII • NR. 8 • 19. 2. 1933

AIZ

AUS DEM INHALT:

15 JAHRE IM DIENSTE DER ARBEITER UND BAUERN

Einheitsfront gegen Faschismus • Verheißungen - Erfüllungen
6 Tage - 13 Tote • Schmuggel • Preisaufgabe u. a. m.

Vereint kämpfen!

3

Schließt die Reihen
gegen Faschismus und Reaktion!
WÄHLT KOMMUNISTEN LISTE

Montage: JOHN HEARTFIELD

DURCH LICHT ZUR NACHT

Also sprach Dr. Goebbels: Lasst uns aufs neue Brände entfachen, auf dass die Verblendeten nicht erwachen!

AM 10. MAI WERDEN IN DEUTSCHLAND ALLE MISSLIEBIGEN BÜCHER VERBRANNT

THROUGH LIGHT TO NIGHT

Thus spake Dr. Goebbels: Let us start new fires so that the dazzled do not awake!

ON 10 MAY IN GERMANY ALL ODIOUS BOOKS ARE TO BE BURNED

Joseph Goebbels (1897–1945) became minister of public enlightenment and propaganda in 1933 (see 16/34, 19/34, 20/34, 50/34, 1/35, 9/35, 12/35, 14/35, 16/35, 19/35, 3/36, 7/36, 23/36, 4/37, 23/37). The Reichstag burns in the background. The writing on the can – "Deterding-Goering & Co / prima / Brandstifter-Oel" (Deterding-Göring & Co. / first-class / arsonist's oil) – refers to Henry Deterding, a Dutch oil millionaire and Nazi supporter (see 2/37), and the prominent Nazi Hermann Göring, who was accused by Communists of having masterminded the Reichstag Fire in February 1933 to justify emergency actions against the Left (see 23/33).

Some of the books in the fire were published by Malik Verlag, the leftist publishing house run by Wieland Herzfelde, and Heartfield had designed their jackets: Ilja Ehrenburg, *Die Heiligsten Güter* (The most sacred possessions; 1931); M. Iljin , *Fünf Jahre, die die Welt verändern* (Five years that changed the world; 1932); Theodor Plivier, *Der Kaiser ging, Die Generäle Bleiben* (The Kaiser goes, the generals remain; 1932). In the version of the montage that appeared in Herzfelde's *John Heartfield: Leben und Werk* in 1962 (p. 158), Johannes R. Becher's *Ein Mensch unserer Zeit* (A man of our time; 1930) was added to the fire. Becher (1891–1958) was a Communist writer whose books were also burned by the Nazis. Heartfield's discreet addition of his book probably registered Becher's contemporary importance in the German Democratic Republic. From 1950 he had been a member of the central committee of the ruling Communist Party, and from 1954 to 1958 he was minister of culture. The lyric of the national anthem of the GDR is a Becher poem.

AIZ

Erscheint wöchentlich einmal. • Preis Kč 1·60, 30 Gr., 30 Schweizer Rappen, 20 Pfg.
In Nordamerika und Kanada 10 Cents • V. b. b. • Jahrgang XII • Nummer 18 • 10. Mai 1933

AM 10. MAI WERDEN IN DEUTSCHLAND ALLE MISSLIEBIGEN BÜCHER VERBRANNT

DURCH LICHT ZUR NACHT

Also sprach Dr. Goebbels: Lasst uns aufs neue Brände entfachen, auf dass die Verblendeten nicht erwachen!

HITLERS PROGRAMM

Das Volk wäre glücklich angeschmiert,
jetzt müssen die Häuser angeschmiert werden!

Hitler in seiner Programmrede am 1. Mai: "Zur Behebung
der Arbeitslosigkeit wollen wir die Häuser wieder in
Ordnung bringen."

HITLER'S PROGRAM

The people are now happily swindled,
next the houses must be daubed!

Hitler in his policy speech on 1 May: "To do away with
unemployment, we want to put the houses in order again."

Anschmieren means both to swindle someone and to daub. See also
6/34 and Fig. 4, the original artwork for this montage.

HITLERS PROGRAMM

Hitler in seiner Programmrede am 1. Mai: „Zur Behebung der Arbeitslosigkeit wollen wir die Häuser wieder in Ordnung bringen." Fotomontage: John Heartfield

Das Volk wäre glücklich angeschmiert, jetzt müssen die Häuser angeschmiert werden!

339

Dem Kongreß der Antifaschisten in Kopenhagen

Hooh-ruck!
Setzt die Nazis unter Druck!
Packt an
Mann für Mann,
Bis die Fahne niederkracht.
Einig seid Ihr eine Macht!

On the occasion of the Congress of Anti-Fascists in Copenhagen

Heave!
Put the Nazis under pressure!
Lend a hand
Man for man,
Until the flag crashes down.
Be united as one power!

This issue carried a two-page report (pp. 360–61) on the congress of Scandinavian anti-Fascist organizations held in Copenhagen in June 1933.

Fotomontage: John Heartfield

Hooh-rück!
Setzt die Nazis unter Druck!
Packt an
Mann für Mann,
Bis die Fahne niederkracht.
Einig seid Ihr eine Macht!

Dem Kongreß der Antifaschisten in Kopenhagen

Mit seinen Phrasen will er die Welt vergasen

Der Mann, der die deutsche Verfassung beschwor, spricht jetzt von Frieden. Er wird ihn halten wie seinen Eid.

With his empty phrases he wants to gas the world

The man who swore on the German constitution speaks now of peace. He will uphold it as he has his oath.

The symbol of disarmament used by the League of Nations was a *Friedensengel* (angel of peace).

Mit seinen Phrasen will er die Welt vergasen

Fotomontage: John Heartfield

Der Mann, der die deutsche Verfassung beschwor, spricht jetzt von Frieden. Er wird ihn halten wie seinen Eid.

Morgan spricht: "Der Staat bin ich"

"Es hat ja gar keinen Sinn, daß ich Steuern abführe, denn letzten Endes laufen die Steuern doch immer in meine Tresors."

Eine amerikanische Untersuchungskommission stellte fest, daß der Multimilliardär J. P. Morgan seit Jahren keine Einkommensteuer zahlte

Morgan speaks: "I am the state"

"There is no point in my paying taxes, when in the end the taxes always flow into my treasury."

An American investigative commission established that the multibillionaire J. P. Morgan had not been paying income tax for years

---

Heartfield was referring to John Pierpont Morgan, Jr. (1867–1943). "Der Staat bin ich" is a translation of "L'état c'est moi," the assertion Louis XIV is purported to have made before the Parlement de Paris in 1665. Pipes labeled "Einkommensteuer" (income tax) link the pockets of a global work force to the Morgan Trust headquarters in New York.

Morgan spricht: »Der Staat bin ich«

"Es hat ja gar keinen Sinn, daß ich Steuern abführe, denn letzten Endes laufen die Steuern doch immer in meine Tresors."

MORGAN TRUST BUILDING

Fotomontage: John Heartfield

Eine amerikanische Untersuchungskommission stellte fest, daß der Multimilliardär J. P. Morgan seit Jahren keine Einkommensteuer zahlte

Das Kreuz war noch nicht schwer genug

Zur Gründung der deutschen Staatskirche

Der Katholik Adolf Hitler organisierte die evangelische deutsche Staatskirche und ernannte einen Reichsbischof

The cross was not yet heavy enough

On the foundation of the German state church

The Catholic Adolf Hitler organized the Evangelical German state church and nominated a Reich bishop

---

Hitler attempted to merge Catholics and Protestants into a single state church. On 14 July 1933 the Reichstag recognized a constitution for the new state church, and on 23 July Hitler's nominee Ludwig Müller was appointed Reich bishop (see also 3/34).

The starting point for Heartfield's montage (see Fig. 6, the original artwork) was a photograph of a painting by the Danish artist Bertel Thorwaldsen (1770–1844), who is best known as a sculptor and a leader of the neoclassical movement. Thorwaldsen's ecclesiastical art was especially popular in the nineteenth century. The Nazi is Rudolf Diehls, founder of the Gestapo (see also 7/34).

**UNVERÄNDERT REGIERT IN DEUTSCHLAND
DAS KLASSENGESETZ
ALLES MITGLIEDER DER NSDAP**

1 HEINRICH GEORGE, Schauspieler. 2 PRINZ AUGUST WILHELM (Auwi). 3 Der EX-KRONPRINZ. 4 SCHMID-DÜSSELDORF, preußischer Kommissar für Sonderaufträge. 5 Dr. ROBERT LEY, Gewerkschaftskommissar. 6 RUST, Kultusminister.

**CLASS LAW STILL RULES IN GERMANY
ALL MEMBERS OF THE NSDAP**

1 HEINRICH GEORGE, actor. 2 PRINCE AUGUST WILHELM (Auwi). 3 The EX-CROWN PRINCE. 4 SCHMID-DÜSSELDORF, Prussian commissioner for special tasks. 5 Dr. ROBERT LEY, commissioner for trade unions. 6 RUST, minister for culture.

Heinrich George (1893–1946), a film star whose career began in the twenties, enthusiastically supported Nazism and pursued a successful film and theatrical career under the Third Reich. Prince August Wilhelm (1887–1949), nicknamed "Auwi," was the fourth son of Kaiser Wilhelm II. He joined the NSDAP and SA in 1929. The ex-Crown Prince Wilhelm (1882–1951) was the oldest son of the Kaiser. He publicly supported Hitler's candidacy for president in 1932. Carl Christian Schmid (born 1886) was governor of Düsseldorf in 1933. For Robert Ley, see 19/34. Bernhard Rust (1883–1945), Reich minister for science, education, and popular culture from 1934 to 1945, was responsible for purging the schools and universities.

(pages 130–31)

Zur Gründung der deutschen Staatskirche

Der Katholik Adolf Hitler organisierte die evangelische deutsche Staatskirche und ernannte einen Reichsbischof

Fotomontage: John Heartfield

Das Kreuz war noch nicht schwer genug

UNVERÄNDERT REGIERT IN DE
ALLES MITGLIED

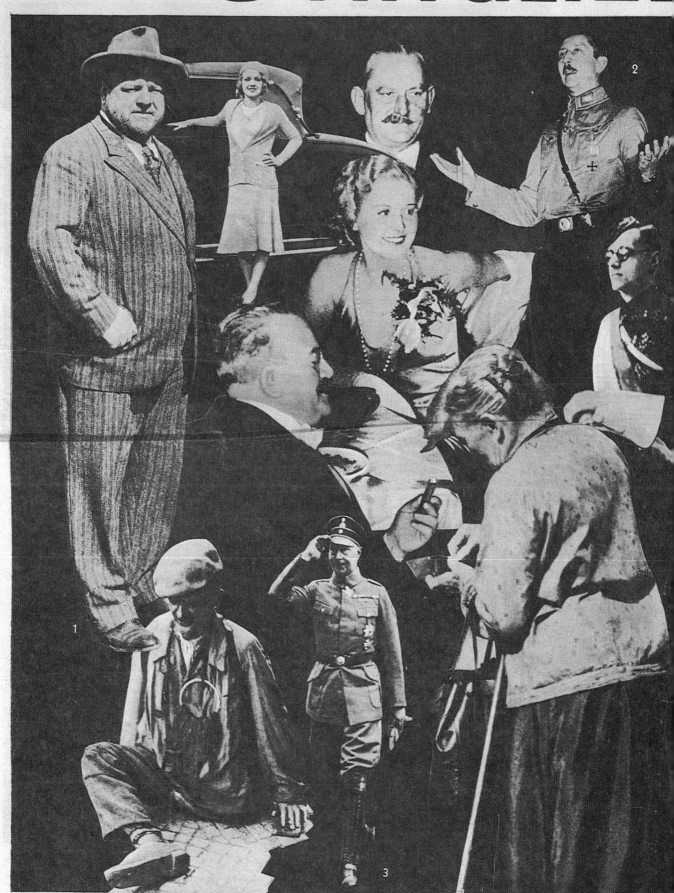

1 HEINRICH GEORGE, Schauspieler. 2 PRINZ AUGUST WILHELM (Auwi). 3 Der EX-KRONPRINZ. 4 SCHMID-DÜSSELDORF, preußischer Kommissar für Sonderaufträge. 5 Dr. ROBERT LEY, Gewerkschaftskommissar. 6 RUST, Kultusminister.

Fotomontage: John Heartfield

ALLES IN SCHÖNSTER ORDNUNG!

Daladier, *französischer Ministerpräsident:* "Ich habe von Beginn der Weltwirtschaftskonferenz an eine günstige Entwicklung der Probleme feststellen können. Die Verhandlungen scheinen fester umrissenen Lösungen entgegen zu gehen, als man hoffen konnte."

MacDonald, *Vorsitzender der Konferenz:* "Ich kann in ehrlicher Überzeugung erklären, daß das Ergebnis der Konferenz sehr befriedigend ist."

Sechs Millionen Sack Kaffee werden vernichtet.
Sao Paolo, 18. Juni. (Tel.-Komp.)
Das staatliche Kaffeeinstitut in Sao Paolo hat die brasilianische Regierung dringend gebeten, ihm die Vernichtung von sechs Millionen Sack Kaffee zu gestatten, um Platz für die neue Ernte zu gewinnen, die man auf 20 Millionen Sack schätzt.

NEVILLE CHAMBERLAIN, engl. Schatzkanzler
CORDELL HULL, amerik. Delegationsführer
RAMSAY MACDONALD

EVERYTHING'S FINE!

Daladier, *French premier:* "From the beginning of the World Economic Conference I could recognize a reasonable approach to the problems. The negotiations seem to be moving toward more concrete solutions than one could have hoped for."

MacDonald, *chairman of the conference:* "I can with genuine conviction announce that the outcome of the conference is very satisfactory."

Six million sacks of coffee are being destroyed.
São Paolo, 18 June. (tel.-com.)
The State Coffee Institute in São Paolo has urgently entreated the Brazilian government to permit the destruction of six million sacks of coffee to make room for the new harvest, which is estimated to be twenty million sacks.

NEVILLE CHAMBERLAIN, English chancellor of the exchequer
CORDELL HULL, leader of the American delegation
RAMSAY MACDONALD

Edouard Daladier (1884–1970), leader of the Radical Socialist Party, was premier of France in 1933, 1934, and 1938–40. For Labour Party leader and British Prime Minister James Ramsay MacDonald, see 5/30. Neville Chamberlain (1869–1940), a Conservative, served as chancellor of the exchequer in Great Britain from 1931 to 1937 and as prime minister from 1937 to 1940. Cordell Hull (1871–1955) was Roosevelt's secretary of state from 1933 to 1944. (In the montage Chamberlain is incorrectly identified as Hull and Hull as Chamberlain.)

The article on the page facing the montage, "Wirrwar der Weltwirtschaft" (Muddle of the world economy), concluded that the only solution for the capitalist crisis was war against the one society not based on the profit motive, the Soviet Union. The article that began on the next page, "Zwei Konferenzen: Zwei Welten!" (Two conferences: Two worlds!), compared the London World Economic Conference unfavorably with a conference convened in Moscow to discuss the Five Year Plan.

ALLES IN SCHÖNSTER ORDNUNG!

Sechs Millionen Sack Kaffee werden vernichtet.

Sao Paolo, 18. Juni. (Tel.-Komp.) Das staatliche Kaffeeinstitut in Sao Paolo hat die brasilianische Regierung dringend gebeten, ihm die Vernichtung von sechs Millionen Sack Kaffee zu gestatten, um Platz für die neue Ernte zu gewinnen, die man auf 20 Millionen Sack schätzt.

NEVILLE CHAMBERLAIN, engl. Schatzkanzler   CORDEL HULL, amerik. Delegationsführer   RAMSAY MACDONALD   Fotomontage: John Heartfield

Daladier, *französischer Ministerpräsident:* „Ich habe von Beginn der Weltwirtschaftskonferenz an eine günstige Entwicklung der Probleme feststellen können. Die Verhandlungen scheinen fester umrissenen Lösungen entgegen zu gehen, als man hoffen konnte."

MacDonald, *Vorsitzender der Konferenz:* „Ich kann in ehrlicher Überzeugung erklären, daß das Ergebnis der Konferenz sehr befriedigend ist."

So ward aus Hugenberg der Hugenzwerg

"Hitler, Hitler, gib mir meine Legionen wieder!"

Hugenbergs Schwanengesang

Gestern noch auf hundert Sesseln
heute sitz' ich in den Nesseln
morgen machen sie mich kalt
… deutsche Treue wird nicht alt!

Thus Hugenberg the mountain became Hugenberg the dwarf

"Hitler, Hitler, give me back my legions!"

Hugenberg's swan song

Yesterday still on a hundred easy chairs
today I am in hot water
tomorrow they will kill me
… German loyalty is short-lived!

Alfred Hugenberg (1865–1951) was a German industrialist and newspaper and film magnate who used his influence in the communications industries to preach nationalism. He became leader of the Deutschnationale Volkspartei (German National People's Party) in 1928. From 1929 to 1933 his party engaged in tactical alliances with the Nazis. On 30 January 1933 he was appointed Hitler's first minister of economics and agriculture, but in June he was forced to resign and his party was broken up as a result of Nazi pressure. The writing on the balloons summarizes Hugenberg's political career. "Harzburger Front," for example, refers to the meeting he convened at Harzburg in 1931. The aim was to create an alliance of nationalists to oust Chancellor Brüning (see also 10/30, 14/33). The initiative failed when Hitler refused to give his support. The phototext report facing the montage illustrated Nazi pressure on Hugenberg's German National People's Party: the headquarters were raided and party functionaries arrested.

The German title plays with the rhyme of *Berg* (mountain) and *Zwerg* (dwarf). The second line alludes to Emperor Augustus's plea to his commander Varus after the Romans were defeated by the Germans in the Teutoburger Wald in 9 A.D. In nationalist mythology, this was the first significant display of German military prowess.

In the swan song, "sich in die Nesseln setzen" means literally to sit in the nettles; "jemanden kalt machen" is literally to make someone cold.

"Hitler, Hitler, gib mir meine Legionen wieder!"

Hugenbergs Schwanengesang

Gestern noch auf hundert Sesseln
heute sitz' ich in den Nesseln
morgen machen sie mich kalt
... deutsche Treue wird nicht alt!

Fotomontage: John Heartfield

So ward aus Hugenberg der Hugenzwerg

"Die Nation steht geschlossen hinter mir"

Ich kenne keine Parteien mehr,
Ich kenne nur noch Gefangene!

Konzentrationslager Deutschland

"The nation stands united behind me"

I no longer know parties,
I know only captives!

Concentration camp Germany

The subtitle rephrases Kaiser Wilhelm's remark on the outbreak of the First World War: "Ich kenne keine Parteien mehr, ich kenne nur noch Deutsche" (I no longer know parties, I know only Germans). See also 6/32.

This montage preceded a feature article on Nazi arrests throughout Germany, "In Deutschland nichts neues!" (All quiet on the German front!), an allusion to Erich Maria Remarque's antiwar novel of 1929, *Im Westen nichts Neues* (All quiet on the Western Front).

On Hitler's left is Paul Löbe (1875–1967), a Social Democratic member of parliament (1920–33) and president of the Reichstag (1920–32). Löbe was temporarily interned in 1933. On Hitler's right is ex-Chancellor Heinrich Brüning (see also 10/30). In July 1933 Brüning gave up his chairmanship of the Catholic Center Party and in 1934 he left the country.

„Die Nation steht geschlossen hinter mir"

Ich kenne keine Parteien mehr,
Ich kenne nur noch Gefangene!

Weil er sich aufs Programm der NSDAP berief

"Dir werden wir unsern "Sozialismus" im Konzentrationslager schon beibringen"

Reichsminister Dr. Frick:
*"Der Herr Reichskanzler hat eindeutig festgestellt, daß die
Revolution abgeschlossen ist. Wer weiterhin noch von einer
Fortsetzung der Revolution oder von einer zweiten
Revolution redet, muß sich darüber klar sein, daß er sich
damit gegen den Führer selbst auflehnt und entsprechend
behandelt wird"*

*Dreizehnhundert rebellische SA-Leute sind im
Konzentrationslager Wilsede in der Lüneburger Heide
untergebracht. Bei einem gemeinsamen "Fluchtversuch aus
dem Lager" wurden 13 SA-Männer von SS erschossen.*

*Bei Gleiwitz O/S schoß SS auf SA-Männer, die gemeinsam
mit den Arbeitern streikten. Drei SA-Leute wurden getötet.*

Because he referred to the NSDAP program

"We will soon teach our 'Socialism' to you in the
concentration camp"

Reich Minister Dr. Frick:
*"The honorable Reich Chancellor has clearly declared that
the revolution is over. Whoever talks further about a
continuation of the revolution or about a second revolution
must realize that he thereby rebels against the Führer himself
and will be dealt with accordingly."*

*Thirteen hundred rebellious SA men have been placed in the
Wilsede concentration camp on the Lüneburg Heath. In a
joint "escape attempt from the camp" thirteen SA men were
shot by the SS.*

*In Gleiwitz, Upper Silesia, SS men shot at SA men who were
on strike with the workers. Three SA men were killed.*

Wilhelm Frick (1877–1946) was Reich minister of the interior from
1933 to 1943. He was responsible for measures against opponents
of the régime, including those members of the SA who demanded a
"second revolution," or the extension of the *socialist* side of National
Socialism. For Frick, see also 22/33, 47/34. On Hitler's continuing
purge of the SA, see 28/34.

Weil er sich aufs Programm der NSDAP berief

Reichsminister Dr. Frick:

*„Der Herr Reichskanzler hat eindeutig festgestellt, daß die Revolution abge-
schlossen ist. Wer weiterhin noch von einer Fortsetzung der Revolution
oder von einer zweiten Revolution redet, muß sich darüber klar sein, daß er
sich damit gegen den Führer selbst auflehnt und entsprechend behandelt wird".*

*Dreizehnhundert rebellische SA-Leute sind im Konzentrationslager Wilsede in der
Lüneburger Heide untergebracht. Bei einem gemeinsamen „Fluchtversuch aus dem
Lager" wurden 13 SA-Männer von SS erschossen.*

*Bei Gleiwitz O/S schoß SS auf SA-Männer, die gemeinsam mit den Arbeitern streikten.
Drei SA-Leute wurden getötet.*

Fotomontage
John Heartfield

„Dir werden wir unsern »Sozialismus« im Konzentrationslager schon beibringen"

DER KRIEG

Ein Gemälde von Franz v. Stuck. Zeitgemäß montiert
von John Heartfield

THE WAR

A painting by Franz von Stuck. A timely montage by
John Heartfield

Heartfield added the swastika-shaped lightning flash and the
photograph of Hitler to the painting *Der Krieg* (1894) by the German
painter Franz von Stuck (1863–1928), one of Hitler's favorite
painters. *Der Krieg* was at the time on display in Munich. The
montage was linked to the title and contents of the article on the next
page, "'Gen Ostland woll'n wir reiten!' Das Dritte Reich rüstet zum
Krieg" ("Against the East we want to ride!" The Third Reich arms for
war). The article suggested that Nazi Germany was preparing for a
war of intervention against the Soviet Union. In *Mein Kampf* (1925)
Hitler had said he wanted to revive the "Drang nach Osten" (Drive to
the East), the policy carried out by the Teutonic knights in the
thirteenth and fourteenth centuries.

DER KRIEG

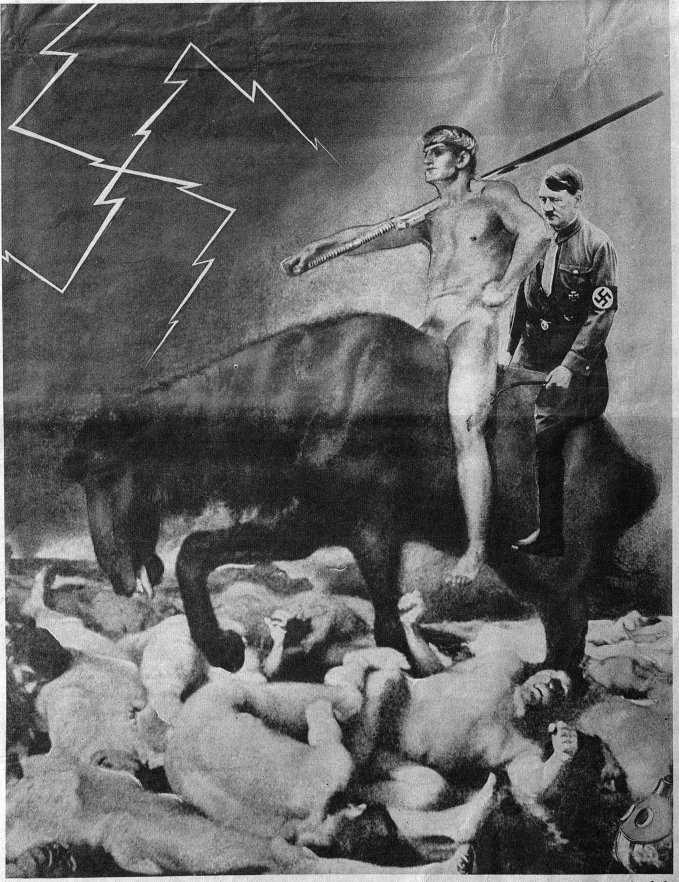

Ein Gemälde von Franz v. Stuck. Zeitgemäß montiert von John Heartfield

DAS MÖRDERKREUZ

Wo ihr dies Zeichen seht, denkt daran:
Für euch ist das Blut der Genossen geflossen.
Ihre brechenden Augen sprechen:
IHR MÜSST UNS RÄCHEN!

RÜCKSEITE DES SCHUTZUMSCHLAGES FÜR DAS
BRAUNBUCH. SIEHE SEITE 522

THE MURDERER'S CROSS

Wherever you see this sign, think of the following:
For you the blood of the comrades flowed.
Their glazed eyes speak:
YOU MUST AVENGE US!

BACK COVER OF THE DUSTJACKET FOR THE BROWN BOOK.
SEE PAGE 522.

The title is an ironic reference to the *Mutterkreuz*, the cross of honor
given to German mothers. The unidentified corpse is that of August
Bassy, an agricultural worker and active anti-Fascist who was
murdered by the SA in 1932. Regular readers would have recognized
the photograph from "Hitlers Menschenjäger" (Hitler's manhunter),
an article that appeared in *AIZ* in 1932 (11, no. 10, pp. 218–19).

This montage illustrated the dustjacket of *Das
Braunbuch* (The brown book), published by Willi Münzenberg (see
1/32), which presented a Communist view of how the Reichstag
was set on fire. It also became part of a set of four propaganda
postcards by Heartfield on the theme of the Reichstag Fire (see
also 25/33, 27/33, 30/33, 32/33).

DAS MÖRDERKREUZ

Wo ihr dies Zeichen seht, denkt daran:
Für euch ist das Blut der Genossen geflossen.
Ihre brechenden Augen sprechen:
IHR MÜSST UNS RÄCHEN!

RÜCKSEITE DES SCHUTZUMSCHLAGES FÜR DAS BRAUNBUCH. SIEHE SEITE 522   FOTOMONTAGE: JOHN HEARTFIELD

WERKZEUG IN GOTTES HAND?
SPIELZEUG IN THYSSENS HAND!

"Der Führer fühlt sich bei der Vollbringung seiner Aufgabe als Werkzeug in Gottes Hand".
(Kube, Preußischer Staatsrat, Oberpräsident der Mark Brandenburg, Führer der Nationalsozialisten im Preußischen Landtag)

Der Großindustrielle Fritz Thyssen, Eigentümer eines Vermögens von 125 Millionen Mark, Leiter eines der größten deutschen Trusts, wurde zum Wirtschaftsdiktator des wichtigsten deutschen Industrie-gebiets, Rheinland-Westfalen, ernannt.

INSTRUMENT IN GOD'S HAND?
TOY IN THYSSEN'S HAND!

"In the fulfillment of his task, the Führer perceives himself as God's instrument."
(Kube, Prussian Council, president of Mark Brandenburg, leader of the National Socialists in the Prussian Landtag)

The industrial magnate Fritz Thyssen, owner of a fortune of 125 million marks and director of one of the largest German trusts, was proclaimed economic dictator of the most important German industrial region, Rhineland-Westphalia.

Fritz Thyssen (1873–1951) headed the largest steel trust in Germany. He joined the Nazi Party in 1931 and was an important mediator between Hitler and other Rhineland industrialists.

The Thyssen portrait (minus Heartfield's additions of a cigar and swastika tie pin) had appeared in the previous issue of *AIZ* (12, no. 30 [3 August 1933], pp. 516–17) in an article entitled "Der Feldzug gegen die zweite Revolution" (The campaign against the second revolution) whose theme was the Nazi Party's abandonment of its anticapitalist commitments.

V. b. b. - Erscheint wöchentlich einmal. - Preis: 1,60 Kč, 30 Gr., 1,25 Frs., 30 Rp., 20 Pfg., 10 Cts. - Jahrgang XII. - Nr. 31. - 10. August 1933.

A.I.Z.

WERKZEUG IN GOTTES HAND?
SPIELZEUG IN THYSSENS HAND!

„Der Führer fühlt sich bei der Vollbringung seiner Aufgabe als Werkzeug in Gottes Hand".
(Kube, Preußischer Staatsrat, Oberpräsident der Mark Brandenburg, Führer der Nationalsozialisten im Preußischen Landtag)

Der Großindustrielle Fritz Thyssen, Eigentümer eines Vermögens von 125 Millionen Mark, Leiter eines der größten deutschen Trusts, wurde zum Wirtschaftsdiktator des wichtigsten deutschen Industriegebiets, Rheinland-Westfalen, ernannt.   Fotomontage: John Heartfield

Bekenntnis eines teutschen Übermenschen

DER DICHTER RUDOLF BINDING AN ROMAIN ROLLAND:

"Wir geben zu, daß in Deutschland Menschenjagden veranstaltet werden auf solche Menschen, die wir für nichtdeutsch zu erklären uns anmaßen. Wir bekennen und nehmen nicht zurück, daß um der Abkunft, des Glaubens, der Gesinnung und Meinung willen der Mensch verfemt, verunrechtet, ja gemartert und gemordet wird. Wir räumen ein, daß Deutschland keinen Raum hat für Marxisten, Juden, Pazifisten, Humanisten und ähnliches Gelichter. Das mag schwer sein für die Opfer, aber Gott sei Dank, deutsche Seele, deutsches Blut ist in der Lage, die Leiden anderer heroisch zu ertragen. Und was besagen die Leiden einzelner Gruppen gegenüber der herrlichen Tatsache, daß unser Volk wieder Volk wurde, daß die deutsche Seele Auferstehung, Neugeburt, vaterländischen Höhenflug feiert. Wir sind deutsch, was brauchen wir edel zu sein?"

Creed of a Teutonic superman

THE POET RUDOLF BINDING TO ROMAIN ROLLAND:

"We admit that in Germany manhunts are carried out against such people as we dare to declare non-German. We confess and do not retract the belief that over questions of descent, belief, perceptions and views, a man is outlawed, deprived of citizenship and indeed tortured and murdered. We concede that Germany has no space for Marxists, Jews, pacifists, humanists and similar riffraff. That may be hard for the victims, but thank God, the German soul and German blood are in a position to endure heroically the sufferings of others. And what do the sufferings of individual groups matter against the wonderful fact that our people has become a people again, that the German soul celebrates resurrection, new birth and elation in the Fatherland? We are German; why do we need to be noble?"

The German poet and novelist Rudolf Georg Binding (1867–1938) defended the Third Reich against foreign critics in works like *Antwort eines Deutschen an die Welt* (A German's reply to the world) of 1933. Romain Rolland (1866–1944) was a French writer with Communist sympathies. He denounced the Nazi régime in a publicized letter of 14 May 1933 to the editor of the *Kölnische Zeitung*. The passage attributed to Binding here has not been verified.

Bekenntnis eines teutschen Übermenschen

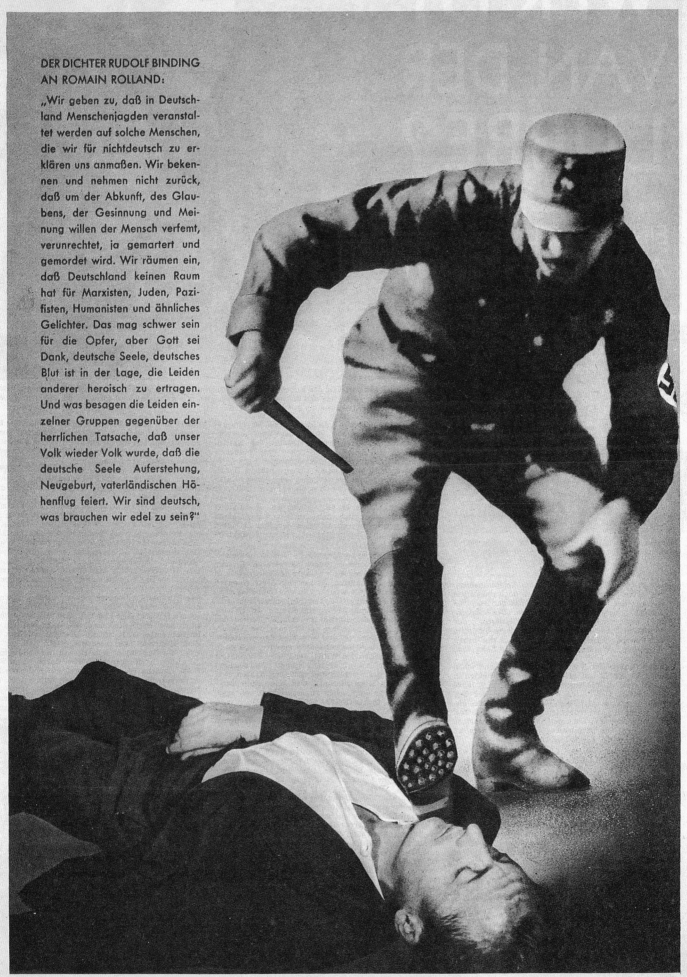

DER DICHTER RUDOLF BINDING
AN ROMAIN ROLLAND:

„Wir geben zu, daß in Deutschland Menschenjagden veranstaltet werden auf solche Menschen, die wir für nichtdeutsch zu erklären uns anmaßen. Wir bekennen und nehmen nicht zurück, daß um der Abkunft, des Glaubens, der Gesinnung und Meinung willen der Mensch verfemt, verunrechtet, ja gemartert und gemordet wird. Wir räumen ein, daß Deutschland keinen Raum hat für Marxisten, Juden, Pazifisten, Humanisten und ähnliches Gelichter. Das mag schwer sein für die Opfer, aber Gott sei Dank, deutsche Seele, deutsches Blut ist in der Lage, die Leiden anderer heroisch zu ertragen. Und was besagen die Leiden einzelner Gruppen gegenüber der herrlichen Tatsache, daß unser Volk wieder Volk wurde, daß die deutsche Seele Auferstehung, Neugeburt, vaterländischen Höhenflug feiert. Wir sind deutsch, was brauchen wir edel zu sein?"

Fotomontage: John Heartfield

**"Spieglein, Spieglein an der Wand,
wer ist der Stärkste im ganzen Land?"
"Die Krise."**

**"Mirror, mirror on the wall,
who is the strongest in the whole country?"
"The crisis."**

The caption is of course an allusion to the evil stepmother's question in the German fairy tale "Schneewittchen" (Snow White).

V. b. b. - Erscheint wöchentlich einmal. - Preis: 1,60 Kč, 30 Gr., 1,25 Frs.,
30 Rp., 20 Pfg., 10 Cts. - Jahrgang XII. - Nr. 33. - 24. August 1933.

AIZ

„Spieglein, Spieglein an der Wand,
wer ist der Stärkste im ganzen Land?"
„Die Krise."

Fotomontage: John Heartfield

NEUER LEHRSTUHL AN DEN DEUTSCHEN
UNIVERSITÄTEN
VÖLKISCHE TIEFENSCHAU

Ein Professor Vitlawopsky von der Universität Heidelberg hat festgestellt, daß das menschliche Hühnerauge, allerdings nur das germanische, befähigt ist, in die Zukunft zu schauen. Hitler hat sogleich nach Bekanntwerden der Entdeckung des genialen Forschers die Überführung von 1300 Hühneraugenoperateuren ins Konzentrationslager angeordnet.

NEW PROFESSORIAL CHAIR IN GERMAN
UNIVERSITIES
THE PROFOUND VIEW OF THE PEOPLE

A Professor Vitlawopsky of the University of Heidelberg asserted that the human corn, but only the Germanic variety, is qualified to see into the future. After being made aware of this discovery of the genial researcher, Hitler immediately ordered that 1300 corn surgeons be interned in concentration camps.

In the Third Reich the adjective *völkisch* had national, racial, and anti-Semitic connotations. Similarly, *das Volk* suggested the nation or the race, rather than just the people (see also 30/36). The German word for corn is *Hühnerauge*, which is literally a chicken's eye. Thus only the German corn has a "profound view" and can "see into the future." The phrases on the blackboard are "Gesichtsloser Fuß des Untermenschen" (Faceless foot of the subhuman) and "Idealer Tiefenschaufuß" (Ideal foot with a profound view). Note also the credit line: "Original-Aufnahme aus dem teutonischen Busch von John Heartfield" (Original photograph from the Teutonic backwoods by John Heartfield).

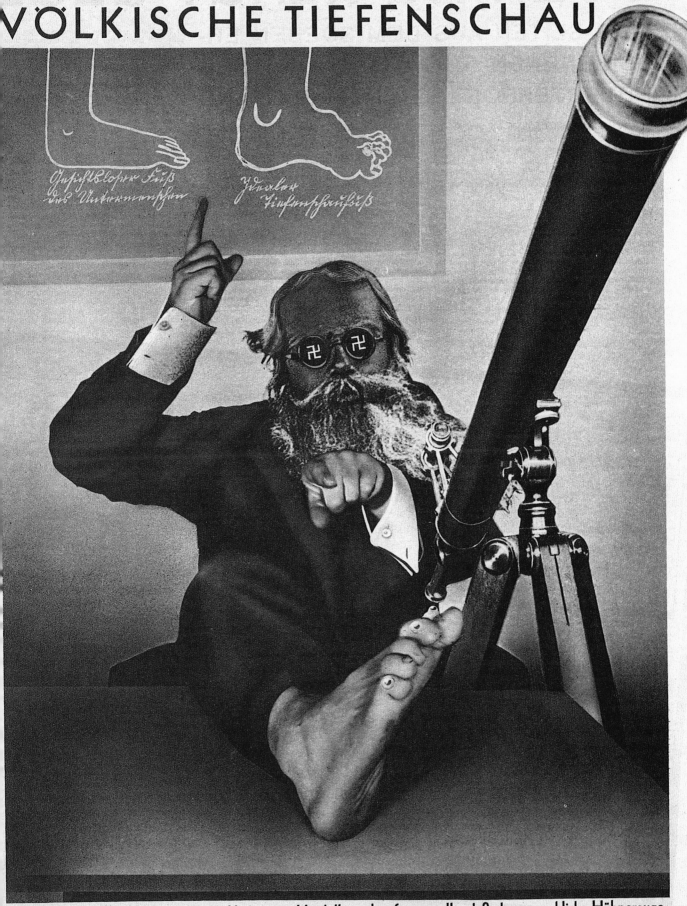

NEUER LEHRSTUHL AN DEN DEUTSCHEN UNIVERSITÄTEN
VÖLKISCHE TIEFENSCHAU

Ein Professor Vitlawopsky von der Universität Heidelberg hat festgestellt, daß das menschliche Hühnerauge, allerdings nur das germanische, befähigt ist, in die Zukunft zu schauen. Hitler hat sogleich nach Bekanntwerden der Entdeckung des genialen Forschers die Überführung von 1300 Hühneraugenoperateuren ins Konzentrationslager angeordnet.

Original-Aufnahme aus dem teutonischen Busch von John Heartfield.

DIE WANZE ALS KAMMERJÄGER
"Ich werde mein Haus doch noch
von Ungeziefer rein kriegen!"
(33 Deutschen, darunter Heinrich Mann, Prof. E. J. Gumbel,
Willy Münzenberg, Wilhelm Piek, Ernst Toller, Kurt
Tucholski, Lion Feuchtwanger, wurde die
Staatsangehörigkeit aberkannt.)

THE BUG AS VERMIN EXTERMINATOR
"I'll get my house clear of vermin yet!"
(33 Germans, among them Heinrich Mann, Prof. E. J.
Gumbel, Willy Münzenberg, Wilhelm Piek, Ernst Toller, Kurt
Tucholski, Lion Feuchtwanger, were deprived of citizenship.)

"NAZI-FLIT / Marke Frick Deutsches Erzeugnis" (NAZI-FLIT / Frick
brand, German product) is written on the spray can. The human bug
is Wilhelm Frick, who was Reich minister of the interior (see 15/33).
Heinrich Mann (1871–1950) was a novelist with Communist
sympathies. Emil Julius Gumbel (1891–1966) was a mathematician
and pacifist. Willi Münzenberg was a Communist propagandist and
publisher of *AIZ* (see 1/32). Wilhelm Pieck (1876–1960) was a
German Communist leader. Ernst Toller (1893–1939) was a writer
and pacifist. Kurt Tucholsky (1890–1935), a writer opposed to
nationalism and militarism, had coproduced with Heartfield the
satirical phototext book *Deutschland, Deutschland über alles*,
published by Münzenberg in 1929. Leon Feuchtwanger (1884–1958)
was a Jewish novelist.

AIZ

V. b. b. - Erscheint wöchentlich einmal. - Preis: 1,60 Kč, 30 Gr., 1,25 Frs., 30 Rp., 20 Pfg., 10 amer. Cts., 15 holl. Cts. - Jahrgang XII. - Nr. 35. - 7. September 1933.

DIE WANZE ALS KAMMERJÄGER

„Ich werde mein Haus doch noch von Ungeziefer rein kriegen!"

(33 Deutschen, darunter Heinrich Mann, Prof. E. J. Gumbel, Willy Münzenberg, Wilhelm Piek, Ernst Toller, Kurt Tucholski, Lion Feuchtwanger, wurde die Staatsangehörigkeit aberkannt.)

Fotomontage: John Heartfield

GOERING
DER HENKER DES DRITTEN REICHS

In Leipzig werden am 21. September neben dem Provok-ateur Lubbe, vier Unschuldige – Opfer eines der ungeheuerlichsten Justizverbrechen – vor Gericht stehen. Der wahre Reichstagsbrandstifter, Goering, wird nicht vor den Schranken erscheinen.

Fotomontage: John Heartfield // Umschlagbild des "Braun-buchs über Reichstagsbrand und Hitlerterror" // Das Gesicht Goerings ist einer Originalfotografie entnommen und wurde nicht retuschiert.

GÖRING
THE EXECUTIONER OF THE THIRD REICH

In Leipzig on 21 September, next to the agent provocateur Lubbe, four innocent men – victims of one of the most outrageous judicial crimes – will stand trial. The true Reichstag arsonist, Göring, will not appear before the bar.

Photomontage: John Heartfield // Jacket illustration of the "Brown Book about the Reichstag Fire and Hitler Terror" // Göring's face is taken from an original photograph and has not been retouched.

Hermann Göring (1893–1946) held various positions in the Third Reich, including prime minister and minister of the interior for Prussia and head of the air force. He also became the minister with responsibility for economic preparations for war. See 25/33, 26/33, 27/33, 30/33, 31/33, 32/33, 33/33, 4/34, 39/34, 1/35, 6/35, 8/35, 26/35, 3/36, 5/36, 7/36, 17/36, 28/36, 38/36, 15/37, 25/37.

This was the cover of a special issue titled "Reichstags-brandprozess / Gegenprozess" (Reichstag Fire trial / countertrial). The Reichstag Fire occurred on 27 February 1933, shortly after Hitler became chancellor. The Nazis sought to prove that the fire was the first stage in a planned Communist putsch. The Communists claimed that Göring, who acted as chief prosecutor at the trial, was behind the attempt to discredit and repress the Left. A Dutch worker, Marinus van der Lubbe, and various Communists, most notably Georgi Dimitrov, were prosecuted. See also 5/33, 17/33, 25/33, 30/33, 31/33, 33/33, 4/34, 8/35, 14/35, 28/36, 34/36.

Note that Göring is wearing a "Blue Max" inscribed "Pour le Profit," instead of "Pour le Mérite." Heartfield also put this medal around the necks of a hyena (1/32) and Hitler (6/32).

AIZ

Erscheint wöchentlich einmal — Preis: 1.60 Kč, 30 Gr., 1.25 Frs., 30 Rp., 20 Pfg., 10 amer. Cts., 15 holl. Cts — Jahrgang XII. - Nr. 36. - 14. September 1933

DEUTSCHEN VOLKE

Pour le Profit

GOERING
DER HENKER
DES DRITTEN REICHS

In Leipzig werden am 21. September neben dem Provokateur Lubbe, vier Unschuldige — Opfer eines der ungeheuerlichsten Justizverbrechen — vor Gericht stehen. Der wahre Reichstagsbrandstifter, Goering, wird nicht vor den Schranken erscheinen.

Fotomontage: John Heartfield // Umschlagbild des „Braunbuchs über Reichstagsbrand und Hitlerterror" // Das Gesicht Goerings ist einer Originalfotografie entnommen und wurde nicht retuschiert.

SONDERNUMMER: REICHSTAGSBRAND   PROZESS/GEGENPROZESS

Deutsche Eicheln 1933

German acorns 1933

The montage preceded "Wie sie die Jugend vergiften" (How they poison the young), an article concerning the Nazi militarization of children. The acorns are intended to suggest both young Germans and war preparations.

Deutsche
Eicheln
1933

Fotomontage John Heartfield

DER GALGENGRUSS

Zum Hitler-Gruß hebt seinen Arm
Göring, Preußens Generalgendarm.
Sein Arm ist wie ein Galgen,
der Galgen wie sein Arm,
der brandgeschwärzt
und blutbefleckt
sich über Deutschland streckt.

Doch es kommt das Gericht,
das an den höchsten Galgen
hängt dieses Galgengesicht!

THE GALLOWS SALUTE

In the Hitler salute he raises his arm
Göring, Prussia's top gendarme.
His arm is like a gallows,
the gallows like his arm,
black from fire
and stained with blood
stretching across Germany.

But a court will one day
from the highest gibbet
hang this gangster!

This montage was followed by a two-page report on the Leipzig trial
and the London countertrial (see 23/33), "London und Leipzig –
Wahrheit und Lüge" (London and Leipzig – truth and lie). The image
was also made into a propaganda postcard (see also 17/33, 27/33,
30/33, 32/33).

DER GALGENGRUSS

Zum Hitler-Gruß hebt seinen Arm
Göring, Preußens Generalgendarm.
Sein Arm ist wie ein Galgen,
der Galgen wie sein Arm,
der brandgeschwärzt
und blutbefleckt
sich über Deutschland streckt.

Doch es kommt das Gericht,
das an den höchsten Galgen
hängt dieses Galgengesicht!

Fotomontage John Heartfield

Freie Zeugenvernehmung in Leipzig

Free hearing of witnesses in Leipzig

For the Reichstag Fire trial that began in Leipzig in September 1933, see 23/33.

AIZ

Freie
Zeugenvernehmung
in Leipzig

Fotomontage John Heartfield

Zum Brandstifter-Prozess in Leipzig

Sie winden sich und drehen sich und nennen sich deutsche Richter

At the arsonist trial in Leipzig

They twist and turn and call themselves German judges

The colloquial expression "sich winden wie ein Aal" (literally, to wriggle like an eel) means to try energetically to avoid telling the truth. The snakes are in the shape of the paragraph sign used in German law books.

This montage related directly to the issue's cover, which showed the accused, Dimitrov (see 23/33, 30/33), with two guards, and was titled "Dimitroff vor Gericht: In diesem Prozess bin ich nicht der Schuldner, sondern der Gläubiger!" (Dimitrov before the court: In this trial I am not the debtor, but the creditor!).

The image was also used for a postcard (see also 17/33, 25/33, 30/33, 32/33).

Zum Brandstifter-Prozess in Leipzig

Fotomontage John Heartfield

Sie winden sich und drehen sich und nennen sich deutsche Richter

HITLER ERZÄHLT MÄRCHEN

I.

Das Dritte Reich ist ein pazifistisches Reich:

Seine Soldaten
sind keine Soldaten,
sie sind Engel
des ewigen
Hitlerfriedens,
nur die Flügel
sind getarnt.

HITLER TELLS FAIRY TALES

I.

The Third Reich is a pacifist Reich

Her soldiers
aren't really soldiers,
they are angels
of Hitler's eternal peace,
only their wings
are camouflaged.

AIZ

Seine Soldaten
sind keine Soldaten,
sie sind Engel
des ewigen
Hitlerfriedens,
nur die Flügel
sind getarnt.

Fotomontage John Heartfield

GLEICHE BRÜDER
GLEICHE MÖRDER

Das Schwarzhemd zum Braunhemd:
"Dir gebührt der Dolch! – Du hast uns im Meuchelmord übertroffen."

Berlin, 19. Oktober
Die italienische faschistische Partei hat dem Stellvertreter Hitlers, Rudolf Hess, einen Ehrendolch überreichen lassen.

LIKE BROTHERS
LIKE MURDERERS

The Blackshirt to the Brownshirt:
"You deserve the dagger! – You have surpassed us in assassination."

Berlin, 19 October
The Italian Fascist Party had a prize dagger presented to Hitler's representative, Rudolf Hess.

The title rephrases the proverbial saying "Gleiche Brüder, gleiche Kappen" (literally, like brothers, like caps), which is akin to like father, like son, or birds of a feather flock together. Rudolf Hess (1894–1988) became deputy leader of the Nazi Party in April 1933. The Nazi depicted is Julius Streicher, founder of the anti-Semitic newspaper *Der Stürmer* and its editor from 1923 to 1945 (see also 23/34, 11/35).

A radically altered version of the montage appeared in Wieland Herzfelde's *John Heartfield: Leben und Werk* (p. 173). The Italian Blackshirt and all the text were removed, and the montage was given a new title: *EIN PANGERMANE: Der Schoß ist fruchtbar noch, aus dem das kroch* (A Pan-German: The womb from which that crept is still fertile). Heartfield was suggesting that conditions for the reemergence of Fascism still existed in the Federal Republic of Germany (but not, of course, in the German Democratic Republic).

AIZ

GLEICHE BRÜDER GLEICHE MÖRDER

Berlin, 19. Oktober.
Die italienische faschistische Partei hat dem Stellvertreter
Hitlers, Rudolf Hess, einen Ehrendolch überreichen lassen.

Das Schwarzhemd zum Braunhemd:
„Dir gebührt der Dolch! – Du hast uns im Meuchelmord übertroffen."

Fotomontage: John Heartfield

DER RICHTER
DER GERICHTETE

DIMITROFF

MINISTERPRÄSIDENT GÖRING

Roter Strolch / Verbrecher / Gesindel / Gauner / an den
Galgen!

THE JUDGE
THE JUDGED

DIMITROV

PRIME MINISTER GÖRING

Red tramp / criminal / scum / swindler / to the gallows!

Georgi Dimitrov (1882–1949), a Bulgarian, was working for the
Communist International in Moscow when he was arrested in Berlin
in February 1933 and accused of involvement in the Reichstag Fire
(see 23/33). He was acquitted and deported to the Soviet Union,
where he played a key role in the adoption of a new Popular Front
strategy to defeat Fascism in 1935. See 13/35, 14/35.

The montage related directly to the cover, which showed
Göring, the chief prosecutor, addressing the court. An accompanying
text entitled "Warten Sie nur, Sie Gauner!" (Just you wait, you
swindler!) reported the exchanges between Göring and Dimitrov
during the trial. Heartfield extracted and reverse-printed the cover
photograph of Göring and reduced his speech to a stream of abuse
aimed at Dimitrov. After studying the cover, the reader turned the
page and saw the montage with a miniscule Göring literally put in his
place before a monumental Dimitrov.

Heartfield used this montage as one of a series of four
postcards (see also 17/33, 25/33, 27/33, 32/33).

DER RICHTER
DIMITROFF

Fotomontage: John Heartfield

MINISTERPRÄSIDENT GÖRING

DER GERICHTETE

DER HENKER UND DIE GERECHTIGKEIT

Göring im Reichstagsbrand-Prozeß: Für mich ist das Recht etwas Blutvolles

THE EXECUTIONER AND JUSTICE

Göring at the Reichstag Fire trial: For me the law is a lively affair

---

Blutvoll (lively) means literally full of blood; it also calls to mind *glutvoll,* which means passionate or glowing (from *Glut,* the word for heat or glowing fire). On the Reichstag Fire trial, see 23/33.

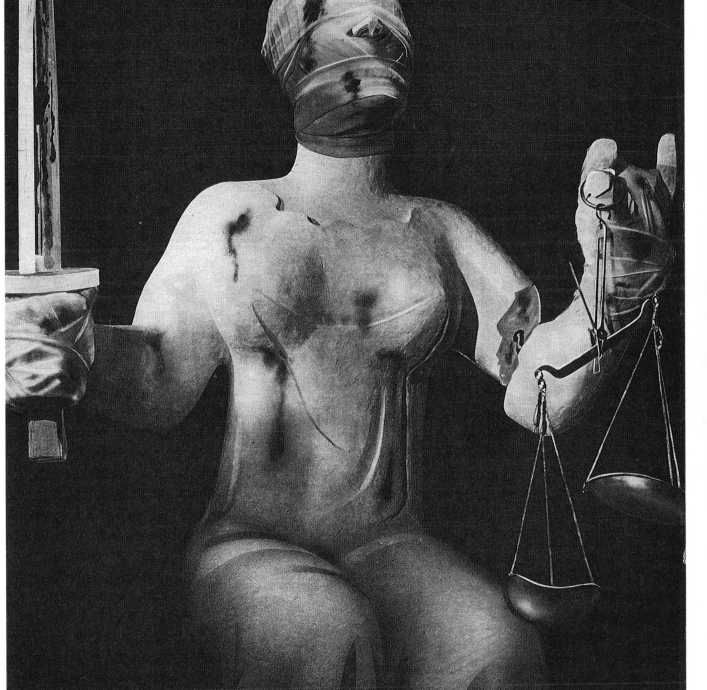
Fotomontage: John Heartfield

DER HENKER UND DIE GERECHTIGKEIT

Göring im Reichstagsbrand-Prozeß: **Für mich ist das Recht etwas Blutvolles**

FRIEDE AUF ERDEN?

Kein Friede auf Erden, solange die Armen ärmer werden!

PEACE ON EARTH?

No peace on earth, as long as the poor become poorer!

Heartfield's montage was to be read in conjunction with the cover (p. 833), titled "UND FRIEDE AUF ERDEN!" (And peace on earth!), which showed the guns of an American battleship and reminded readers that during the season of goodwill the politicians were preparing for the coming world slaughter.

Facing the montage was the article "Eine Waffe im Kampf gegen den Faschismus" (A weapon in the struggle against Fascism), on the four *AIZ* montages about the Reichstag Fire trial that had then become available as postcards (see 17/33, 25/33, 27/33, 30/33).

FRIEDE AUF ERDEN?

Fotomontage: John Heartfield

Kein Friede auf Erden, solange die Armen ärmer werden!

Das Urteil der Welt!

In seinen Zügen steht geschrieben, was das Gericht verschwiegen hat.

The judgment of the world!

His features reveal what the court remained silent about.

The montage was again related to the cover, which showed Dimitrov's sister, mother, and wife waiting for the *Urteilsverkündung* (passing of judgment) at the end of the Reichstag Fire trial in Leipzig (see 23/33, 30/33). The reader turned the page and was confronted with Heartfield's montage. Immediately following the montage was an article about the trial called "Dimitroffs grosser Tag" (Dimitrov's great day).

The portrait of Göring was taken from the cover photograph of the *AIZ* issue published 26 October 1933 (12, no. 42, p. 705), which in turn had been taken from the hunting magazine *Wild und Hund.* The original photograph showed Göring with a dead elk. The photograph was reverse-printed and the smoke and flames painted on.

Das Urteil der Welt!

Montiert John Heartfield

In seinen Zügen steht geschrieben,
was das Gericht verschwiegen hat!

**Ab 1. Januar
neue Briefmarken im Dritten Reich**

5 Tausend Tote 5

Dritte Reichspest

**From 1 January
new postage stamps in the Third Reich**

5 thousand dead 5

Third Reich plague

Reichspest plays with the similarity of *Post* (post) and *Pest* (plague).

Ab 1. Januar
neue Briefmarken im Dritten Reich

5 Tausend Tote 5

Dritte Reichspest

Fotomontage: John Heartfield

Das erneuerte Horst-Wessel-Lied:

Die Preise hoch,
Kartelle fest geschlossen!
Die Krupp und Vögler
scheffeln den Profit.
Wer nicht pariert,
wird totgeschossen –
Und für den Sozialismus
sorgt Herr Schmitt…

Kanonenkönig
KRUPP

Generaldirektor
VÖGLER

Heil Hitler

The renewed Horst-Wessel-Song:

Up the prices,
Firmly close the trusts!
Krupp and Vögler
Rake in the profit.
Whoever does not obey
Is shot dead –
And Herr Schmitt
Looks after Socialism…

Cannon King
KRUPP

Managing Director
VÖGLER

Heil Hitler

This was the cover for a special issue offering a "balance sheet" of the Third Reich. The "Horst-Wessel-Lied" was a marching song composed by the young SA leader Horst Wessel (1907–1930). Killed in a Berlin brawl, Wessel ended up a martyr to the Nazi cause and his song became a Party anthem. Gustav Krupp von Bohlen und Halbach (1870–1950), here called the "Cannon King," was head of the Krupp armaments firm and actively supported Hitler from 1933 on (see also 28/34). Albert Vögler (1877–1945) was a steel magnate who generously funded Hitler. Kurt Schmitt (1886–1950) was Hitler's first minister of economics (see 25/34).

The corpse is a reverse-printed detail from the cover of the 5 June 1932 issue of *AIZ* (no. 23, p. 529). The dead man is Oskar Kaufmann, who was shot by police in Waltershausen during a demonstration of the unemployed against reductions in welfare payments. Heartfield used the same image in 18/34.

SONDERNUMMER
BILANZ
DES DRITTEN REICHS
1933

AIZ

V. b. b. - Erscheint wöchentlich einmal.
Preis: 1,60 Kč, 40 Gr., 1,25 Frs., 30 Rp.,
20 Pfg., 10 amer. Cts., 15 holl. Cts.
Jahrgang XIII. - Nr. 2. - 11. Januar 1934

Heil Hitler!

Kanonenkönig
KRUPP

Das erneuerte Horst-Wessel-Lied:

Die Preise hoch,
Kartelle fest geschlossen!
Die Krupp und Vögler
scheffeln den Profit.
Wer nicht pariert,
wird totgeschossen –
Und für den Sozialismus
sorgt Herr Schmitt…

Generaldirektor
VÖGLER

Fotomontage: John Heartfield

Der Reichsbischof richtet das Christentum aus

"He, der Mann da, das Kruzifix etwas weiter nach rechts!"

Reichsbischof Müller

The Reich Bishop dresses Christendom

"Hey, the man over there, the cross a bit more to the right!"

Reich Bishop Müller

Ludwig Müller (1883–1946) was a leader of the Association of German Christians, a neopagan church that aimed to combine Christianity and Nazi ideology. He was made a Reich bishop in July 1933. A similar photograph of Müller appeared in "Die 10 Minuten Schule der AIZ – Was ist Religion?" (*AIZ*'s 10-minute school – What is religion?) in the 4 January 1934 issue of *AIZ* (13, no. 1, p. 14). The caption included another of Müller's characteristic expressions: "Die deutschen Christen sind die SA Jesu!" (German Christians are the SA of Jesus!).

Der Reichsbischof richtet das Christentum aus

Reichsbischof Müller

„He, der Mann da, das Kruzifix etwas weiter nach rechts!"

Fotomontage: John Heartfield

LUBBES GRAB

"Verdammt, je tiefer wir ihn vergraben,
desto mehr kommt die Wahrheit ans Licht!"

LUBBE'S GRAVE

"Damn, the deeper we bury him,
the more the truth comes to light!"

Marinus van der Lubbe was sentenced to death at the Reichstag Fire trial (see 23/33) and was subsequently beheaded. The figure in the center is Göring, the true arsonist according to the Communists. He is flanked by a German judge and Hitler.

LUBBES GRAB

Fotomontage: John Heartfield

„Verdammt, je tiefer wir ihn vergraben, desto mehr kommt die Wahrheit ans Licht!"

ARBEITERFÜHRER DES DRITTEN REICHS
ODER:
DER BOCK ALS GÄRTNER

"Gefolgschaft, mal herhören! Unser Führer hat bestimmt:
Ab heute bin ICH euer Führer, weil ich euer Chef bin und
den Profit einstecke."

WORKERS' LEADER OF THE THIRD REICH
OR:
THE GOAT AS GARDENER

"Followers, stop talking and listen! Our Führer has decided:
Starting today I am your leader, because I am your boss and
pocket the profit."

"Den Bock zum Gärtner machen" means to make the goat the
gardener, in other words, to give someone a task which he exploits
for his own ends.

Hitler's Labor Charter, prescribing cooperation between
labor and capital, was published in January and came in force on 1
May 1934. The montage was followed by an article on Nazi labor
policy entitled "Jeder Betrieb eine Kaserne" (Every plant a barracks).

ARBEITERFÜHRER DES DRITTEN REICHS
ODER:
DER BOCK ALS GÄRTNER

Fotomontage: John Heartfield

»Gefolgschaft, mal herhören! Unser Führer hat bestimmt:
Ab heute bin ICH euer Führer, weil ich euer Chef bin und den Profit einstecke.«

NACH EINEM JAHR

Fassade unverändert – Kater und Pleitegeier nicht mehr wegzuleugnen

AFTER ONE YEAR

Facade unchanged – tomcats and vultures of bankruptcy no longer deniable

---

Kater is a tomcat, and also a hangover. *Pleitegeier*, a compound of *Pleite* (bankruptcy) and *Geier* (vulture), means both the threat of bankruptcy and a bankrupt. The montage suggests that the German eagle has turned into a vulture.

The subject is Hitler's house-painting program, already satirized in 6/33.

NACH EINEM JAHR

Fotomontage: John Heartfield

Fassade unverändert – Kater und Pleitegeier nicht mehr wegzuleugnen

Ihre Angst nimmt zu
Ihr Terror nimmt zu

Diehls, Chef der Geheimen Staatspolizei (ehem. Demokrat): Melde meinem Führer gehorsamst: Keinerlei Anlaß sich wegen Erstarkung der KPD zu beunruhigen. 60 Millionen Geiseln fest in unserer Hand. Jederzeit auf der Flucht erschießbar

Vier der besten Söhne des deutschen Proletariats, JOHN SCHEER, Mitglied des Zentralkomitees der KPD, ERICH STEINFURTH, EUGEN SCHÖNHAAR, RUDOLF SCHWARZ, führende Mitglieder der kommunistischen Partei Deutschlands, sind auf Befehl Goerings von der Geheimen Staatspolizei "auf der Flucht erschossen" worden. Die deutsche Arbeiterklasse wird diesen Gemordeten besonders gedenken, an dem Tag, da sie Gericht halten wird über die Mörder und ihre Anstifter.

Their fear increases
Their terror increases

Diehls, chief of the Gestapo (formerly Democrat): I report most obediently to my Führer: absolutely no reason to worry about the strengthening of the KPD. 60 million hostages firmly under control. At any time they can be shot while escaping

Four of the best sons of the German proletariat, JOHN SCHEER, member of the central committee of the KPD, ERICH STEINFURTH, EUGEN SCHÖNHAAR, RUDOLF SCHWARZ, leading members of the German Communist Party, on the orders of Göring, were "shot while escaping" by the Gestapo. The German working class will especially remember these murdered people on the day it judges the murderers and their ringleaders.

Rudolf Diehls (1900–1957) defected from the Social Democrats to the Nazis in 1933. He was the founder and first leader of the Gestapo (see also 10/33).

AIZ.

Vier der besten Söhne des deutschen Proletariats, JOHN SCHEER, Mitglied des Zentralkomitees der KPD, ERICH STEINFURTH, EUGEN SCHÖNHAAR, RUDOLF SCHWARZ, führende Mitglieder der kommunistischen Partei Deutschlands, sind auf Befehl Goerings von der Geheimen Staatspolizei „auf der Flucht erschossen" worden. Die deutsche Arbeiterklasse wird diesen Gemordeten besonders gedenken, an dem Tag, da sie Gericht halten wird über die Mörder und ihre Anstifter.

Ihre Angst nimmt zu
Ihr Terror nimmt zu

Diehls, Chef der Geheimen Staatspolizei (ehem. Demokrat): Melde meinem Führer gehorsamst: Keinerlei Anlaß sich wegen Erstarkung der KPD zu beunruhigen. 60 Millionen Geiseln fest in unserer Hand. Jederzeit auf der Flucht erschießbar

WIEN...

Das alte Wort der pariser Kommune ward wieder lebendig:
"PLATZ DEM ARBEITER!
TOD DEN HENKERN!"

VIENNA...

The old saying of the Paris Commune came back to life:
"MAKE WAY FOR THE WORKER!
DEATH TO THE EXECUTIONERS!"

In February 1934 there were clashes between troops and workers on Socialist-controlled housing estates in Vienna. The troops gained control after five days. The *AIZ* issue in which this montage was published contained a two-page report on the unrest (pp. 116–17). According to Socialist mythology from Marx onward, the short-lived Paris Commune, a popular insurrection that grew out of the French defeat in the Franco-Prussian War of 1870–71, was the first concrete instance of workers' control.

AIZ

V. b. b. · Erscheint wöchentlich einmal.
Preis: 1,60 Kč, 40 Gr., 1,25 Frs., 30 Rp.,
20 Pfg., 10 amer. Cts., 15 holl. Cts
Jahrgang XIII. Nr. 8. · 22. Februar 1934

WIEN...

Das alte Wort der pariser Kommune ward wieder lebendig:

„PLATZ DEM ARBEITER! TOD DEN HENKERN!"

Fotomontage: John Heartfield

**Die alte Welt hat ihre Pleitegeier
Österreich hat einen mit zwei Köpfen**

In Wien wurde der Doppeladler wieder eingeführt

**The old world has its vultures of bankruptcy
Austria has one with two heads**

In Vienna the double-headed eagle was reintroduced

Engelbert Dollfuß (1892–1934), appointed Austrian chancellor in 1932, was responsible for the army's shelling of workers' estates in Vienna in February 1934 (see 8/34). Emil Fey (1896–1938) was his vice-chancellor. See also 11/34, 13/34.

  The *Doppeladler* (double-headed eagle) is a reference to the dual monarchy of Austria-Hungary, which collapsed in 1918. The bird wears a Christian cross and the Austrian *Krukenkreuz* (cross potent). For an explanation of *Pleitegeier,* see 6/34.

Dollfuß

Major Fey

In Wien wurde der Doppeladler wieder eingeführt

Die alte Welt hat ihre Pleitegeier
Österreich hat einen mit zwei Köpfen

Fotomontage: John Heartfield

Der alte Wahlspruch im "neuen" Reich:
BLUT UND EISEN

The old motto in the "new" Reich:
BLOOD AND IRON

Otto von Bismarck (1815–1898) delivered his "blood and iron"
speech before the Prussian House of Deputies in 1886. He claimed
that if Prussia's expansionist policies were to be successful the king
must be given maximum military powers: "Mit Reden und
Schützenfesten und Liedern macht sie sich nicht, sie macht sich nur
durch Blut und Eisen" (This policy does not succeed through
speeches and shooting matches and songs, but through blood and
iron). See also 3/37.

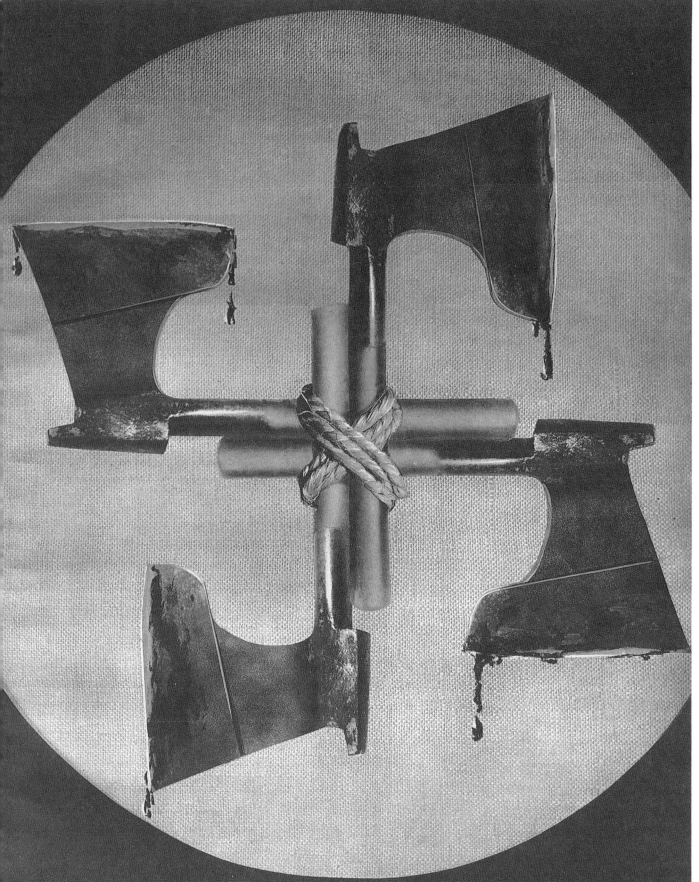

Fotomontage: John Heartfield

Der alte Wahlspruch im „neuen" Reich:

BLUT UND EISEN

DER UNTERSCHIED

Wer die Verfassung schützt, die
der Reichskanzler beschworen hat,
WIRD GEKÖPFT.

Wer die Verfassung schützt, die
der Bundeskanzler beschworen hat,
WIRD GEHÄNGT.

THE DIFFERENCE

Whoever protects the constitution, which
the Reich chancellor has sworn to uphold,
WILL BE BEHEADED.

Whoever protects the constitution, which
the chancellor of the Republic has sworn to uphold,
WILL BE HANGED.

Heartfield was comparing Hitler's Germany with Dollfuß's Austria
(see also 8/34, 9/34, 13/34).

DER UNTERSCHIED

Wer die Verfassung schützt, die der Reichskanzler beschworen hat, WIRD GEKÖPFT.

Wer die Verfassung schützt, die der Bundeskanzler beschworen hat, WIRD GEHÄNGT.

SOWJETAUFBAU UND NAZIAUFBAU

Die Sowjetunion ist eine der größten Industriemächte der
Welt geworden

Die Sammelaktionen haben riesenhafte Ausmaße
angenommen

SOVIET CONSTRUCTION AND NAZI CONSTRUCTION

The Soviet Union has become one of the greatest industrial
powers in the world

Fundraising campaigns have reached enormous proportions

The left section consists of a cropped photograph of the construction
of a silo in Tashkent. The photograph appeared in *AIZ* in 1931 (10,
no. 9, p. 169) as evidence of Socialist construction. The right section
shows collection boxes for various Nazi charities.

SOWJETAUFBAU UND NAZIAUFBAU

Die Sowjetunion ist eine der größten Industriemächte der Welt geworden

Die Sammelaktionen haben riesenhafte Ausmaße angenommen

"O, du mein humanes Österreich!"

Je größer das Kaliber, umso größer die Humanität

Wien, Sonntag   Reichspost 11. März 1934
…nicht unbekannt sein. Die Kanonen waren übrigens,
gerade weil sie die Entscheidung beschleunigten und so der
Zahl der Opfer eine Grenze setzten, die humanste der zur
Verwendung gekommenen Waffen.

"Oh, my humane Austria!"

The greater the caliber, the greater the humanity

Vienna, Sunday   Reichspost 11 March 1934
…not be unknown. Because they accelerated the showdown
and thus limited the number of victims, the cannons were the
most humane of the weapons used.

"Säuglings-Munition" (baby ammunition) and the names of Dollfuß
and Major Fey (chancellor and vice-chancellor of Austria) are
inscribed on the shells (see also 9/34, 11/34). There had been clashes
between workers and troops in Vienna in February (see 8/34).

»O, du mein humanes Österreich!«

Wien, Sonntag   Reichspost   11. März 1934

nicht unbekannt sein. Die Kanonen waren übrigens   der zur Verwendung gekommenen Waffen.
gerade weil sie die Entscheidung beschleunigten und so
der Zahl der Opfer eine Grenze setzten, die humanste

Je größer das Kaliber, umso größer die Humanität

Fotomontage: John Heartfield

Hjalmar oder Das wachsende Defizit

"Ich lasse sie auf keinen Fall fallen!"

Die Presse meldet, daß der Reichsbankpräsident Dr. Hjalmar Schacht, um das Vertrauen maßgeblicher Kreise zu stärken, die Änderung seines Namens in Hjalmar Helfersich beantragt hat.
(Der seinerzeitige Reichsbankpräsident Helfferich schuf nach dem Inflationsgeschäft die sogenannte Rentenmark.)

Hjalmar or The growing deficit

"I certainly won't let it fall!"

The press announces that the Reichsbank president Dr. Hjalmar Schacht, in order to bolster the confidence of the most influential circles, has applied to change his name to Hjalmar Helfersich.
(After the inflation business, the then Reichsbank president Helfferich created the so-called Rentenmark.)

Financier Horace Greely Hjalmar Schacht (1877–1970) was president of the Reichsbank from 1923 to 1930 and from 1933 to 1939. Under the Third Reich he also held various ministerial posts. Heartfield was playing on the similarity of *helfersich* (literally, helps himself) and the surname of Karl Helfferich (1872–1924), a former Reichsbank president.

AIZ

Die Presse meldet,
daß der Reichsbankpräsident
Dr. Hjalmar Schacht, um das Vertrauen maßgeblicher Kreise zu stärken,
die Änderung seines Namens in
Hjalmar Helfersich beantragt hat.

(Der seinerzeitige Reichsbankpräsident Helfferich schuf
nach dem Inflationsgeschäft die sogenannte Rentenmark.)

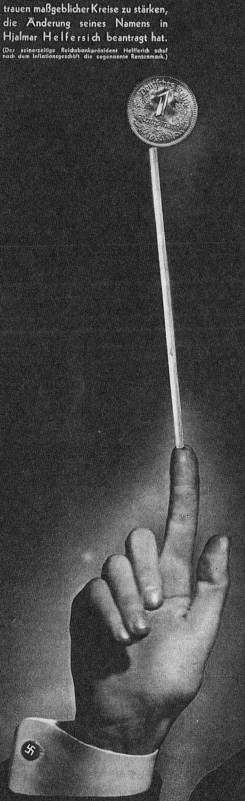

„Ich lasse sie auf keinen Fall fallen!"

CHOR DER RÜSTUNGSINDUSTRIE:
"EIN FESTE BURG IST UNSER GENF"

WILLST DU RÜSTUNGSAUFTRÄGE, SO FINANZIERE
FRIEDENSKONFERENZEN

CHOIR OF THE ARMS INDUSTRY:
"A MIGHTY FORTRESS IS OUR GENEVA"

IF YOU WANT ARMS DEALS, THEN FINANCE PEACE
CONFERENCES

The title is an adaption of the first line of Martin Luther's hymn "Ein
feste Burg ist unser Gott" (A mighty fortress is our God) of 1529. On
the shells are the names of major arms manufacturers.

In Wieland Herzfelde's *John Heartfield: Leben und Werk*
(p. 180), the montage has a new title, *Gesang der Ewig-Gestrigen:
Wir beten an die Macht der Bomben* (Hymn of the forces of
yesterday: We worship the power of the bomb), paraphrasing yet
another hymn, "Wir beten an die Macht der Liebe" (We worship the
power of love).

Fotomontage: John Heartfield

AIZ

WILLST DU
RÜSTUNGSAUFTRÄGE,
SO FINANZIERE
FRIEDENSKONFERENZEN

Vickers Ltd.

Krupp & Co.

Bethlehem Steel Company

Schneider-Creuzot

CHOR DER RÜSTUNGSINDUSTRIE:
»EIN FESTE BURG IST UNSER GENF«

MIMIKRY

Nachdem alle Versuche, die nationalsozialistischen Ideen in die Arbeiterschaft zu tragen, erfolglos geblieben waren, ist Göbbels auf einen letzten verzweifelten Einfall gekommen: er hat den "Führer" überredet, fortan, wenn er vor Arbeitern spricht, sich einen Karl Marx-Bart umzuhängen.

Zeitungsmeldung vom 8. April 1934:
"Die diesjährige Maiplakette der Nationalen Arbeitsfront trägt neben einem Goethekopf und dem Adler mit Hakenkreuz auch die bolschewistischen Symbole Hammer und Sichel, offenbar um auf diese Weise die dem Regime immer noch ablehnend gegenüberstehenden Arbeiter zu gewinnen."

MIMICRY

When all attempts to convey National Socialist ideas to the working class failed, Goebbels had one last desperate idea: he persuaded the "Führer" to wear a Karl Marx beard in the future when addressing workers.

Newspaper report of 8 April 1934:
"Beside Goethe's bust and the eagle with swastika, this year's National Labor Front May Day medal also shows the Bolshevik symbols of hammer and sickle, apparently in an effort to win over the workers who are still opposed to the régime."

The Nazis tried to appropriate May Day from the Socialists, making it an official holiday called National Labor Day.

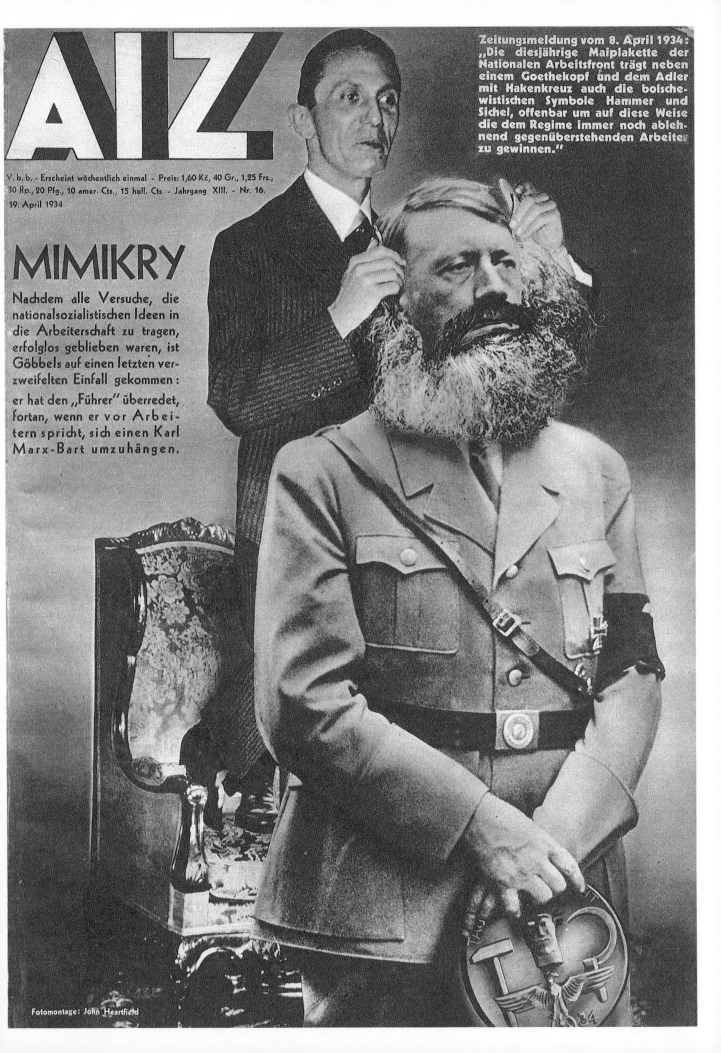

AIZ

V. b. b. - Erscheint wöchentlich einmal - Preis: 1,60 Kč, 40 Gr., 1,25 Frs.,
30 Rp., 20 Pfg., 10 amer. Cts., 15 holl. Cts. - Jahrgang XIII. - Nr. 16.
19. April 1934

Zeitungsmeldung vom 8. April 1934:
„Die diesjährige Maiplakette der Nationalen Arbeitsfront trägt neben einem Goethekopf und dem Adler mit Hakenkreuz auch die bolsche-wistischen Symbole Hammer und Sichel, offenbar um auf diese Weise die dem Regime immer noch ablehnend gegenüberstehenden Arbeiter zu gewinnen."

MIMIKRY

Nachdem alle Versuche, die nationalsozialistischen Ideen in die Arbeiterschaft zu tragen, erfolglos geblieben waren, ist Göbbels auf einen letzten ver-zweifelten Einfall gekommen: er hat den „Führer" überredet, fortan, wenn er vor Arbei-tern spricht, sich einen Karl Marx-Bart umzuhängen.

Fotomontage: John Heartfield

ERSTER MAI

Am 1. Mai, am Tag der für eine neue, sozialistische Welt kämpfenden Arbeiterklasse, sind die Gedanken der Werktätigen aller Länder bei ihren Brüdern, den Arbeitern und Bauern der Sowjetunion und den befreiten Kulis der jungen kraftvoll wachsenden chinesischen Räterepublik.

FIRST OF MAY

On 1 May, the day of the working class fighting for a new socialist world, the thoughts of working people of all countries are with their brothers, the workers and peasants of the Soviet Union and the liberated coolies of the young, increasingly powerful Chinese soviet republic.

This issue of *AIZ* (pp. 260–61) contained an article entitled "Rote Fahnen über China" (Red flags over China), about the emergence of Chinese soviets.

AIZ

V. b. b. - Erscheint wöchentlich einmal - Preis: 1,60 Kč, 40 Gr., 1,25 Frs., 30 Rp., 20 Pfg., 10 amer. Cts., 15 holl. Cts. - Jahrgang XIII. - Nr. 17. - 26. April 1934

Am 1. Mai, am Tag der für eine neue, sozialistische Welt kämpfenden Arbeiterklasse, sind die Gedanken der Werktätigen aller Länder bei ihren Brüdern, den Arbeitern und Bauern der Sowjetunion und den befreiten Kulis der jungen kraftvoll wachsenden chinesischen Räterepublik.

ERSTER MAI

Zur Intervention des Dritten Reichs

gegen die Internationale Karikaturen-Ausstellung im Kunstverein Mánes in Prag

Je mehr Bilder sie weghängen,
umso sichtbarer wird die Wirklichkeit!

Der deutsche Gesandte in Prag protestierte in mehreren Verbalnoten gegen Fotomontagen und Karikaturen, die seine FÜHRER darstellen. Auf die Intervention hin wurden einige Bilder aus der Ausstellung behördlich entfernt.

On the occasion of the intervention of the Third Reich

against the international caricature exhibition at the Mánes Art Association in Prague

The more pictures they remove,
the more visible becomes the reality!

The German envoy in Prague protested verbally on a number of occasions against photomontages and caricatures which depict his FÜHRER. As a result of his intervention several pictures were officially withdrawn from the exhibition.

For each picture removed there is a sign, handwritten in Gothic script: "Auf Einspruch der deutschen Gesandtschaft entfernt" (Withdrawn due to the objection of the German embassy). The image of the corpse also appears in 2/34.

A photograph of Heartfield's contribution to the exhibition, prior to censorship, had been published in the 19 April issue of *AIZ* (13, no. 16, p. 242). The next issue, dated 26 April, carried an article on the scandal entitled "John Heartfield," along with Rodchenko's photograph of the artist (see Fig. 12). The article began by asking, "Which of our readers does not yet know him?" and continued:

> Everyone knows him, if not by his appearance, then from his photomontages, those furious lampoons that inspire the friend and wound the foe, and that make laughter into a devastating weapon. John Heartfield's photomontages – which it is our pride and joy to be able to count among the characteristic features of *AIZ* – are the truest kind of art, great art, as they inspire the revolutionary fantasy of the masses and their will to fight for a better world. Heartfield's photomontages are at the moment the center of a protest which the German and Austrian envoys are waging against an exhibition of caricatures on the premises of the "Mánes" Art Association, an exhibition in which the montages of John Heartfield are recognized as the best section. The public flocking in by the thousands, the most famous artists, the most celebrated critics, have let Heartfield know through their enthusiastic approval that he is a great artist – though in the diplomatic notes of the Austrian and German envoys the photomontages are said to be inartistic, sorry efforts. Given the artistic standards the swastika and the cross potent have achieved, this aesthetic judgment by both excellencies should be taken as the sole decisive judgment for now and posterity. (*AIZ* 13, no. 17, p. 272)

Die Väter des Arbeitsgesetzes in Nöten

MOTTO: "VATER WERDEN IST NICHT SCHWER, VATER SEIN DAGEGEN SEHR"

"WIE BRINGEN WIR IHM DAS LOHNABFÜHRMITTEL NUR BEI?"

Zeitungsmeldung: "Das Inkrafttreten des Arbeitsgesetzes, das am 1. Mai erfolgen sollte, wurde auf unbestimmte Zeit verschoben."

Dr. LEY
Führer der deutschen Arbeitsfront

GOEBBELS

The fathers of the labor law in difficulty

MOTTO: "TO BECOME A FATHER IS NOT DIFFICULT, TO BE A FATHER IS VERY MUCH SO"

"JUST HOW DO WE GET HIM TO TAKE THE WAGE LAXATIVE?"

Newspaper report: "The effective date of the labor law, which should have been 1 May, has been postponed indefinitely."

Dr. LEY
Leader of the German Labor Front

GOEBBELS

The montage plays with the double meaning of *abführen:* to pay out and to loosen the bowels. *Lohn-Abführmittel* is, literally, a wage laxative.

     Dr. Robert Ley (1890–1945) was leader of the German Labor Front from 1933 to 1945 (see also 11/33). His tasks involved suppressing independent trade unions.

AIZ

Die Väter des Arbeits-
gesetzes in Nöten

MOTTO: »VATER WERDEN IST NICHT SCHWER,
VATER SEIN DAGEGEN SEHR«

Zeitungsmeldung: »Das Inkrafttreten des Arbeitsgesetzes, das am
1. Mai erfolgen sollte, wurde auf unbestimmte Zeit verschoben.«

Dr. LEY
Führer der deutschen Arbeitsfront

Lohn-
Abführ-
mittel

GOEBBELS

»WIE BRINGEN WIR IHM DAS LOHNABFÜHRMITTEL NUR BEI?«

Fotomontage: John Heartfield

DR. GOEBBELS, DER GESUNDBETER

"60 MILLIONEN ANTRETEN ZUM NACHBETEN!"

MIR IST NICHT MIES!
DIR IST NICHT MIES!
IHM IST NICHT MIES!
IHR IST NICHT MIES!
ES IST NICHT MIES!

"Die Reichspropagandaleitung der NSDAP hat eine umfassende Versammlungs-Propagandaaktion angeordnet gegen die Miesmacher und Kritikaster, gegen die Gerüchtemacher und Hetzer. Die Versammlungen werden alle erfassen bis in das letzte Dorf hinein, mit jeder Woche in ihrem Tempo stärker, in der Unerbittlichkeit der Forderungen härter, an Durchschlagskraft und Erfolgen alle bisher durchgeführten Aktionen in den Schatten stellend."
(Völkischer Beobachter)

"Eben in diesen Tagen schleichen sie umher und tuscheln jedem Willigen oder Harmlosen einen mageren Witz vom "Apotheker Coué" in die Ohren." (Fränkische Tageszeitung)

DR. GOEBBELS, THE FAITH HEALER

"60 MILLION FALL IN TO CHANT!"

I DON'T FEEL LOUSY!
YOU DON'T FEEL LOUSY!
HE DOESN'T FEEL LOUSY!
SHE DOESN'T FEEL LOUSY!
IT DOESN'T FEEL LOUSY!

"The Reich propaganda leadership of the NSDAP has ordered a comprehensive meeting-and-propaganda action against the killjoys and faultfinders, against the rumor-mongers and agitators. The meetings will cover everybody in the last remaining village, each week more dynamic, more demanding, putting the decisiveness and success of all previous actions in the shade." (Völkischer Beobachter)

"Even these days they creep about and whisper in the ears of every willing or naive person a poor joke about 'Pharmacist Coué.'" (Fränkische Tageszeitung)

More than two thousand meetings were held during the two-month campaign. "Pharmacist Coué" is Emile Coué (1857–1926), a French pharmacist and therapist who developed the idea that the repetition of key ideas (e.g., I feel healthy) could have real effects, making a sick person well. During the campaign Goebbels was compared to Coué.

"Mir ist mies" means I feel lousy, "etwas mies machen" is to run something down, and a *Miesmacher* is someone who always complains, a killjoy. *Miesmacher* was one of the catchwords Goebbels used regularly during the campaign. See also 27/34, *Meck und Mies im Dritten Reich* (Meck and Mies in the Third Reich).

Dr. GOEBBELS, DER GESUNDBETER

MIR IST NICHT MIES!
DIR IST NICHT MIES!
IHM IST NICHT MIES!
IHR IST NICHT MIES!
ES IST NICHT MIES!

MIES!
MIES!
MIES!
MIES!
MIES!
MIES!

„Die Reichspropagandaleitung der
NSDAP hat eine umfassende Versammlungs-Propagandaaktion angeordnet gegen die Miesmacher
und Kritikaster, gegen die Gerüchtemacher und Hetzer. Die Versammlungen werden alle erfassen
bis in das letzte Dorf hinein, mit jeder Woche in ihrem Tempo stärker,
in der Unerbittlichkeit der Forderungen härter, an Durchschlagskraft und Erfolgen alle bisher durchgeführten Aktionen in den Schatten
stellend."   (Völkischer Beobachter)

„Eben in diesen Tagen schleichen sie
umher und tuscheln jedem Willigen
oder Harmlosen einen mageren
Witz vom »Apotheker Coué« in die
Ohren."   (Fränkische Tageszeitung)

MIR IST NICHT MIES!
DIR IST NICHT MIES!
IHM IST NICHT MIES!
IHR IST NICHT MIES!
ES IST NICHT MIES!

DIR IST NICHT MIES!
ES IST NICHT MIES!
IHM IST NICHT MIES!

Fotomontage: John Heartfield

»60 MILLIONEN ANTRETEN ZUM NACHBETEN!«

LENINS VISION WARD WIRKLICHKEIT

Am 12. April, 12 Uhr, verließ der hunderttausendste Traktor der stalingrader Traktorenwerke das Fließband.

Vor 15 Jahren sagte Lenin auf dem 8. Parteitag der Bolschewiki: "Wenn wir morgen 100 000 erstklassige Traktoren liefern, sie mit Benzin und Traktorführern versehen könnten (ihr wißt wohl, daß dies einstweilen Fantastik ist), so würde der Mittelbauer sagen, ich bin für den Kommunismus. Doch um dies zu erzielen, muß man erst die internationale Bourgeoisie besiegen, man muß sie zwingen, uns diese Traktoren zu geben, oder aber unsere Produktivität muß so gehoben werden, daß wir sie selber liefern können."

Und in 15 Jahren beharrlicher bolschewistischer Arbeit ist das Ziel Lenins verwirklicht, ja übertroffen worden: über 200 000 Traktoren – alle aus Sowjet-Werken – sind auf den Feldern der Kollektiv-Wirtschaften und Sowjetgüter in Betrieb.

LENIN'S VISION BECAME REALITY

On 12 April at 12 o'clock, the 100,000th tractor left the assembly line of the Stalingrad tractor factory.

Fifteen years ago, Lenin said at the 8th Party Congress of the Bolsheviks: "If tomorrow we deliver 100,000 first-class tractors and are able to supply them with petrol and tractor drivers (you well know that this is fantasy at present), then the middle-class peasant would say: I am for Communism. In order to achieve this, one must first defeat the international bourgeoisie and must compel it to give us tractors, or on the other hand our productivity must increase to such a level that we can provide them ourselves."

And after 15 years of persistent Bolshevik work, Lenin's goal has been realized, even surpassed: over 200,000 tractors – all from Soviet factories – are in operation on the fields of collective farms and Soviet estates.

The Five Year Plans of Josef Stalin (1879–1953) were attempts to revolutionize Soviet industry and agriculture. He frequently sought to legitimize his actions with reverential allusions to Lenin. The symbolic significance of the tractor was also suggested by *AIZ*'s appeal to readers in 1930 (9, no. 6, p. 118) for contributions to provide "an *AIZ* tractor for the Soviet Union." For the original artwork for this montage, see Fig. 7.

Fotomontage: John Heartfield

LENINS VISION
WARD WIRKLICHKEIT

Am 12. April, 12 Uhr, verließ der hunderttausendste Traktor der stalingrader Traktorenwerke das Fließband.

Vor 15 Jahren sagte Lenin auf dem 8. Parteitag der Bolschewiki: »Wenn wir morgen 100 000 erstklassige Traktoren liefern, sie mit Benzin und Traktorführern versehen könnten (ihr wißt wohl, daß dies einstweilen Fantastik ist), so würde der Mittelbauer sagen, ich bin für den Kommunismus. Doch um dies zu erzielen, muß man erst die internationale Bourgeoisie besiegen, man muß sie zwingen, uns diese Traktoren zu geben, oder aber unsere Produktivität muß so gehoben werden, daß wir sie selber liefern können.«

Und in 15 Jahren beharrlicher bolschewistischer Arbeit ist das Ziel Lenins verwirklicht, ja übertroffen worden: über 200 000 Traktoren — alle aus Sowjet-Werken — sind auf den Feldern der Kollektiv-Wirtschaften und Sowjetgüter in Betrieb.

WIE IM MITTELALTER...

...SO IM DRITTEN REICH

AS IN THE MIDDLE AGES...

...SO IN THE THIRD REICH

The top panel reads: "Aufs Rad geflochtener Mann in einer alten Stiftskirche in Tübingen" (A man broken on the wheel in an old collegiate church in Tübingen). The bottom panel, with its allusion to the Pietà, incorporates a studio photograph of the German actor Erwin Geschonnek.

WIE IM MITTELALTER . . .

Aufs Rad geflochtener
Mann in einer alten
Stiftskirche in Tübingen.

. . . SO IM DRITTEN REICH

GESPRÄCH IM BERLINER ZOO

"Herr Streicher schreibt, die Juden seien Tiere und so weiter –
Da sperrt man sie wohl nächstens in den Zoo?"

Da sprach der weise Marabu: "Iwoo!
Man setzt sie auf die Kirchturmspitzen, denn das ist viel
gescheiter".

Der Affe drauf: "Erkläre mir, wieso?"

"Die Juden sind die besten Blitzableiter."

TALK IN THE BERLIN ZOO

"Herr Streicher writes that the Jews are animals and so on –
Will they soon be locked up in the zoo?"

Said the wise marabou: "Phoo!
They are to be placed on church spires. That's much
cleverer."

Then the monkey: "Explain, why?"

"The Jews are the best lightning conductors."

The monkey is reading the anti-Semitic newspaper *Der Stürmer*, edited
by Julius Streicher (see also 29/33, 11/35). It is the "Ritualmord-
Nummer" (Ritual murder issue), with the headline "Jüdischer
Mordplan gegen die nichtjüdische Menschheit" (Jewish murder plot
against non-Jewish humanity). That particular issue of *Der Stürmer*
had been attacked in "Ritualmordmärchen und Pogromhetze!" (Ritual
murder fairy tales and pogrom rabble rousing!), an article published in
AIZ on 24 May (13, no. 21, pp. 328–29).

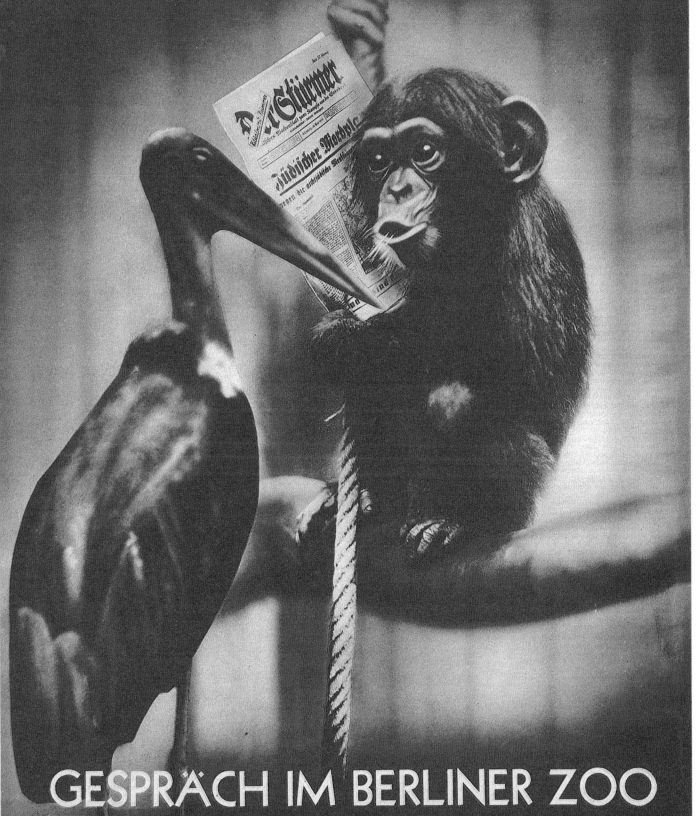

GESPRÄCH IM BERLINER ZOO

„Herr Streicher schreibt, die Juden seien Tiere und so weiter –
Da sperrt man sie wohl nächstens in den Zoo?"

Da sprach der weise Marabu: „Iwoo!
Man setzt sie auf die Kirchturmspitzen, denn das ist viel gescheiter".

Der Affe drauf: „Erkläre mir, wieso?"

„Die Juden sind die besten Blitzableiter."

Fotomontage: John Heartfield

Die Nachtleuchter tagen in Brüssel

Wo die hinleuchten, wirds duster!

Der Executivausschuß der Zweiten Internationale tagte in Brüssel.

DIE TAGNACHTLAMPE
von Christian Morgenstern

Korf erfindet eine Tagnachtlampe,
die, sobald sie angedreht,
selbst den hellsten Tag
in Nacht verwandelt.

Als er sie vor des Kongresses Rampe
demonstriert, vermag
niemand, der sein Fach versteht,
zu verkennen, daß es sich hier handelt –

(Finster wird's am hellerlichten Tag,
und ein Beifallssturm das Haus durchweht)
(Und man ruft dem Diener Mampe:
"Licht anzünden") – daß es sich hier handelt

um das Faktum: daß gedachte Lampe,
in der Tat, wenn angedreht,
selbst den hellsten Tag
in Nacht verwandelt.

The dimwits meet in Brussels

Where their light shines, things become dark!

The executive committee of the Second International met in Brussels.

THE DAY AND NIGHT LAMP
by Christian Morgenstern

Korf invents a day and night lamp
which as soon as it is turned on
changes the brightest day
into night.

When he demonstrates it
before the conference stage,
no one who knows his subject
can deny, that he finds it quite –

(The sunlit day becomes dark,
and a storm of applause blows through the hall)
(And someone calls to the servant Mampe:
"Turn on the light") – that he finds it quite

evident that the invented lamp,
when turned on, does in fact
change the brightest day
into night.

The montage shows Social Democratic leaders Friedrich Adler (1879–1960) of Austria, Emile Vandervelde (see 4/30) of Belgium, Otto Wels (1873–1939) of Germany, and Hendrik de Man (1885–1953) of Belgium (the latter with his name misspelled and his nationality incorrectly identified). Wels holds a *Nachtleuchter*, which can mean either candlestick or dimwit. The figure on the right demands, "Neu beginnen!" (Start afresh!), which was a slogan of the Second International. The poet Christian Morgenstern (1871–1914) was known for his nonsense verse, of which this is an example.

Die Nachtleuchter tagen in Brüssel

Der Exekutivausschuß der Zweiten Internationale tagte in Brüssel.

DIE TAGNACHTLAMPE
von Christian Morgenstern

Korf erfindet eine Tagnachtlampe,
die, sobald sie angedreht,
selbst den hellsten Tag
in Nacht verwandelt.

Als er sie vor des Kongresses Rampe
demonstriert, vermag
niemand, der sein Fach versteht,
zu verkennen, daß es sich hier handelt —

(Finster wird's am hellerlichten Tag,
und ein Beifallssturm das Haus durchweht)
(Und man ruft dem Diener Mampe:
„Licht anzünden") — daß es sich hier handelt

um das Faktum: daß gedachte Lampe,
in der Tat, wenn angedreht,
selbst den hellsten Tag
in' Nacht verwandelt.

Neu beginnen!

Vandervelde
(Belgien)

Otto Wels
(Deutschland)

Friedrich Adler
(Österreich)

Henrik de Man
(Holland)

Wo die hinleuchten, wirds duster!

IDYLLE IM DRITTEN REICH

Szene aus dem deutschen Kriminalfilm "DER VIER-
JAHRESPLAN"

"An den Auslandsbörsen erfuhr die Mark eine weitere
empfindliche Abschwächung. In Paris sind "Effektenmark"
schon für 2,35 frs., "Touristenmark" für 4 frs. (offizieller
Kurs 6,05 frs.) zu haben.

Schmitt   Schacht
(Wirtschaftsminister)   (Finanzminister)

IDYLL IN THE THIRD REICH

Scene from the German detective film "THE FOUR YEAR
PLAN"

"On the foreign exchanges the mark experienced a further
severe weakening. In Paris 'Effektenmark' are to be had for
2.35 frs., 'Touristenmark' for 4 frs. (official rate 6.05 frs.)."

Schmitt   Schacht
(Minister of Economics)   (Finance Minister)

Hitler's first Four Year Plan was launched in 1934. Kurt Schmitt
(1886–1950) was Hitler's first minister of economics (see also 2/34).
For Schacht, see 14/34.

IDYLLE IM
DRITTEN REICH

„An den Auslandsbörsen erfuhr die Mark eine weitere empfindliche Abschwächung. In Paris sind „Effektenmark" schon für 2,35 frs., „Touristenmark" für 4 frs. (offizieller Kurs 6,05 frs.) zu haben.

Schmitt
(Wirtschaftsminister)

Schacht
(Finanzminister)

Fotomontage: John Heartfield

Szene aus dem deutschen Kriminalfilm »DER VIER-JAHRESPLAN«

DER PAKT VON VENEDIG

"Schluß mit dem Friedensgegurre! Stillgestanden!
Wegtreten!"

THE VENICE PACT

"End the cooings about peace! Attention! Break ranks!"

Hitler and Benito Mussolini (1883–1945) met for the first time in
Venice in June 1934.

DER PAKT VON VENEDIG

Fotomontage: John Heartfield

»Schluß mit dem Friedensgegurre! Stillgestanden! Wegtreten!«

MECK UND MIES IM DRITTEN REICH

"Na, MECK, deine Flügel verkleinern sich täglich!"
"Ja, MIES, die Devisendeckung ist kläglich."
"Dein Bauch ist auch nicht mehr prall und rund!"
"Der Rohstoffersatz richtet uns zu Grund."
"Lebst aber noch sichtlich auf großen Füßen."
"Reiß nicht dein Maul auf, du wirst es noch büßen."
"Beklecker dir nur nicht die weiße Weste.
Es kommt bald ganz anders. Dann aber feste!"
"Das geht mir zu weit! Ich baue auf Papen,
Der räumt jetzt auf mit Hitlers Satrapen."
"Bei dir piepst's wohl? Der hat doch schon einmal regiert
Und uns prompt in die Hitlerei geführt."
"Ja aber – was sonst? Bolschewismus droht!"
"Na und? Der bringt Friede, Arbeit und Brot."
Da hat es dem MECK die Stimme verschlagen.
Und MIES ging weg, um es weiter zu sagen.

MECK AND MIES IN THE THIRD REICH

"Well, MECK, your wings are getting smaller daily!"
"Yes, MIES, the foreign currency reserve is pitiful."
"Your belly is no longer firm and round!"
"The ersatz raw material is running us into the ground."
"But you obviously still live extravagantly."
"Shut up, you'll pay for that."
"Only don't stain your white waistcoat.
Soon everything will be completely different. Quite definitely!"
"That's going too far! I'm backing Papen,
Who is now doing away with Hitler's satraps."
"Are you off your head? He has already governed once
And promptly led us into the Hitler era."
"Yes but – what else? Bolshevism threatens!"
"So what? It brings peace, work and bread."
That left MECK speechless.
And MIES went away, to spread the word.

In Wieland Herzfelde's fable "Meck" and "Mies" stand for the mythical Meckerer (Grumbler) and Miesmacher (Grouser), who spread rumors and skepticism (see also 20/34). Note that Meck holds a copy of the *Meckernburger Tagblatt*, an allusion to the *Mecklenburger Tagesblatt*. Mies holds the *Miesmacher Anzeiger;* the *Miesbacher Anzeiger* existed from 1875 to 1945 and was a favorite newspaper of the Nazis' in the twenties because of its sharp criticism of the Weimar Republic. For Von Papen, see 15/32, 33/34, 42/34.

"Auf großem Fuß leben," in line 5, means literally to live on a big foot.

MECK UND MIES
IM DRITTEN REICH

„Na, MECK, deine Flügel verkleinern sich täglich!"

„Ja, MIES, die Devisendeckung ist kläglich."

„Dein Bauch ist auch nicht mehr prall und rund!"

„Der Rohstoffersatz richtet uns zu Grund."

„Lebst aber noch sichtlich auf großen Füßen."

„Reiß nicht dein Maul auf, du wirst es noch büßen."

„Beklecker dir nur nicht die weiße Weste.
Es kommt bald ganz anders. Dann aber feste!"

„Das geht mir zu weit! Ich baue auf Papen,
Der räumt jetzt auf mit Hitlers Satrapen."

„Bei dir piepst's wohl? Der hat doch schon einmal regiert
Und uns prompt in die Hitlerei geführt."

„Ja aber — was sonst? Bolschewismus droht!"

„Na und? Der bringt Friede, Arbeit und Brot."

Da hat es dem MECK die Stimme verschlagen.
Und MIES ging weg, um es weiter zu sagen.

Fotomontage: John Heartfield   Fabel von W. Herzfelde

TREUE UM TREUE
GRUSS VOM FÜHRER

LOYALTY FOR LOYALTY
GREETINGS FROM THE FÜHRER

Ernst Röhm (1887–1934) is shown being executed with Krupp guns (see 3/33, 2/34). Röhm, who created the SA from his own private force in 1921, was an early supporter of Hitler. In 1931, as chief of staff, he took command of both the SS and the SA, and in 1933 he became state commissar and secretary of state of Bavaria. His populist demagogy offended some of the powerful groups courted by Hitler, such as the Rhineland industrialists. He was accused of conspiracy to overthrow Hitler and executed without a trial.

The elimination of the SA leaders on 30 June 1934, "the Night of the Long Knives," was the lead story in the issue this montage appeared in. An article entitled "Köpfe rollen" (Heads roll; p. 434) included a photograph of Hitler and Krupp. The caption read: "Der Führer und sein Führer" (i.e., Hitler and the man behind him, Krupp). The accompanying text noted that Hitler had visited Krupp a few days before the purge and concluded: "Herr von Krupp dürfte nicht verfehlt haben, seinem 'Führer' den Wunsch der Schwerindustrie mitzuteilen: die SA ist überflüssig!" (Herr von Krupp will not have failed to convey to his "Führer" the wish of heavy industry: The SA is superfluous!).

TREUE UM TREUE

MODELL KRUPP 1934

MODELL KRUPP 1934

MODELL KRUPP 1934

GRUSS VOM FÜHRER

30. JUNI 1934
HEIL HITLER!

30 JUNE 1934
HEIL HITLER!

An article in this issue (p. 450), "Nach der Nacht der Langen Messer"
(After the Night of the Long Knives), offered further analysis of the
SA purge (see 28/34).

30. JUNI 1934

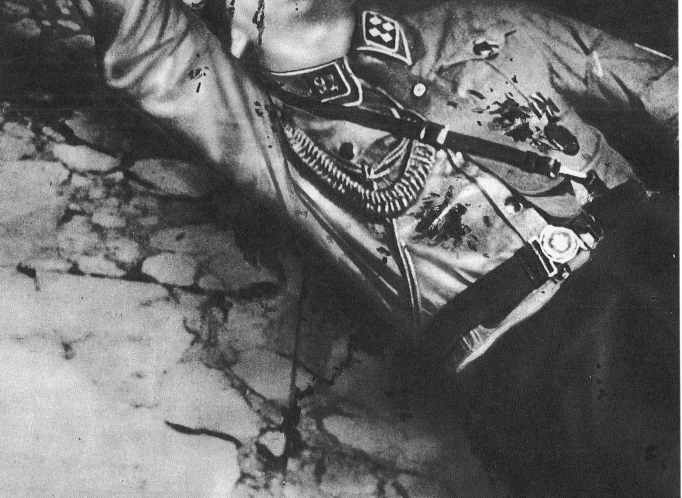

HEIL HITLER!

Fotomontage: John Heartfield

**Faschismus sein letzter Retter –
Krieg sein letzter Ausweg!**

SONDERNUMMER 1914–1934

Hitler treibt zum Krieg! SIEHE INNENSEITEN!

**Fascism his final savior –
war his final resort!**

SPECIAL ISSUE 1914–1934

Hitler drives toward war! SEE INSIDE!

This was the front cover of a special issue commemorating the outbreak of World War I (see also 38/34); 31/34 was the back cover, creating a diptych.

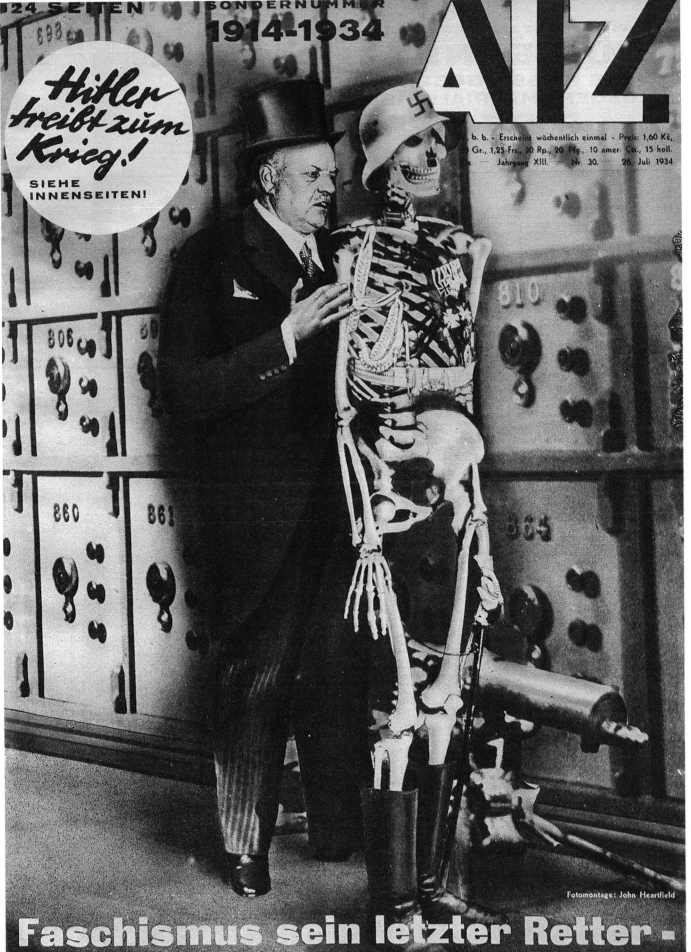

24 SEITEN · SONDERNUMMER
1914–1934

AIZ

Hitler treibt zum Krieg!

SIEHE
INNENSEITEN!

b. b. · Erscheint wöchentlich einmal · Preis: 1,60 Kč,
Gr., 1,25 Frs., 30 Rp., 20 Pfg., 10 amer. Cts., 15 holl.
s. — Jahrgang XIII. — Nr. 30. — 26. Juli 1934

Fotomontage: John Heartfield

Faschismus sein letzter Retter –
Krieg sein letzter Ausweg!

SCHLUSS DAMIT!

PROFITWIRTSCHAFT   FASCHISMUS
KRISE   KRIEG

STOP IT!

PROFIT ECONOMY   FASCISM
CRISIS   WAR

This inscription on the cross in the "Profit Economy" section reads:
"Hier ruhen 20 Millionen Arbeitslose" (Here rest 20 million
unemployed).This was the back cover of the issue. See 30/34, which
was the front.

PROFITWIRTSCHAFT   FASCHISMUS

KRIEG

KRISE

SCHLUSS DAMIT!

Fotomontage: John Heartfield

Die Toten, der großen Idee gestorben, werden Millionen Vorbild sein!

Das Henkerbeil arbeitet ohne Unterlaß im Dritten Reich. Eben wurde in Stuttgart der Jungkommunist Minnich enthauptet. Vor ihm waren ein halbes Hundert Genossen geköpft worden. Unter ihnen – vor einem Jahr – Lütgens und die anderen Helden von Altona; auch die zu Pfingsten hingerichteten tapferen hamburger Revolutionäre Dettmer, Schmidt, Fischer und Wehrenberg. Fischers letzter Brief ist jetzt bekannt geworden. In diesem Brief schrieb er, der dem Tode Geweihte, an Frau und Kinder:

Wenn ich auch falle, die Fahne wird stehen, trotzig und stark.
Hermann Fischer

The dead, who died for the great idea, will be a model for millions!

The executioner's ax works without a pause in the Third Reich. In Stuttgart the Young Communist Minnich was beheaded recently. Before him some fifty comrades were decapitated. Among them – a year ago – Lütgens and the other heroes of Altona; also the valiant Hamburg revolutionaries Dettmer, Schmidt, Fischer and Wehrenberg were executed at Whitsuntide. Fischer's last letter has now become known. In this letter, written shortly before death, he wrote to wife and children:

Even if I die, the flag will stand defiant and strong.
Hermann Fischer

The words on the flag are "Für ein freies sozialistisches Räte-Deutschland!" (For a free socialist soviet Germany!).

Die Toten, der großen Idee gestorben, werden Millionen Vorbild sein!

Für ein freies sozialistisches Räte-Deutschland!

Das Henkerbeil arbeitet ohne Unterlaß im Dritten Reich. Eben wurde in Stuttgart der Jungkommunist Minnich enthauptet. Vor ihm waren ein halbes Hundert Genossen geköpft worden. Unter ihnen — vor einem Jahr — Lütgens und die anderen Helden von Altona; auch die zu Pfingsten hingerichteten tapferen hamburger Revolutionäre Dettmer, Schmidt, Fischer und Wehrenberg. Fischers letzter Brief ist jetzt bekannt geworden. In diesem Brief schrieb er, der dem Tode Geweihte, an Frau und Kinder:

Wenn ich auch falle, die Fahne wird stehen, trotzig und stark.

Hermann Fischer

Fotomontage: John Heartfield

HERR VON PAPEN,
ein Gesandter, doch kein Geschickter

Treu seiner diplomatischen Gewohnheit
hat Herr v. Papen seine für Wien bestimmte Aktenmappe
schon im vorhinein verloren

Hier ist sie!

Herr von Papen organisierte im Krieg als Militärattaché der
deutschen Botschaft in Amerika Spionagedienst und
Sabotageakte. Er mußte, weil er eine Aktenmappe mit
kompromittierendem Material in der Untergrundbahn liegen
ließ, das Land verlassen. Unterwegs nach Deutschland ließ
er in den Händen englischer Behörden weiteres belastendes
Material, u.a. die Namen der deutschen Agenten in USA.
Ein drittes Mal verlor er eine Diplomatenmappe mit sehr
wichtigen Dokumenten in der Türkei.

MR. VON PAPEN,
an ambassador, but not a clever one

True to his diplomatic form
Mr. von Papen lost his briefcase destined for Vienna before
he even got there

Here it is!

During the war, Mr. von Papen, as military attaché of the
German embassy, organized the secret service and acts of
sabotage in America. He had to leave the country because
he left a briefcase with compromising material in the subway.
En route to Germany he left in the hands of English authorities
further incriminating material, among other things the names
of German agents in America. A third time he lost a
diplomatic bag with very important documents in Turkey.

In July 1934 there had been a failed National Socialist putsch in
Vienna; this issue of *AIZ* carried a report (pp. 506–9). Von Papen
(see 15/32, 27/34, 42/34) had been named ambassador to Austria on
26 July. The contents of his briefcase, including a highly confidential
letter from Hitler, provided concrete evidence of Nazi interference in
Austrian affairs.

Gesandter, the usual word for envoy or diplomat, means
literally the person sent (*senden* is to send). *Geschickter*, a clever
person, is derived from *schicken*, also meaning to send. The phrase
"ein Gesandter, doch kein Geschickter" therefore has two levels of
meaning: an ambassador, but not a clever one, and a person sent,
but not sent.

HERR VON PAPEN,
ein Gesandter, doch kein Geschickter

Herr von Papen organisierte im Krieg als Militärattaché der deutschen Botschaft in Amerika Spionagedienst und Sabotageakte. Er mußte, weil er eine Aktenmappe mit kompromittierendem Material in der Untergrundbahn liegen ließ, das Land verlassen. Unterwegs nach Deutschland ließ er in den Händen englischer Behörden weiteres belastendes Material, u. a. die Namen der deutschen Agenten in USA. Ein drittes Mal verlor er eine Diplomatenmappe mit sehr wichtigen Dokumenten in der Türkei.

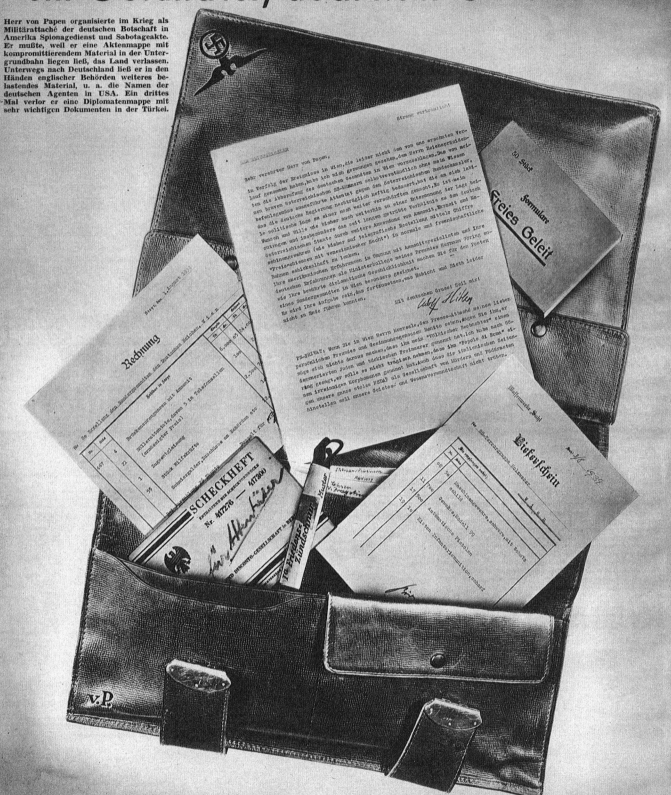

Treu seiner diplomatischen Gewohnheit
hat Herr v. Papen seine für Wien bestimmte Aktenmappe schon im vorhinein verloren
Hier ist sie!

Fotomontage: John Heartfield

DEUTSCHE NATURGESCHICHTE

METAMORPHOSE

"Matamorphose", (griechisch μορφí– Gestalt) bedeutet: 1.
In der Mythologie: die Verwandlung von Menschen in
Bäume, Tiere, Steine u.s.w. 2. In der Zoologie: die
Entwicklung mancher Tiere über Larvenformen und Puppen,
beispielsweise Raupe, Puppe, Schmetterling. 3. In der
Geschichte der weimarer Republik: die geradlinige Folge
EBERT–HINDENBURG–HITLER.

DEUTSCHER TOTENKOPF-FALTER

(Acherontia atropos germanica) in seinen drei
Entwicklungsstufen: Raupe, Puppe, Falter

GERMAN NATURAL HISTORY

METAMORPHOSIS

"Metamorphosis" (Greek μορφή – form) means: 1. In
mythology: the transformation of humans into trees, animals,
stones and so on. 2. In zoology: the development of some
animals through forms of larvae and chrysalis, for example,
caterpillar, chrysalis, butterfly. 3. In the history of the
Weimar Republic: the succession in a straight line
EBERT–HINDENBURG–HITLER.

GERMAN DEATH'S-HEAD MOTH

(Acherontia atropos germanica) in its three stages of
development: caterpillar, chrysalis, moth

Friedrich Ebert (1871–1925), a Social Democrat, was president of
the Weimar Republic from 1919 to 1925. Paul von Hindenburg (see
also 6/30) was president from 1925 to 1934. Hitler declared himself
Führer, combining the posts of chancellor and president, on 2
August 1934, the day Hindenburg died. This issue, published two
weeks later, included an assessment titled "Hindenburg – Legende
und Wirklichkeit" (Hindenburg – legend and reality; pp. 524–25,
532). The withered oak branch symbolizes Germany.

DEUTSCHE NATURGESCHICHTE

DEUTSCHER TOTENKOPF-FALTER
(Acherontia atropos germanica) in seinen
drei Entwicklungsstufen: Raupe, Puppe, Falter

METAMORPHOSE

»Metamorphose«, (griechisch μορφή - Gestalt) bedeutet: 1. In der Mythologie: die Verwandlung von Menschen in Bäume, Tiere,
Steine u. s. w. 2. In der Zoologie: die Entwicklung mancher Tiere über Larvenformen und Puppen, beispielsweise Raupe, Puppe,
Schmetterling. 3. In der Geschichte der weimarer Republik: die geradlinige Folge EBERT — HINDENBURG — HITLER.

Fotomontage: John Heartfield

SEIN KAMPF MIT SEINEM "KAMPF"

"Fort mit Schaden! Hauptsache: die russischen Seiten bleiben drin".

Die "nationale Befreiung Deutschlands", feierlich versprochen in Hitlers "Mein Kampf", macht Fortschritte: SÜDTIROL wurde schon vor Jahren aus dem "unveränderlichen Programm der NSDAP" gestrichen; der POLNISCHE KORRIDOR ist längst "kein Streitpunkt mehr"; DANZIG – regiert von National-sozialisten – "gliedert sich in den polnischen Wirtschaftsraum ein"; an der SAAR gibt es – nach Hitlers eigenen Worten – "keine territorialen Fragen mehr"; und jetzt mußte "der Führer" von seinen Anschlußforderungen auf ÖSTERREICH abrücken! Die "Sklavenketten von Versailles", die Adolf Hitler immer wieder zu zerbrechen versprach, sind somit heil geblieben, dafür wurde Blatt für Blatt seines Buches "Mein Kampf" zerrissen.

HIS STRUGGLE WITH HIS "STRUGGLE"

"Good riddance! Main point: the Russian pages remain."

The "national liberation of Germany," solemnly promised in Hitler's "Mein Kampf," makes progress: SOUTH TYROL has already been struck out of the "unchangeable program of the NSDAP" years ago; the POLISH CORRIDOR has long been "no more a point of dispute"; DANZIG – ruled by National Socialists – "integrates itself into the Polish economic territory"; on the SAAR, there is – in Hitler's own words – "no longer a territorial question," and now the "Führer" has had to dissociate himself from the demands for union with AUSTRIA! The "slave chains of Versailles," which Adolf Hitler continuously promised to smash, have thus remained intact. Instead his book "Mein Kampf" was torn up page by page.

Hitler did, of course, briefly fulfill some of the promises he made in *Mein Kampf* (Part 1, 1925) to reverse the terms of the Treaty of Versailles of 1919: restoration of German authority in Saarland (1935), union with Austria (1938), and union with Danzig (1939).

AIZ

V. b. b. — Erscheint wöchentlich einmal Preis: 1,60 Kč, 40 Gr., 1,25 Frs., 30 Rp.,
20 Pfg., 10 amer. Cts., 15 holl. Cts. - Jahrgang XIII. - Nr. 34. - 23. August 1934

SEIN KAMPF MIT SEINEM „KAMPF"

Die „nationale Befreiung Deutschlands", feierlich versprochen in Hitlers „Mein Kampf", macht Fortschritte:
SÜDTIROL wurde schon vor Jahren aus dem „unveränderlichen Programm der NSDAP" gestrichen; der
POLNISCHE KORRIDOR ist längst „kein Streitpunkt
mehr"; DANZIG — regiert von Nazionalsozialisten —
„gliedert sich in den polnischen Wirtschaftsraum ein";
an der SAAR gibt es — nach Hitlers eigenen Worten —
„keine territorialen Fragen mehr"; und jetzt mußte „der
Führer" von seinen Anschlußforderungen auf ÖSTER-
REICH abrücken! Die „Sklavenketten von Versailles",
die Adolf Hitler immer wieder zu zerbrechen versprach, sind somit heil geblieben, dafür wurde Blatt
für Blatt seines Buches „Mein Kampf" zerrissen.

„Fort mit Schaden! Hauptsache: die russischen Seiten bleiben drin".

Fotomontage: John Heartfield

FÜNF MILLIONEN NEIN

ZU LEICHT BEFUNDEN!
Das Blut und die Tränen wiegen mit!

FIVE MILLION NOS

STILL TOO LIGHT!
Blood and tears weigh too!

On 2 August Hitler declared himself Führer. In the referendum concerning his new powers that was held on 19 August, almost 90 percent of the votes were favorable. The text on the ballot reads: "Stimmst Du, deutscher Mann, / und Du, deutsche Frau, / der in diesem Gesetz getroffenen Regelung zu? / Ja   Nein" (Do you approve, German man, / and you, German woman, / of the arrangement contained in this law? / Yes   No). Note the Nazi use of the familiar form *Du*. One ballot has been defaced with the name of Thälmann, the KPD (German Communist Party) leader imprisoned by the Nazis (see also 37/34).

AIZ

V. b. b. — Erscheint wöchentlich einmal Preis: 1,60 Kč, 40 Gr., 1,25 Frs., 30 Rp.,
20 Pfg., 10 amer. Cts., 15 holl. Cts. - Jahrgang XIII. - Nr. 35. - 30. August 1934

Fotomontage: John Heartfield

FÜNF MILLIONEN NEIN

TERROR

ZU LEICHT BEFUNDEN!
Das Blut und die Tränen wiegen mit!

THÄLMANN,

DAS IST EINE FAHNE! DIE GROSSE, HEILIGE SACHE DER
MENSCHHEIT! DIE IDEE! (André Gide)

THÄLMANN MUSS GEWONNEN WERDEN WIE EINE
SCHLACHT! (Henri Barbusse)

THÄLMANN,

THAT IS A FLAG! THE GREAT, HOLY CONCERN OF
HUMANITY! THE IDEA! (André Gide)

THÄLMANN MUST BE WON LIKE A BATTLE! (Henri Barbusse)

Ernst Thälmann (1886–1944), leader of the German Communist
Party, was arrested and interned in 1933 (see also 15/36). The last
line is a quote from Henri Barbusse (1874–1951), a writer who like
André Gide (1869–1951) had Communist sympathies at the time.

V. b. b. — Erscheint wöchentlich einmal Preis: 1,60 Kč, 40 Gr., 1,25 Frs., 30 Rp., 20 Pfg., 10 amer. Cts., 15 holl. Cts. - Jahrgang XIII. - Nr. 36. - 6. September 1934

AIZ.

THÄLMANN,
DAS IST EINE FAHNE!
DIE GROSSE, HEILIGE
SACHE DER MENSCH-
HEIT! DIE IDEE! (André Gide)

Fotomontage: John Heartfield

THÄLMANN MUSS GEWONNEN WERDEN WIE EINE SCHLACHT!

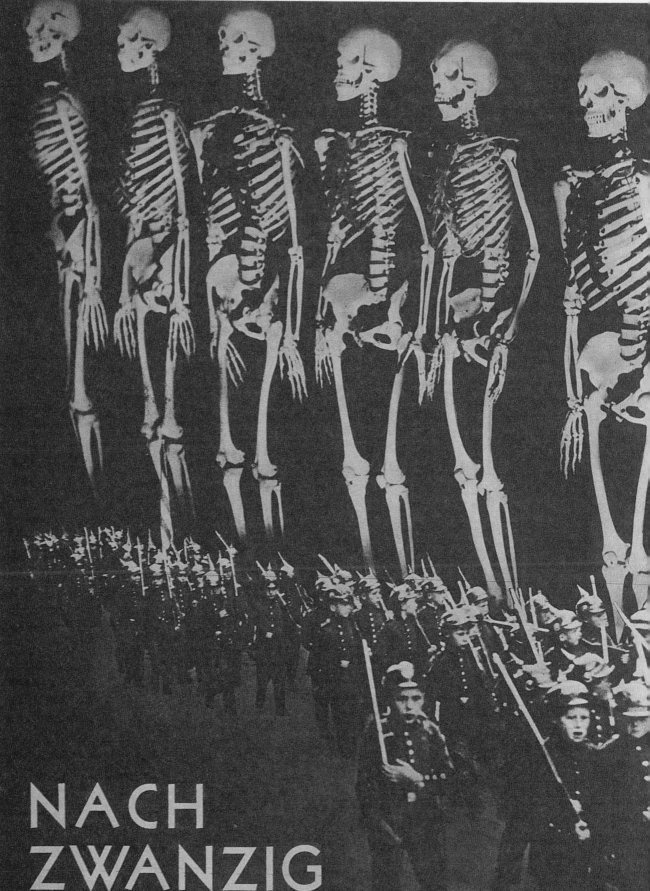

NACH
ZWANZIG
JAHREN!

Fotomontage: John Heartfield

„Sogar dreijährigen Kindern muß, wenn sie Krieg spielen, die Handhabung des Gewehres und des Säbels ernsthaft beigebracht und das Gefühl eingeflößt werden, daß der Krieg angenehm ist und daß man den Krieg lieben muß.“

(Aus der in Charbin erscheinenden japanischen Zeitung »Charbin Simbun«.)

NACH ZWANZIG JAHREN!

"Sogar dreijährigen Kindern muß, wenn sie Krieg spielen, die Handhabung des Gewehres und des Säbels ernsthaft beigebracht und das Gefühl eingeflößt werden, daß der Krieg angenehm ist und daß man den Krieg lieben muß." (Aus der in Charbin erscheinenden japanischen Zeitung "Charbin Simbun".)

TWENTY YEARS LATER!

"Even three-year-old children, when they play at war, must be solemnly taught the proper handling of the gun and the saber, and the feeling that war is pleasant and that we must love war must be instilled." (From the Japanese newspaper in Kharbin "Kharbin Simbun.")

This issue commemorated the twentieth anniversary of the outbreak of World War I (see also 30/34). On the right is General Karl Litzmann (1850–1936), a veteran of World War I and from 1929 an active member of the Nazi Party. His presence suggests that the militaristic attitudes that sacrificed a generation still survived in the Third Reich. The quotation, encouraging militarism in young children, is from the *Harbin Shimbun,* a contemporary Japanese newspaper published in the Manchurian city of Harbin (or Kharbin), which had been occupied by the Japanese since 1932. Heartfield was therefore not only commemorating the start of World War I but also warning of the possibility of another war started by Germany or Japan.

       The same image, but with different text, had been displayed in the window of Herzfelde's Berlin bookshop in 1924 to mark the tenth anniversary of the start of World War I (see Herzfelde, *John Heartfield,* p. 367, no. 125).

(pages 250–51)

Das tausendjährige Reich

"Die deutsche Lebensform ist für das nächste Jahrtausend endgültig bestimmt." – "In den nächsten tausend Jahren findet in Deutschland keine Revolution mehr statt."

Adolf Hitler auf dem nürnberger Parteitage

The Thousand Year Reich

"The German way of life has been conclusively ordained for the next millennium." – "In the next thousand years no further revolution will take place in Germany."

Adolf Hitler at the Nürnberg party rally

Using skat cards, Heartfield presented an anatomy of the Third Reich: the lowest cards of the different suits depict the German people suffering from economic autarky and propaganda; the higher face cards represent the alliance of capital and the Nazi state. At the summit of his studio construction of cards (see Fig. 11, the original artwork) is the pro-Nazi industrialist Thyssen (see 18/33) as the king of bells (money bags here). At the lower right is Hitler the drummer ("Der Trommler") as the knave of leaves. The knaves in the center represent, in order of ascending importance, Feldjäger (military police); Schwarze Reichswehr (Nazi army); SA (Sturmabteilung, or Brownshirts, with a bleeding heart alluding to "the Night of the Long Knives" [see 28/34]); SS (Schutzstaffel, or Blackshirts, with the word *Ersatz* on the acorn); and Reichswehr (army). At the lower left is the seven of leaves, inscribed: "Deutsche Buche in die deutsche Pfeife" (German beech into the German pipe), a reference to economic autarky. The eight of acorns is inscribed: "Die Deutsche Eichel / Das Volkskraftnahrungsmittel des III. Reiches / Friedensschalmei" (The German acorn / The remedy of the Third Reich for building up the strength of the people / The shawm of peace). The ten of shells has the text "Dr. Goebbels / Ia Propaganda-schellen / Bestes Mittel gegen Hunger u. Arbeitslosigkeit / Atta Troll" (Dr. Goebbels / 1st class propaganda bells / Best remedy against hunger and unemployment / Atta Troll [the German dancing bear in Heinrich Heine's satirical verse epic of 1843]). To the eight of hearts is added, "Volksgemeinschaftsherzen / Luxusausgabe für Wirtschafts-führer / Einfache Ausgabe für Gefolgschaft" (National community hearts / Luxury edition for the economic leadership / Ordinary edition for the work force). The next card shows Göring as "Der blutige Hermann" (Bloody Hermann), a beastlike figure grasping images of a prison and an ax.

Fotomontage: John Heartfield

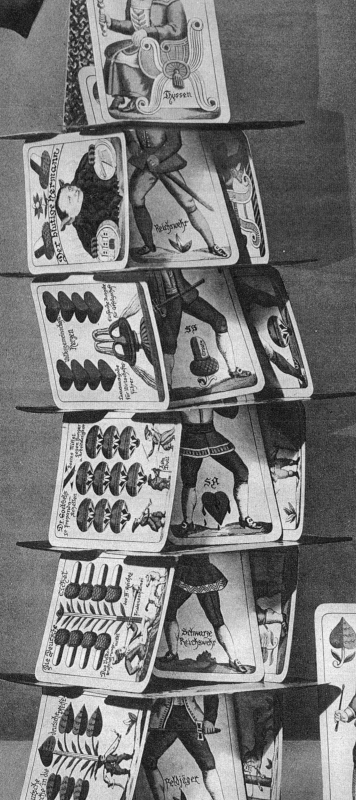

„Die deutsche Lebensform ist für
das nächste Jahrtausend endgültig
bestimmt." — „In den nächsten
tausend Jahren findet in Deutschland keine Revolution mehr statt."

Adolf Hitler auf dem nürnberger Parteitage

Das tausendjährige Reich

JEDEM KRIEGSOPFER SEIN EHRENKREUZ!

Die Hitler-Regierung hat ein Gesetz erlassen, nach dem "im Verwaltungswege" die bisher gesetzlich verankert gewesene Unterstützung den Kriegsopfern und den Hinterbliebenen beliebig gekürzt werden kann. Den Betroffenen werden "EHRENKREUZE" verliehen.

A CROSS OF HONOR FOR EVERY WAR VICTIM!

The Hitler government has passed a law according to which "through administrative action" the support of war victims and surviving dependents, until now a legal obligation, can be cut at will. Those affected will be awarded "CROSSES OF HONOR."

The inscription on one of the crosses reads: "Ernst Hampel / gestorben durch Renten-Entzug / ausgezeichnet mit / dem / Ehrenkreuz" (Ernst Hampel / dead as a result of the withdrawal of a pension / decorated with / the / cross of honor).

This issue carried a related article (pp. 620–21): "Der Dank des III. Reichs ist euch gewiss…" (The thanks of the Third Reich is assured you…).

Die Hitler-Regierung hat ein Gesetz erlassen, nach dem „im Verwaltungswege" die bisher gesetzlich verankert gewesene Unterstützung den Kriegsopfern und den Hinterbliebenen beliebig gekürzt werden kann. Den Betroffenen werden „EHRENKREUZE" verliehen.

JEDEM KRIEGSOPFER SEIN EHRENKREUZ!

Alle Fäuste zu einer geballt,
Zeigt dem Faschismus eure Gewalt!
Was sie in Frankreich, im Saarland gekonnt:
Antifaschisten in einer Front,
Überall muß es so werden!

All fists clenched into one,
Show Fascism your power!
What they were able to do in France, in Saarland:
Anti-Fascists in one front,
Everywhere it must become like that!

This was the cover of a special issue (*Sondernummer*) on
"antifaschistische Aktionseinheit" (anti-Fascist united action).

V. 8. 8. — Erscheint wöchentlich einmal Preis: 1,00 Kč, 40 Gr., 1,25 Frs., 50 Rp.,
20 Pfg., 10 amer. Cts., 15 holl. Cts. - Jahrgang XIII. - Nr. 40. - 4. Oktober 1934

AIZ

SONDERNUMMER:
Antifaschistische
Aktionseinheit

Alle Fäuste zu *einer geballt,*

Zeigt dem Faschismus eure Gewalt!
Was sie in Frankreich, im Saarland gekonnt:
Antifaschisten in einer Front,
Überall muß es so werden!

Herr von Papen auf dem Jagdpfad

Herr Papen fuhr wohl auf die Pirsch,
Halali – Halali – Sieg-Heil!
Doch nicht zu jagen Reh und Hirsch,
Halali – Halali – Sieg-Heil!
Nach andrem Wildpret stand sein Sinn,
Drum fuhr er zu Freund Gömbös hin
Adolfs allzeit bereiter
Herrenreiter.
Er pirscht nicht nur im Walde frisch,
Halali – Halali – Sieg-Heil!
Sein Jagdfeld ist der grüne Tisch,
Halali – Halali – Sieg-Heil!
"Freund Gömbös, laß das Reh dem Bock,
komm in den polnisch-deutschen Block!"
Sprach Adolfs allzeit gewandter
Sondergesandter.
"Ich weiß ein prächtig Jagdrevier,
Halali – Halali – Sieg-Heil!
Gen West- und Ostland reiten wir,
Halali – Halali – Sieg-Heil!
Heissa! Auf Tschech, Franzos und Russ –
Das erst ist wahrer Jagdgenuß!"
Rief Adolfs allzeit reger
Sonntagsjäger.
Nicht immer hat ein Jäger Glück,
Halali – Halali – ei weih!
Schon mancher Schuß schlug bös zurück.
Halali – Halali – ei weih!
Und der zur Treibjagd fröhlich blies,
Dem Bären Haut und Haare ließ:
Adolfs weltweit gereister
Jägermeister!

"Die Jagdreise von Papens nach Ungarn diente hochpolitischen Zwecken. Es wurden mit Gömbös vor dessen warschauer Reise die auf Einreihung Ungarns in den deutsch-polnischen Block abzielenden Vorschläge der Wilhelmstraße besprochen. Herr von Papen erklärte den Pressevertretern, er sei mit seinem Aufenthalt in Ungarn sehr zufrieden. Sein Jagdausflug sei trefflich gelungen."
Aus den Zeitungen vom 3. Oktober 1934.

Mr. von Papen on the hunting track

Mr. Papen did indeed go deerstalking,
Tallyho – Tallyho – Sieg-Heil!
Yet not to hunt deer and stag,
Tallyho – Tallyho – Sieg-Heil!
Other prey was on his mind,
Therefore he journeyed to friend Gömbös,
Adolf's ever ready
Gentleman rider.
He stalks not only in the woods so fresh,
Tallyho – Tallyho – Sieg-Heil!
His hunting ground is the green table,
Tallyho – Tallyho – Sieg-Heil!
"Friend Gömbös, leave the doe to the buck,
come into the Polish-German bloc!"
Spoke Adolf's ever clever
Special envoy.
"I know a splendid game preserve,
Tallyho – Tallyho – Sieg-Heil!
Toward western and eastern lands we ride,
Tallyho – Tallyho – Sieg-Heil!
Hurrah! After Czechs, French and Russians –
That is the real pleasure of hunting!"
Cried Adolf's ever lively
Sunday hunter.
A hunter does not always have luck,
Tallyho – Tallyho – oh Christ!
Many a shot has viciously returned.
Tallyho – Tallyho – oh Christ!
And he who joyfully called for the hunt
Left skin and hair to the bears:
Adolf's world-traveler
Master of hounds!

"Von Papen's hunting trip to Hungary had highly political aims. Before Gömbös's journey to Warsaw, they discussed the Wilhelmstraße proposals concerning the incorporation of Hungary into the German-Polish bloc. Mr. von Papen announced to the representatives of the press that he was very satisfied with his stay in Hungary. His hunting excursion was a brilliant success."
From the newspapers of 3 October 1934.

In June 1934 Germany and Poland had signed a ten-year nonaggression pact. Von Papen (see 15/32, 27/34, 33/34) was appointed German ambassador to Austria on 26 July. Gyula Gömbös von Jáfka (1886–1936), prime minister of Hungary from 1932 to 1936, was sympathetic to the Fascists in Germany and Italy. "In memoriam 30 Juni" is a reference to the SA purge (see 28/34, 29/34). The map shows diplomatic trips from Berlin to neighboring cities. Wilhelmstraße, the street where the Reich Chancellery was located, was a synonym for the German government.

Herr von Papen auf dem Jagdpfad

Herr Papen fuhr wohl auf die Pirsch,
Halali — Halali — Sieg-Heil!
Doch nicht zu jagen Reh und Hirsch,
Halali — Halali — Sieg-Heil!
Nach andrem Wildpret stand sein Sinn,
Drum fuhr er zu Freund Gömbös hin
Adolfs allzeit bereiter
Herrenreiter.

Er pirscht nicht nur im Walde frisch,
Halali — Halali — Sieg-Heil!
Sein Jagdfeld ist der grüne Tisch,
Halali — Halali — Sieg-Heil!
„Freund Gömbös, laß das Reh dem Bock,
komm in den polnisch-deutschen Block!"
Sprach Adolfs allzeit gewandter
Sondergesandter.

„Ich weiß ein prächtig Jagdrevier,
Halali — Halali — Sieg-Heil!
Gen West- und Ostland reiten wir,
Halali — Halali — Sieg-Heil!
Heissa! Auf Tschech, Franzos und Russ —
Das erst ist wahrer Jagdgenuß!"
Rief Adolfs allzeit reger
Sonntagsjäger.

Nicht immer hat ein Jäger Glück,
Halali — Halali — ei weih!
Schon mancher Schuß schlug bös zurück.
Halali — Halali — ei weih!
Und der zur Treibjagd fröhlich blies,
Dem Bären Haut und Haare ließ:
Adolfs weltweit gereister
Jägermeister!

„Die Jagdreise von Papens nach Ungarn diente hochpolitischen Zwecken. Es wurden mit Gömbös vor dessen warschauer Reise die auf Einreihung Ungarns in den deutsch-polnischen Block abzielenden Vorschläge der Wilhelmstraße besprochen. Herr von Papen erklärte den Pressevertretern, er sei mit seinem Aufenthalt in Ungarn sehr zufrieden. Sein Jagdausflug sei trefflich gelungen."
Aus den Zeitungen vom 3. Oktober 1934.

Fotomontage John Heartfield

Ruhe herrscht wieder in Barcelona

Giftgas erst schafft wahre Volksgemeinschaft!

In den gestrigen Abendstunden flammten die Kämpfe
in ganz Spanien, namentlich in Katalonien, wieder auf.
General Batet droht, gegen die Aufständischen mit
Giftgasen vorzugehen.
Prager Abendzeitung   Montag, den 8. Oktober 1934.

Quiet rules again in Barcelona

Only poison gas creates true national unity!

Yesterday evening, conflicts flared up again throughout
Spain, particularly in Catalonia. General Batet threatened
to use poison gas against the rebels.

This was a special issue on the crisis in Spain. In 1934 there were
several actions against the new Right government: Socialists called a
general strike, there was a workers' revolt in the Asturias (Oviedo),
and activists in Barcelona sought to create an autonomous Catalonia.
All were suppressed.

   Another version of this montage, with text that reads:
"Wenn wir es alle nicht wollen, wird es nie sein!" (If we all do not
want it, it will never happen!), was produced in 1957 (see Herzfelde,
John Heartfield, p. 237).

Ruhe herrscht wieder in Barcelona

In den gestrigen Abendstunden flammten die Kämpfe in ganz Spanien, namentlich in Katalonien, wieder auf. General Batet droht, gegen die Aufständischen mit Giftgasen vorzugehen.

Montag, den 8. Oktober 1934.

Prager Abendzeitung

Giftgas erst schafft wahre Volksgemeinschaft!

SCHÜTZT DIE SAAR VOR DES HENKERS BEIL
ALLE FÜR DEN STATUS QUO!

DEUTSCHES LAND HALTET FREI
VON DER BRAUNEN BARBAREI

PROTECT THE SAAR FROM THE EXECUTIONER'S AX
ALL FOR THE STATUS QUO!

GERMAN LAND REMAIN FREE
FROM THE BROWN BARBARISM

This montage was part of a special issue on Saarland, which under the terms of the Treaty of Versailles was administered by the League of Nations from 1919 to 1935. In the plebiscite held in January 1935 about the future of Saarland, some 91 percent of the voters favored union with the Third Reich. Communists opposed union, urging a continuation of the status quo. See also 50/34, 51/34, 52/34, 2/35, 3/35, 4/35, 5/35.

V. b. b. — Erscheint wöchentlich einmal. Preis: 1,60 Kč, 40 Gr., 1,25 Frs., 30 Rp., 20 Pfg., 10 amer. Cts., 15 holl. Cts. - Jahrg. XIII. - Nr. 43. - 25. Okt. 1934

AIZ

SONDERNUMMER: SAAR

METTLACH

SAAR

MERZIG

SAAR

DEUTSCHES LAND HALTET FREI
VON DER BRAUNEN BARBAREI

SCHÜTZT DIE SAAR VOR DES HENKERS BEIL

ALLE FÜR DEN STATUS QUO!

Fotomontage: John Heartfield

Ein neuer Mensch – Herr einer neuen Welt

A new man – master of a new world

This special issue celebrated the seventeenth anniversary of the
founding of the Soviet Union.

AIZ

V. 6. 6. — Erscheint wöchentlich einmal. Preis: 1,60 Kč, 40 Gr., 1,25 Frs., 30 Rp., 20 Pfg., 10 amer. Cts., 15 holl. Cts. - Jahrg. XIII. - Nr. 44. - 1. November 1934

Sondernummer:
17 Jahre Sowjetunion

Ein neuer Mensch - Herr einer neuen Welt

EIN GEFÄHRLICHES EINTOPFGERICHT
DEUTSCHES FIXIERBILD 1934

Ihr sollt alle aus einem Topf essen,

denn wir wollen euch alle unter einen Topf pressen.

A DANGEROUS HOT POT
GERMAN PICTURE PUZZLE 1934

You all ought to eat from one pot,

because we want to press you all under one pot.

A *Topf* is a cooking pot. *Eintopf* means stew or hot pot, and the Nazis encouraged the *Eintopfgericht,* the one-pot meal, as an economy measure, with the money saved supposedly going to charity. A *Tophut* (literally, a pot hat) is a cloche. "Alles in einen Topf werfen" (literally, to toss everything in one pot) means to lump everything together. *Pressen* has several meanings, among them press, force, squeeze, oppress, and block (a hat). *Fixierbild* (literally, fixed picture) suggests both *Vexierbild* (picture puzzle) and *Fixiermittel* (photographic fixer). For the original artwork for this montage, see Fig. 3.

EIN GEFÄHRLICHES EINTOPFGERICHT

DEUTSCHES FIXIERBILD 1934

Ihr sollt alle aus einem Topf essen,

denn wir wollen euch alle unter einen Topf pressen.

Fotomontage: John Heartfield

Zu Schillers 175. Geburtstag
10. November 1934

Reichsinnenminister Dr. Frick: "Was hat der Kerl
geschrieben? 'Eine Grenze hat Tyrannenmacht!' Den hätte
ich glatt ausgebürgert."

On the occasion of Schiller's 175th birthday
10 November 1934

Reich Minister of the Interior Dr. Frick: "What did the guy
write? 'Tyranny has bounds!' For that I would have stripped
him of citizenship."

"Tyranny has bounds" is quoted from the verse drama *Wilhelm Tell*
(1803–4) by Friedrich von Schiller (1759–1805). See also 31/37. Frick
(see 15/33) is staring at Gerhard von Kügelgen's portrait of Schiller.

AIZ

F. SCHILLER

Zu Schillers 175. Geburtstag

10. November 1934

Reichsinnenminister Dr. Frick: „Was hat der Kerl geschrieben? »Eine Grenze hat Tyrannenmacht!« Den hätte ich glatt ausgebürgert."

Fotomontage: John Heartfield

Krisenfestes Rindvieh

Nach langwierigen Versuchen ist es endlich gelungen, die ideale Kuh zu züchten. Der Import kostspieliger Rindvieh-vernichtungsmaschinen wird dadurch überflüssig. Das bedeutet einerseits gewaltige Devisenersparnisse für die viehzuchttreibenden Länder, erschwert allerdings anderer-seits den Export der verbliebenen Normalrindviehbestände in die maschinenerzeugenden Länder. Einige Regierungen sind, infolge der Quertreibereien der Exporteure, über die neue Kreuzung bereits gestürzt.

Bildbericht unseres Berichterstatters John Heartfield.

Crisis-free cattle

After lengthy attempts there has finally been success in breeding the ideal cow. The import of costly cow-destruction machines will therefore no longer be necessary. On the one hand, that means great foreign-currency savings for the cow-breeding countries; on the other hand, it makes more difficult the export of the remaining normal cattle stock to the machine-producing countries. Due to the intrigues of the exporters, several governments have already plunged into crisis because of the new crossbreeding.

Picture report by our correspondent John Heartfield.

The destruction of cattle in Denmark because of alleged over-production was presented by *AIZ* as a classic instance of the irrationality of capitalism. See "Das Englische Schwein frisst die dänische Kuh" (The English pig eats the Danish cow; *AIZ* 13, no. 13 [29 March 1934], pp. 200–201) and "Hunger im Lande des Überflusses" (Hunger in the land of plenty; *AIZ* 13, no. 46 [15 November 1934], pp. 750–51).

Krisenfestes Rindvieh

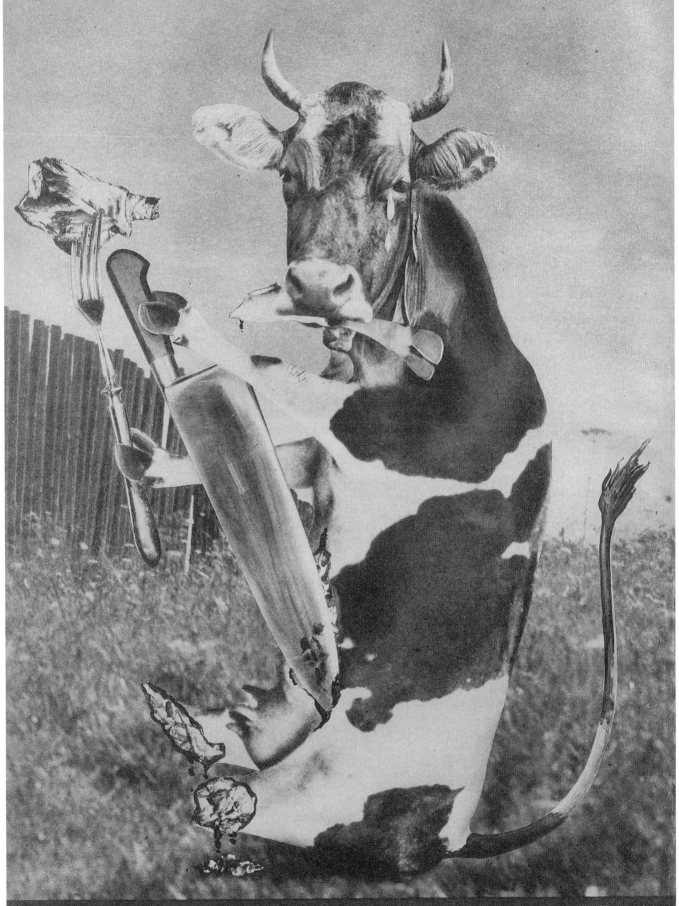

Nach langwierigen Versuchen ist es endlich gelungen, die ideale Kuh zu züchten. Der Import kostspieliger Rindviehvernichtungsmaschinen wird dadurch überflüssig. Das bedeutet einerseits gewaltige Devisenersparnisse für die viehzuchttreibenden Länder, erschwert allerdings andererseits den Export der verbliebenen Normalrindviehbestände in die maschinenerzeugenden Länder. Einige Regierungen sind, infolge der Quertreibereien der Exporteure, über die neue Kreuzung bereits gestürzt.

Bildbericht unseres Berichterstatters John Heartfield.

ZUM MORD DER HOHN!

Gestapo-Briefe an deutsche Frauen

Wiederholt erhielten im Dritten Reich die Frauen unschuldig Erschossener von der Geheimen Staatspolizei ohne vorherige Mitteilung die Asche der Ermordeten im Postpaket oder Brief zugestellt. So erging es z. B. der Frau des katholischen Führers Dr. Klausener.

ADDING INSULT TO MURDER!

Gestapo letters to German wives

Repeatedly in the Third Reich the wives of innocent men shot by the secret state police have, without prior notification, received the ashes of the murdered person in a parcel or letter. This happened for example to the wife of the Catholic leader Dr. Klausener.

This montage appeared in a special issue titled "Frauen Gestern – Heute – Morgen!" (Women yesterday – today – tomorrow!).

Erich Klausener (1885–1934), leader of Catholic Action from 1928 to 1933, served as director of communications in Hitler's first government. He was critical of the régime, however, and in 1934 he was murdered in his office by the SS.

Gestapo-Briefe an deutsche Frauen

Wiederholt erhielten im Dritten Reich die Frauen
unschuldig Erschossener von der Geheimen Staats-
polizei ohne vorherige Mitteilung die Asche der
Ermordeten im Postpaket oder Brief zugestellt.
So erging es z. B. der Frau des katholischen
Führers Dr. Klausener.

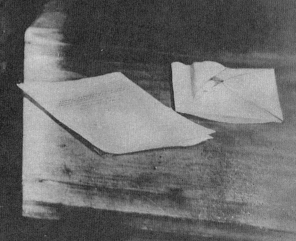

ZUM MORD DER HOHN!

Montiert: John Heartfield

NEUDEUTSCHER KRAFT-AKT

SCHACHT
Reichsbankpräsident

GOERDELER
Reichskommissar für
Preisüberwachung

GOEBBELS
Propagandaminister

"Hallo, Mannen!" schreit Herr Schacht,
"Hoch die Mark! Nicht schlapp gemacht!
Wenn erst Mitte Januar
abgestimmt ist an der Saar,
stürzt sie doch – was macht's dann schon? –
in die schönste Inflation!"

NEW GERMAN STRONG-MAN ACT

SCHACHT
Reichsbank president

GOERDELER
Reich commissioner for
monitoring prices

GOEBBELS
Propaganda minister

"Hello, men!" screams Herr Schacht,
"Up with the mark! Don't give up!
When the vote on the Saar finally takes place
in the middle of January,
it will crash – what will it matter then? –
into the most beautiful inflation!"

The dialogue refers to the Saarland plebiscite, which was held in January 1935 (see 44/34). For Schacht, see 14/34; for Goebbels, see 5/33. Carl Goerdeler (1884–1945) was appointed price commissioner in November 1934.

NEUDEUTSCHER KRAFT-AKT

SCHACHT
Reichsbankpräsident

GOERDELER
Reichskommissar für Preisüberwachung

GOEBBELS
Propagandaminister

„Hallo, Mannen!" schreit Herr Schacht,
„Hoch die Mark! Nicht schlapp gemacht!
Wenn erst Mitte Januar

abgestimmt ist an der Saar,
stürzt sie doch – was macht's dann schon? –
in die schönste Inflation!"

Fotomontage: John Heartfield

"Arbeitsschlacht"

"Wenn wir die Saar in die Finger bekommen, gibt's
Überstunden für uns vom Mordsturm noch und noch!"

"Labor battle"

"When we get our hands on the Saar, there will be plenty of
overtime for us of the homicide unit."

Arbeitsschlacht (labor battle) was Hitler's term to describe all the
measures taken to create work and eliminate unemployment.
Mordsturm (literally, murder storm) is an allusion to the *Sturm-
trupper* (storm troops) who violently enforced Nazi policy. In
National Socialist terminology a *Sturm* was a company or unit. For a
list of montages on Saarland and the plebiscite of 1935, see 44/34.

»Arbeitsschlacht«

Fotomontage: John Heartfield

»Wenn wir die Saar in die Finger bekommen, gibt's Überstunden für uns vom Mordsturm noch und noch!«

DIE RÖCHLING-RECHNUNG

Hitler = Versklavung des Volkes
Versklavung des Volkes = vermehrter Profit
Vermehrter Profit = mein Ideal

also:
Hitler = mein Ideal!

Hermann Röchling, der Eisenkönig an der Saar, wirbt für den Anschluß an das Dritte Reich der Thyssen und Krupp. Was ihn aber nicht hinderte, dem "Erbfeind Frankreich" Panzerplatten zu liefern und Kapital in französischen Unternehmungen zu investieren.

DIE HERREN RECHNEN SO –
DAS VOLK WÄHLT STATUS QUO!

THE RÖCHLING CALCULATION

Hitler = enslavement of the people
Enslavement of the people = increased profit
Increased profit = my ideal

therefore:
Hitler = my ideal!

Hermann Röchling, the Iron King on the Saar, canvasses for union with the Third Reich of the likes of Thyssen and Krupp, which however does not prevent him from supplying armor plate to the "traditional enemy France" and investing capital in French undertakings.

THE RULERS CALCULATE THUS –
BUT THE PEOPLE VOTE STATUS QUO!

This was a special issue on the struggle in Saarland and the plebiscite to be held there in January on the question of union with the Third Reich (see 44/34). The schoolteacher is Hermann Röchling (1872–1955), a Saarland industrialist. Thyssen (see 18/33) and Krupp (see 2/34, 28/34) were powerful Rhineland industrialists.

Erscheint wöchentl. einmal / Preis: 1,00 Kč, 40 Gr., 1,25 Frs., 50 Rp.,
20 Pfg., 10 am. Cts., 15 holl. Cts. / Jahrg. XIII. Nr. 51. / 20. Dez. 34

AIZ

SONDERNUMMER: SAARKAMPF

DIE RÖCHLING-RECHNUNG

Hitler = Versklavung des Volkes

Versklavung des Volkes = vermehrter Profit

Vermehrter Profit = mein Ideal

also:

Hitler = mein Ideal!

Hermann Röchling, der Eisenkönig an der Saar, wirbt für den Anschluß an das Dritte Reich der Thyssen und Krupp. Was ihn aber nicht hinderte, dem „Erbfeind Frankreich" Panzerplatten zu liefern und Kapital in französischen Unternehmungen zu investieren.

DIE HERREN RECHNEN SO —
DAS VOLK WÄHLT STATUS QUO!

O Tannenbaum im deutschen Raum, wie krumm sind deine Äste!

Dem christlichen Tannenbaum wird laut Erlaß des Reichsernährungsministers Darré ab Weihnachten 1934 als artfremdem Eindringling auf deutschem Boden die Fortpflanzung verboten. Erlaubt ist künftighin nur noch der in Walhall gezüchtete braune "Einheitstannenbaum – DRGM".

O Christmas tree in German soil, how bent are thy branches!

By decree of Reich Food Minister Darré, as of Christmas 1934 propagation of the Christian fir tree, an alien intruder, is forbidden on German soil. In future only the brown "standard fir tree DRGM," cultivated in Valhalla, will be allowed.

The carol "O Tannenbaum" (O Christmas tree), based on a German folk tune of the sixteenth century, was written in 1820. Richard-Walther Darré (1895–1953) served as Reich farmers' leader and Reich food minister. He developed a "blood and soil" ideology that celebrated the German peasant and the Nordic race, and he was involved in the Deutsche Glaubensbewegung (German Faith Movement), a neopagan sect that arose during the Third Reich and advocated making Christmas a pagan solstice festival.

DRGM stands for Deutsches Reichs-Gebrauchsmuster (German Reich Registered Design). In Scandinavian mythology Valhalla is the hall in the celestial regions where the souls of heroes slain in battle are borne by the Valkyries, to live forever in bliss.

O Tannenbaum im deutschen Raum, wie krumm sind deine Äste!

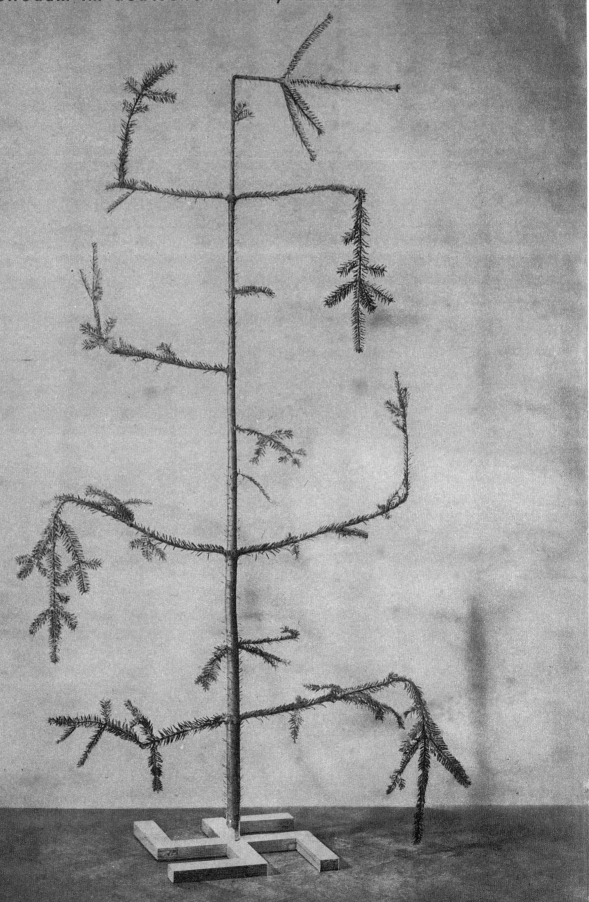

Fotomontage: John Heartfield

Dem christlichen Tannenbaum wird laut Erlaß des Reichsernährungsministers Darré ab Weihnachten 1934 als artfremdem Eindringling auf deutschem Boden die Fortpflanzung verboten. Erlaubt ist künftighin nur noch der in Walhall gezüchtete braune „Einheitstannenbaum - DRGM".

Die drei Weisen aus dem Sorgenland

Und die bilden sich ein:
das geht fünfundzwanzigtausend Jahre so weiter!

The three magi from the Land of Sorrow

And they imagine:
this will continue for twenty-five thousand years!

The three magi – Goebbels, Göring, and Hitler – come not from
Morgenland (the East) but from Sorgenland (the Land of Sorrow),
which, as the signpost says, is the Third Reich, or Nazi Germany.
"Deutsche Wühlmäuse" are chewing the knot securing the high
wire. A *Wühlmaus* (literally, burrowing mouse) is a vole; a *Wühler* is
an agitator.

Die drei Weisen aus dem Sorgenland

DRITTES REICH

Deutsche Wühlmäuse

Und die bilden sich ein:
das geht fünfundzwanzigtausend Jahre so weiter!

Fotomontage: John Heartfield

Der braune Tod vor den Toren

Es greift der Tod das Saarland an;
doch ist's in eure Macht gegeben,
daß er es nicht erwürgen kann:
Wählt status quo! Schützt euer Leben!

The brown death before the gates

Death attacks the Saarland;
yet it lies within your power
to prevent him from strangling it:
Vote for the status quo! Protect your life!

On the Saarland plebiscite, see 44/34.

Der braune Tod vor den Toren

Es greift der Tod das Saarland an;
doch ist's in eure Macht gegeben,
daß er es nicht erwürgen kann:
Wählt status quo! Schützt euer Leben!

Ernst Moritz Arndt,
der deutsche Freiheitsdichter, spricht:

Krieg und Zerstörung wird nicht mangeln,
solange dieser lebt, der mordet, wann er schmeichelt,
lügt, wann er schwört,
Verderben meint, wann er von Frieden klingt,
auf Vernichtung sinnt, wann er von Freundschaft
und Bundesgenossenschaft spricht.
Er hat bis jetzt gespielt, zweideutig und zweifelhaft vielen,
er wird hinfort offener spielen müssen –
seine Larve ist fast zerrissen –
aber desto blutiger und verderblicher wird er spielen.
Er ist Werkzeug der Zerstörung, nicht der Gründung.

Darum stimmt die Saar
für status quo!

Ernst Moritz Arndt,
the German freedom poet, speaks:

War and destruction will not be wanting,
as long as this one lives, who murders when he flatters,
lies when he swears,
sounds doom when he chimes of peace,
plots annihilation when he speaks of friendship
and alliance.
Until now, he has performed most ambiguously and
suspiciously,
henceforth he will have to act more openly –
his mask is almost torn off –
but all the more bloodily and ruinously will he perform.
He is the tool of destruction, not of creation.

Therefore the Saar votes
for the status quo!

Ernst Moritz Arndt (1769–1860) was a German poet and political
writer who actively opposed Napoleon. The final lines refer to the
League of Nations plebiscite held in the Saar in January 1935 (see
also 44/34).

Ernst Moritz Arndt,

der deutsche Freiheitsdichter, spricht:

Krieg und Zerstörung wird nicht mangeln,

solange dieser lebt, der mordet, wann er schmeichelt,

lügt, wann er schwört,

Verderben meint, wann er von Frieden klingt,

auf Vernichtung sinnt, wann er von Freundschaft

und Bundesgenossenschaft spricht.

Er hat bis jetzt gespielt, zweideutig und zweifelhaft vielen,

er wird hinfort offener spielen müssen —

seine Larve ist fast zerrissen —

aber desto blutiger und verderblicher wird er spielen.

Er ist Werkzeug der Zerstörung, nicht der Gründung.

Darum stimmt die Saar

für status quo!

Montfort John Heartfield.

"FREIE" ABSTIMMUNG AN DER SAAR

"DER VÖLKERBUND GARANTIERT DIE FREIHEIT, DIE
AUFRICHTIGKEIT UND GEHEIMHALTUNG DER WAHL."

"FREE" PLEBISCITE ON THE SAAR

"THE LEAGUE OF NATIONS GUARANTEES THE FREEDOM,
HONESTY AND SECRECY OF THE VOTE."

On the Saarland plebiscite, see 44/34. "Deutsche Front: Hilfspolizei," on
the policeman's armband, means German Front: auxiliary police. The
Deutsche Front was the pro-Nazi organization in Saarland. Allan Rohde
was president of the plebiscite commission. "UNERLEDIGTE POST a)
PROTESTE DER EINHEITSFRONT b) MELDUNGEN ÜBER TERROR DER
DEUTSCHEN FRONT" means unanswered mail a) protests of the United
Front b) reports about the terror of the German Front.

Erscheint wöchentlich einmal / Preis 1,60 Kč, 40 Gr., 1,25 Frs., 30 Rp., 20 Pfg., 10 am. Cts., 15 holl. Cts., / Jahrgang XIV / Nummer 4 / 24. Januar 1935

AIZ

„FREIE" ABSTIMMUNG AN DER SAAR

„DER VÖLKERBUND GARANTIERT DIE FREIHEIT, DIE AUFRICHTIGKEIT UND GEHEIMHALTUNG DER WAHL."

Deutsche Front
Hilfspolizei

ALLAN ROHDE, PRÄSIDENT DER ABSTIMMUNGSKOMMISSION
UNERLEDIGTE POST
a) PROTESTE DER EINHEITSFRONT
b) MELDUNGEN ÜBER TERROR DER DEUTSCHEN FRONT

Fotomontage: John Heartfield

HITLERS FRIEDENSTAUBE

"Die Saar wäre glücklich erledigt, jetzt lasse ICH MEINEN Habicht nach Süden vorstoßen."

Montag, den 21. Jänner 1935
Habicht wieder tätig
Wien. (havas.) Das "Neue Wiener Tagblatt" meldet, daß Habicht nach München zurückgekehrt ist und neuerlich die Funktion des "Landesinspekteurs der österreichischen Nationalsozialisten" übernommen hat.

HITLER'S DOVE OF PEACE

"The Saar having been happily disposed of, I now let MY hawk move southward."

Monday, 21 January 1935
Habicht active again
Vienna. (Havas.) The "Neue Wiener Tagblatt" reports that Habicht returned to Munich and has recently taken up the post of "State Inspector of the Austrian National Socialists."

Theodor Habicht (born 1898), whose surname means hawk, was the leader of the illegal Nazi Party in Austria. He had provided arms to the Austrian Nazis prior to his expulsion in June 1933. On the Saarland plebiscite, see 44/34.

Erledigt means disposed of or settled, but it can also mean ruined. The identity tag attached to the hawk's leg is inscribed: "Reichswehr-Brief-Taube" (Reich army carrier pigeon).

HITLERS FRIEDENSTAUBE

AIZ.

Montag, den 21. Jänner 1935

Habicht wieder tätig

Wien. (Havas.) Das „Neue Wiener Tagblatt"
meldet, daß Habicht nach München zurückge-
fehrt ist und neuerlich die Funktion des „Landesinspekteurs der österreichischen Nationalsozialisten" übernommen hat.

„Die Saar wäre glücklich erledigt, jetzt lasse ICH MEINEN Habicht nach Süden vorstoßen."

Fotomontage: John Heartfield

Fantasie zweier Ostpaktjäger

Reichsjägermeister Göring zum polnischen Außenminister
Beck: "Lassen Sie mir den Hals des Bären, Herr Kollege,
dann lasse ich Ihnen den Steiß."

Dem Beispiel Herrn von Papens folgend, der kürzlich nach
Ungarn "jagen" fuhr, hat sich Göring zu einer "diplomatischen
Jagd" in die Urwälder von Bialowieza in Polen begeben.

Fantasy of two Eastern Pact hunters

Reich Master of Hounds Göring to the Polish foreign minister
Beck: "You leave me the neck of the bear, Herr colleague,
and I will leave you the rump."

Following the example of Mr. von Papen, who recently led a
"hunt" into Hungary, Göring has himself set out on a "diplomatic hunt" to the backwoods of Bialowieza in Poland.

Heartfield adapted a photograph of Göring (see 23/33) that appeared
on the cover of the previous issue of *AIZ* (14, no. 5 [31 January
1935], p. 65). Józef Beck (1894–1944), Polish foreign minister from
1932 to 1939, was architect of the German-Polish nonaggression
pact of 1934. The constellation "Grosser Bär" (Great Bear)
represents the Soviet Union. For Heartfield's comment on Von
Papen's "diplomatic hunt," see 42/34.

Fantasie zweier Ostpaktjäger

Dem Beispiel Herrn von Papens folgend, der kürzlich nach Ungarn „jagen" fuhr, hat sich Göring zu einer „diplomatischen Jagd" in die Urwälder von Bialowieza in Polen begeben.

GROSSER BÄR

Reichsjägermeister Göring zum polnischen Außenminister Beck:

„Lassen Sie mir den Hals des Bären, Herr Kollege, dann lasse ich Ihnen den Steiß."

Fotomontage: John Heartfield

Es kommt der Tag...

Die internationale Arbeiterklasse an Rákosi:
"Sind auch stark die Mauern, die dich umgeben,
brüchig ist die Macht, die dich gefangen hält."

The day will come...

The international working class to Rákosi:
"As strong as the walls that surround you may be,
the power that keeps you imprisoned is fragile."

The Hungarian Communist leader Mátyás Rákosi (1892–1971) was
sentenced to life imprisonment in 1935. (In 1940 he was extradited
to Moscow, and in 1944 he returned to Hungary, where he served as
secretary of the Communist Party until the Hungarian revolution
forced him to flee to Moscow in 1956.) The previous issue of *AIZ*
(14, no. 7 [14 February 1935], p. 111) included a report of a Czech
delegation to his trial in Budapest: "Wie wir Rákosi im Gerichtssaal
sahen..." (How we saw Rákosi in the courtroom...).

Es kommt der Tag...

Die internationale Arbeiterklasse an Rákosi:

„Sind auch stark die Mauern, die dich umgeben, brüchig ist die Macht, die dich gefangen hält."

Montiert: John Heartfield.

8/35. **AIZ** 14, NUMBER 9, 28 FEBRUARY 1935, PAGE 129

DAS SPIEL DER NAZIS MIT DEM FEUER

"Wenn die Welt erst brennt, werden wir schon beweisen, daß Moskau der Brandstifter war."

THE NAZIS PLAYING WITH FIRE

"When the world eventually burns, we will manage to prove that Moscow was the arsonist."

Heartfield's cover was immediately followed by a two-page article on the second anniversary of the Reichstag Fire that reiterated the view that the fire was an anti-Communist provocation by the Nazis, masterminded by Göring (see 23/33).

DAS SPIEL DER
NAZIS
MIT DEM FEUER

AIZ

Erscheint wöchentlich einmal / Preis 1,60 Kč, 40 Gr.,
1,25 Frs., 30 Rp., 20 Pfg., 10 am. Cts., 15 holl. Cts.
Jahrgang XIV   Nummer 9   28. Februar 1935

„Wenn die Welt erst brennt, werden wir schon
beweisen, daß Moskau der Brandstifter war."

Fotomontage: John Heartfield

Neue Erfolge der Naziheilkunde:
SENF statt KÄSE

"Weg mit dem weißen Käse! Brauner Senf ist das einzige Heilmittel."

Die Sekte des nationalistischen Wunderdoktors Weißenberg, der gegen alle Leiden weißen Käse verschrieb, wurde verboten.

New success of Nazi medical science:
MUSTARD instead of CHEESE

"Away with white cheese! Brown mustard is the only remedy."

The sect of the nationalist quack Weißenberg, who prescribed white cheese for all complaints, has been banned.

"Dr. Goebbels Heilsenf" (literally, Dr. Goebbels's healing mustard) also suggests "Heil mustard!" "Seinen Senf dazu geben" means to make a stupid, uncalled-for contribution to a discussion. "Brauner Senf" in the subtitle thus means not only brown mustard but also Nazi rubbish. *Käse* (cheese) is also a colloquialism for nonsense, or rubbish.

The religious leader Joseph Weißenberg (1855–1941) was known as "the apostle of white cheese" because he promulgated the view that white cheese had healing properties. An article on Weißenberg and his followers, "Besuch beim Meister des weißen Käse" (A visit to the master of white cheese) was published in *AIZ* on 16 October 1932 (11, no. 42, pp. 992–93), and a note in the 21 February 1935 issue (14, no. 8, p. 114) had informed readers that his sect had been banned, even though it supplied followers to the Nazi movement.

Neue Erfolge der Naziheilkunde: SENF statt KÄSE

Die Sekte des nationalistischen Wunderdoktors Weißenberg, der gegen alle Leiden
weißen Käse verschrieb, wurde verboten.

Dr. Goebbels
Heilsenf

„Weg mit dem weißen Käse! Brauner Senf ist das einzige Heilmittel."

Fotomontage: John Heartfield

DIAGNOSE

"Wodurch zog sich der Mann denn die Rückgratsverkrümmung zu?"
"Das sind die organischen Folgen des ewigen "Heil Hitler!""

DIAGNOSIS

"How did the man get this curvature of the spine?"
"That is the organic result of the endless 'Heil Hitler!'"

Heartfield made no further contributions to *AIZ* until 15 August 1935
(11/35). In the interim he was in France, mainly for an exhibition at
the Maison de la Culture in Paris. Heartfield-style montages,
produced by the magazine's designer Hermann Leupold under the
pseudonym Karl Vaněk, continued to appear, however (see, for
example, *AIZ* 14, nos. 17, 20, 22–24, 26–28, 29, 31, 32).

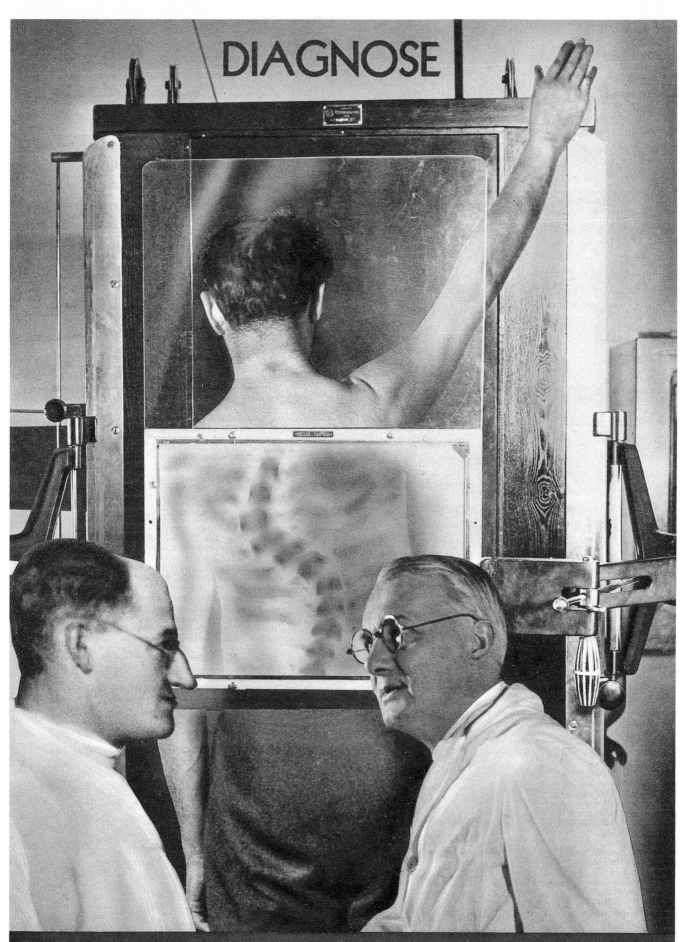

DIAGNOSE

„Wodurch zog sich der Mann denn die Rückgratsverkrümmung zu?"
„Das sind die organischen Folgen des ewigen »Heil Hitler!«"

Fotomontage: John Heartfield

11/35. **AIZ** 14, NUMBER 33, 15 AUGUST 1935, PAGE 528

HITLERS BESTER FREUND

STREICHER, DER SCHÄNDER DEUTSCHLANDS

"DER STÜRMER IST DIE EINZIGE ZEITSCHRIFT DIE ADOLF
HITLER VON A–Z LIEST"
JULIUS STREICHER

HITLER'S BEST FRIEND

STREICHER, THE VIOLATOR OF GERMANY

"THE STORMTROOPER IS THE ONLY NEWSPAPER ADOLF
HITLER READS FROM A TO Z"
JULIUS STREICHER

Julius Streicher (1885–1946) founded the anti-Semitic newspaper *Der Stürmer* and was its editor from 1923 to 1945 (see also 29/33, 23/34). The swastika is formed from *Der Stürmer* headlines: "Rasseschänder Judenschwein" (Race violator Jewish pig), "Ritualmorde…" (Ritual murders), "Der Judengeruch" (The Jewish stench), "Frauen und Mädchen die Juden sind euer Verderben!" (Women and girls the Jews are the ruin of you!), "Judenfreundinnen…Schächtung…" (Girlfriends of Jews…Ritual slaughter…).

In Nazi terminology the word *Schänder* (rapist or violator) described any Jewish male involved in a sexual relationship with a non-Jewish German woman; cohabitation between German Aryans and Jews was *Rassenschande* (race defilement); and interracial marriage was *Blutschande* (incest; literally, blood shame).

HITLERS BESTER FREUND

Raffenſchänder Judenſchwein

Der Judengeruch

Frauen und Mädchen die Juden ſind Euer Verderben!

Ritualmorde zum

Judenfreundinnen o

Schächtung d

„DER STÜRMER
IST DIE EINZIGE
ZEITSCHRIFT DIE
ADOLF HITLER
VON A–Z LIEST"
JULIUS STREICHER

Montiert: John Heartfield.

STREICHER, DER SCHÄNDER DEUTSCHLANDS

Auch ein Propagandaminister

Hitler: "Goebbels, Goebbels, gib mir meine Millionen wieder!"

Die Gestapo hat am 3. August acht hohe Funktionäre des Propagandaministeriums verhaftet. Die oberflächliche Einvernahme hat Unterschleife in Millionenhöhe hinreichend erwiesen.   Prager Presse 10. August 1935

Jeder Beobachter in Deutschland, der nur ein wenig ins Volk zu horchen vermag, muß feststellen, daß Hitler seit der Saarabstimmung Millionen Anhänger verloren hat. Pressemeldung, August 1935

Also a propaganda minister

Hitler: "Goebbels, Goebbels, give me back my millions!"

On 3 August the Gestapo arrested eight high functionaries of the propaganda ministry. Superficial examination was sufficient to conclusively prove embezzlement amounting to millions.   Prager Presse 10 August 1935

Every observer in Germany who is able to listen even a little to the people must agree that Hitler has lost millions of followers since the Saar plebiscite.   Press report, August 1935

For an explanation of "Give me back my millions!" see 13/33.

Auch ein Propagandaminister

Die Gestapo hat am 3. August acht hohe Funktionäre des Propagandaministeriums verhaftet. Die oberflächliche Einvernahme hat Unterschleife in
Millionenhöhe hinreichend erwiesen.   Prager Presse 10. August 1935

Jeder Beobachter in Deutschland, der nur ein wenig ins Volk zu horchen
vermag, muß feststellen, daß Hitler seit der Saarabstimmung Millionen
Anhänger verloren hat.   Pressemeldung, August 1935

Hitler: „Goebbels, Goebbels, gib mir meine Millionen wieder!"

Fotomontage: John Heartfield

Nur die geeinte Front der Schaffenden sichert den Frieden!

Only the united front of the productive classes secures the peace!

The montage shows the Red Army joining the popular forces of the world to defeat the aggressive dogs of Japanese and German Fascism. This issue (p. 576) carried a report on the Seventh World Congress of the Communist International, which had taken place in Moscow from 25 July to 20 August. The report advocated a Popular Front, in which the Soviet Union would play a key role, as a means to defeat Fascism.

Erscheint wöchentlich einmal. — Preis: 1,60 Kč, 40 Gr.,
1,25 Frs., 2,20 belg Frs., 30 Rp., 20 Pfg., 10 amerik. Cts.,
4 Dinar. — Jahrg. XIV. — Nr. 36. — 5. September 1935

AIZ

Nur die geeinte Front der Schaffenden sichert den Frieden!

Fotomontage: John Heartfield

DAS NEUESTE:
Der Reichstag brannte in Moskau!

"Eine politische Bewegung, die darauf ausgeht, ein ganzes
Land dem Wahnsinn unterzuordnen, alle Bindungen
moralischer und politischer Art zu zerstören, mit Brand und
Terror die Menschen in Schrecken zu versetzen, um dann in
der allgemeinen Verwirrung die Dinge an sich zu reißen,
verdient die Vernichtung."
Goebbels in seiner Rede vor dem Strafrechtskongreß in Berlin

THE LATEST:
The Reichstag burned in Moscow!

"A political movement that aims to subordinate a whole
country to madness, to destroy all bonds of a moral and
political nature, to frighten people with fire and terrorism,
and to take over in the general confusion, deserves
annihilation."
Goebbels in his speech before the Criminal Law Congress in
Berlin

This issue was published three weeks after the close of the Seventh
World Congress of the Communist International in Moscow (see
13/35). On the Reichstag Fire, see 23/33.

DAS NEUESTE:
Der Reichstag brannte in Moskau!

„Eine politische Bewegung, die darauf ausgeht, ein ganzes Land dem
Wahnsinn unterzuordnen, alle Bindungen moralischer und politischer Art zu
zerstören, mit Brand und Terror die Menschen in Schrecken zu versetzen,
um dann in der allgemeinen Verwirrung die Dinge an sich zu reißen, verdient die Vernichtung."

Goebbels in seiner Rede vor dem Strafrechtskongreß in Berlin

Fotomontage: John Heartfield

Gesang der Antisemiten:

"Was frag' ich viel nach Gut und Geld,
wenn ich kein Jude bin.
Zu werden satt auf dieser Welt
hat nur der Jud' im Sinn.
Mein Führer schlägt die Juden tot
und wendet so des Volkes Not."

Song of the Anti-Semite:

"What do I care about property and money,
when I am no Jew.
Only the Jew aims
to eat his fill in this world.
My Führer beats the Jews to death
and so reverses the misery of the people."

The anti-Jewish Nürnberg Laws were introduced on 15 September
1935.

Gesang der Antisemiten:

"Was frag' ich viel nach Gut und Geld,
wenn ich kein Jude bin.
Zu werden satt auf dieser Welt
hat nur der Jud' im Sinn.
Mein Führer schlägt die Juden tot
und wendet so des Volkes Not."

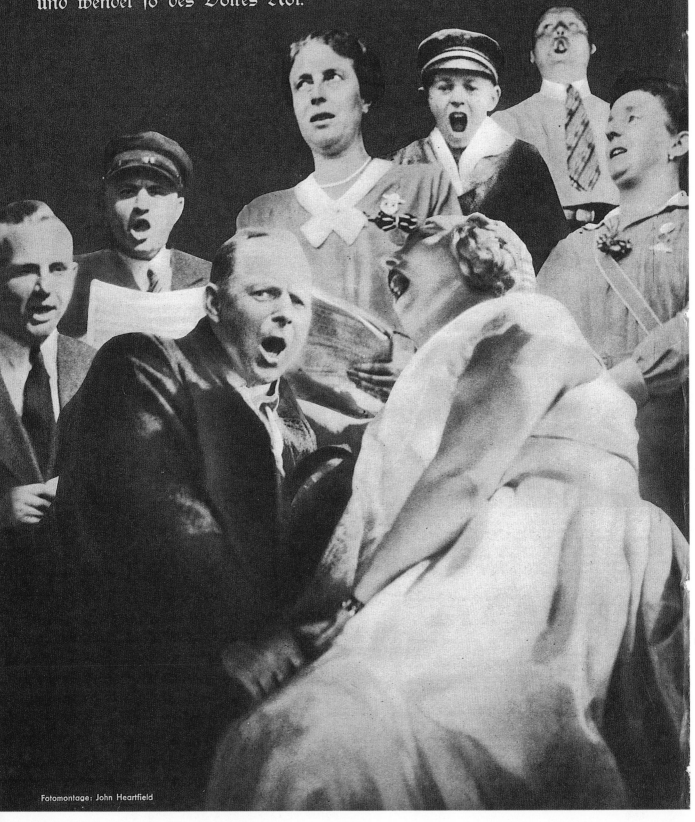

Fotomontage: John Heartfield

KLUMPFÜSSCHENS WUNSCHTRAUM

"HINWEG MIT DIESEN DEGENERIERTEN UNTERMENSCHEN!"

Zur Hetzrede des Propagandaministers Dr. Goebbels gegen die Sowjetunion auf dem Nürnberger Parteitag 1935

LITTLE CLUBFOOT'S WISHFUL THINKING

"AWAY WITH THESE DEGENERATE SUBHUMANS!"

On the occasion of the rabble-rousing speech of Propaganda Minister Dr. Goebbels against the Soviet Union at the Nürnberg party rally 1935

The title refers to Goebbels's physical deformity. He is standing on an unstable pile of books that includes two of the sources for his racist rhetoric: Hitler's *Mein Kampf* (My struggle; 1925–28) and *Der Mythus des zwanzigsten Jahrhunderts* (The myth of the twentieth century; 1930) by Alfred Rosenberg (1893–1946).

    This montage was the back cover of a special issue on the Red Army that began by quoting Stalin: "WIR SIND FÜR DEN FRIEDEN UND WIR VERTEIDIGEN DIE SACHE DES FRIEDENS ABER WIR FÜRCHTEN KEINE DROHUNGEN" (We are for peace and we defend the cause of peace but we fear no threats).

    Wieland Herzfelde gave the montage a new title – *WUNSCHTRAUM DER SELBSTMÖRDER* (A suicide's wishful thinking) – in *John Heartfield: Leben und Werk* (p. 98).

KLUMPFÜSSCHENS WUNSCHTRAUM

Zur Hetzrede des Propagandaministers
Dr. Goebbels gegen die Sowjetunion
auf dem Nürnberger Parteitag 1935

Fotomontage: John Heartfield

„HINWEG MIT DIESEN DEGENERIERTEN UNTERMENSCHEN!"

Nürnberg: 60 Grad im Schatten!

AUFMARSCH DER ROTEN SPORTLER AM JUGENDTAG IN MOSKAU

Herr Führer deklamiert, heiser, aber in vollem Ernst: "Geknechtete Jugend Rußlands, von Juda entehrt und geschändet, Ich bin der kühne Befreier, der dein furchtbares Schicksal wendet!"

Zur Rede Hitlers gegen die Sowjet-Union auf dem Nürnberger Parteitag

Nürnberg: 60 degrees in the shade!

THE PARADE OF RED ATHLETES ON YOUTH DAY IN MOSCOW

Herr Führer declaims, hoarsely, but in utter seriousness: "Enslaved Russian youth, dishonored and violated by Judah, I am the daring liberator who will change your dreadful fate!"

On the occasion of Hitler's speech against the Soviet Union at the Nürnberg party rally

---

AIZ covered the rally in "Die dreifache Kriegserklärung von Nürnberg" (The triple declaration of war from Nürnberg; pp. 626–27). According to *AIZ*, the rally was in effect a declaration of war against the Soviet Union.

Nürnberg: 60 Grad im Schatten!

AUFMARSCH DER ROTEN SPORTLER AM JUGENDTAG IN MOSKAU

Fotomontage: John Heartfield
Zur Rede Hitlers gegen die Sowjet-
Union auf dem Nürnberger Parteitag

Herr Führer deklamiert, heiser, aber in vollem Ernst:

„Geknechtete Jugend Rußlands, von Juda entehrt und geschändet,
Ich bin der kühne Befreier, der dein furchtbares Schicksal wendet!"

Der Platz an der Sonne

"Ich will meinem Volk einen Platz an der Sonne verschaffen!"
Mussolini

The place in the sun

"I want to provide my people with a place in the sun!"
Mussolini

Italy invaded Abyssinia (Ethiopia) on 3 October 1935. See also
25/35, 6/36, 16/36.

Der Platz an der Sonne

**Goebbels-Rezept
gegen die Lebensmittelnot in Deutschland**

"Was? Schmalz und Butter fehlt beim Essen? Ihr könnt ja
eure Juden fressen!"

**Goebbels recipe
against the food shortage in Germany**

"What? Your meals are lacking lard and butter? You can eat
your Jews!"

An article in this issue (pp. 679–81) entitled "Abstieg ins Elend:
Aufstieg zum Wohlstand" (Descent into misery: Ascent to prosperity)
compared the availability and prices of food in the Third Reich and
the Soviet Union.

Goebbels-Rezept
gegen die Lebensmittelnot in Deutschland

AIZ
Das Illustrierte Volksblatt

„Was? Schmalz und Butter fehlt beim Essen? Ihr könnt ja eure Juden fressen!"
Fotomontage: John Heartfield

DER EHRENDOLCH

"IM SINNE DES FÜHRERS"
Königsberg, 17. Oktober. – Ein SA-Mann hatte am 14.
April 1935 einen Arbeiter im Wirtshaus erstochen, weil
der die SA-Uniform "beleidigt" habe. Der Mörder wurde
vom Allensteiner Gericht mit folgender Begründung
freigesprochen: "Die Uniform, das Hoheitszeichen der
Partei, sei eines besonderen Schutzes bedürftig. Ein SA-
Mann in Uniform brauche sich nicht in eine Katzbalgerei
einzulassen, bei der er womöglich verprügelt und die
Uniform besudelt werde. Nicht umsonst habe der Führer
den SA-Männern den Dolch verliehen. Sie seien politische
Soldaten und hätten als solche zu handeln. Bei einem
tätlichen Angriff dürfe sich deshalb der SA-Mann des
Dolches zur Abwehr bedienen, wobei es sich für einen
Soldaten von selbst verstehe, daß diese Abwehr nicht
schwächlich, sondern energisch sei. Es liege ganz im Sinne
des Führers, Beschimpfungen der Uniform rücksichtslos mit
der Waffe abzuwehren."

DAGGER OF HONOR

"ACCORDING TO THE WISHES OF THE FÜHRER"
Königsberg, 17 October. – On 14 April 1935 an SA man
stabbed a worker to death in a tavern because the man had
"insulted" the SA uniform. The murderer was acquitted by
the Allenstein court on the following grounds: "The uniform,
the national emblem of the party, needs exceptional
protection. An SA man does not need to engage in a scuffle
in which he might be thrashed and his uniform soiled. Not
for nothing has the Führer granted every SA man a dagger.
They are political soldiers and must handle themselves as
such. In case of attack, an SA man should use his dagger for
protection, and it goes without saying that a soldier's self-
defense must not be timid, but forceful. This coincides
completely with the wishes of the Führer, to wrecklessly
defend insults against the uniform with the weapon."

The SA dagger is inscribed: "Blut und Ehre!" (blood and honor!).

DER EHRENDOLCH

Blut und Ehre!

»IM SINNE DES FÜHRERS«

Königsberg, 17. Oktober. — Ein SA-Mann hatte am 14. April 1935 einen Arbeiter im Wirtshaus erstochen, weil der die SA-Uniform „beleidigt" habe. Der Mörder wurde vom Allensteiner Gericht mit folgender Begründung freigesprochen: „Die Uniform, das Hoheitszeichen der Partei, sei eines besonderen Schutzes bedürftig. Ein SA-Mann in Uniform brauche sich nicht in eine Katzbalgerei einzulassen, bei der er womöglich verprügelt und die Uniform besudelt werde. Nicht umsonst habe der Führer den SA-Männern den Dolch verliehen. Sie seien politische Soldaten und hätten als solche zu handeln. Bei einem tätlichen Angriff dürfe sich deshalb der SA-Mann des Dolches zur Abwehr bedienen, wobei es sich für einen Soldaten von selbst verstehe, daß diese Abwehr nicht schwächlich, sondern energisch sei. Es liege ganz im Sinne des Führers, Beschimpfungen der Uniform rücksichtslos mit der Waffe abzuwehren."

Fotomontage: John Heartfield

LIED DER HEIL-ARMEE

Auf dem Nürnberger Trichter zu blasen nach der Melodie
"O Monna".

Der Mensch lebt nicht allein von Brot	Heil Hitler!
Wer Deutschland liebt, schlägt Juden tot	Heil Hitler!
Bei uns gibt's keine Roten mehr	Heil Hitler!
Deswegen fürchten wir sie sehr	Heil Hitler!
Wir strafen streng jedweden Spott	Heil Hitler!
Und fürchten nichts als unsern Gott	Heil Hitler!
Wir beten Wotan an und Thor	Heil Hitler!
Und bleiben Christen wie zuvor	Heil Hitler!
Doch Christus ist recht unbeliebt	Heil Hitler!
Weil es nur einen Führer gibt	Heil Hitler!
Die Menschheit krankt noch an Verstand	Heil Hitler!
Ihr fehlt ein kleiner Reichstagsbrand	Heil Hitler!
Den Frieden garantiert der Krieg	Heil Hitler!
Und Wollstra garantiert den Sieg	Heil Hitler!
'ne Kolonie bringt niemand Glück	Heil Hitler!
Doch unsre wollen wir zurück	Heil Hitler!
Und außerdem den Raum in Osten	Heil Hitler!
Das deutsche Schwert darf niemals rosten	Heil Hitler!
Drum halten fest am Alten wir	Heil Hitler!
Wie wir's gelernt beim Münchner Bier	Heil Hitler!
Der Herr regiert, der Knecht bleibt doof	Heil Hitler!
Denn Deutschland ist kein Hühnerhof	Heil Hitler!
Der Herrenmensch braucht Fleisch vom Schwein	Heil Hitler!
Die Masse muß bescheiden sein	Heil Hitler!
Und fehlt ihr hier und dort die Butter	Heil Hitler!
Es wächst ja auch noch Vogelfutter	Heil Hitler!
Wir leben alle schlicht um schlicht	Heil Hitler!
Denn uns genügt ein Topfgericht	Heil Hitler!
Und niemand unterm Hakenkreuz	Heil Hitler!
Besitzt ein Konto in der Schweiz	Heil Hitler!
Nur der ist deutscher Sozialist	Heil Hitler!
Dem's keine Magenfrage ist	Heil Hitler!
Geht's manchem gut, den meisten schlecht	Heil Hitler!
Der Führer macht es allen recht	Heil Hitler!
Und ist er heut noch nicht so weit	Heil Hitler!
Er hat ja tausend Jahre Zeit!	Heil Hitler!

Bitte weiter dichten!	Wieland Herzfelde

SONG OF THE HEIL-ARMY

To be blown on the Nürnberg funnel to the tune of
"O Monna."

Man does not live by bread alone	Heil Hitler!
Whoever loves Germany, beats Jews to death	Heil Hitler!
In our country there are no more Reds	Heil Hitler!
Therefore we are very afraid of them	Heil Hitler!
We severely punish any mockery	Heil Hitler!
And fear nothing but our God	Heil Hitler!
We pray to Wotan and Thor	Heil Hitler!
And remain Christian as before	Heil Hitler!
Yet Christ is fairly unpopular	Heil Hitler!
Because there is only one Führer	Heil Hitler!
Humanity still suffers from intelligence	Heil Hitler!
It lacks a little Reichstag Fire	Heil Hitler!
War guarantees peace	Heil Hitler!
And Wollstra guarantees victory	Heil Hitler!
A colony brings no one luck	Heil Hitler!
Yet we want ours back	Heil Hitler!
And apart from that, space in the East	Heil Hitler!
The German sword must never rust	Heil Hitler!
Therefore we hold fast to the old things	Heil Hitler!
As we learned them while drinking Munich beer	Heil Hitler!
The master rules, the serf remains stupid	Heil Hitler!
For Germany is no chicken run	Heil Hitler!
The ruling man needs meat from swine	Heil Hitler!
The masses must be modest	Heil Hitler!
And should they lack butter here and there	Heil Hitler!
Birdfeed is still growing plentifully	Heil Hitler!
We all live plainly and simply	Heil Hitler!
For a one-pot meal is enough for us	Heil Hitler!
And nobody under the swastika	Heil Hitler!
Has an account in Switzerland	Heil Hitler!
Only the German Socialist	Heil Hitler!
Doesn't worry about his stomach	Heil Hitler!
If it goes well for some, bad for most	Heil Hitler!
The Führer makes everything right	Heil Hitler!
And if today he has not yet got very far	Heil Hitler!
He still has a thousand years!	Heil Hitler!

Please add verse!	Wieland Herzfelde

The title is an allusion not only to the Hitler salute but also to the
Heilsarmee (Salvation Army). For a note on the "Nürnberger
Trichter" (Nürnberg funnel), see 35/36.

LIED DER HEIL-ARMEE

Auf dem Nürnberger Trichter zu blasen
nach der Melodie: „O Monna".

Der Mensch lebt nicht allein von Brot
            Heil Hitler!
Wer Deutschland liebt, schlägt Juden tot
            Heil Hitler!

Bei uns gibt's keine Roten mehr
            Heil Hitler!
Deswegen fürchten wir sie sehr
            Heil Hitler!

Wir strafen streng jedweden Spott
            Heil Hitler!
Und fürchten nichts als unsern Gott
            Heil Hitler!

Wir beten Wotan an und Thor
            Heil Hitler!
Und bleiben Christen wie zuvor
            Heil Hitler!

Doch Christus ist recht unbeliebt
            Heil Hitler!
Weil es nur e i n e n Führer gibt
            Heil Hitler!

Die Menschheit krankt noch an Verstand
            Heil Hitler!
Ihr fehlt ein kleiner Reichstagsbrand
            Heil Hitler!

Den Frieden garantiert der Krieg
            Heil Hitler!
Und Wollstra garantiert den Sieg
            Heil Hitler!

'ne Kolonie bringt niemand Glück
            Heil Hitler!
Doch unsre wollen wir zurück
            Heil Hitler!

Und außerdem den Raum im Osten
            Heil Hitler!
Das deutsche Schwert darf niemals rosten
            Heil Hitler!

Drum halten fest am Alten wir
            Heil Hitler!
Wie wir's gelernt beim Münchner Bier
            Heil Hitler!

Der Herr regiert, der Knecht bleibt doof
            Heil Hitler!
Denn Deutschland ist kein Hühnerhof
            Heil Hitler!

Der
Herrenmensch braucht Fleisch vom Schwein
            Heil Hitler!
Die Masse muß bescheiden sein
            Heil Hitler!

Und fehlt ihr hier und dort die Butter
            Heil Hitler!
Es wächst ja auch noch Vogelfutter
            Heil Hitler!

Wir leben alle schlicht um schlicht
            Heil Hitler!
Denn uns genügt ein Topfgericht
            Heil Hitler!

Und niemand unterm Hakenkreuz
            Heil Hitler!
Besitzt ein Konto in der Schweiz
            Heil Hitler!

Nur der ist deutscher Sozialist
            Heil Hitler!
Dem's keine Magenfrage ist
            Heil Hitler!

Geht's manchem gut, den meisten schlecht
            Heil Hitler!
Der Führer macht es allen recht
            Heil Hitler!

Und ist er heut noch nicht so weit
            Heil Hitler!
Er hat ja tausend Jahre Zeit!
            Heil Hitler!

Bitte weiter dichten!

Wieland Herzfelde

Fotomontage: John Heartfield

DIE LEHRE DES WOLFES

"Der Begriff des "Tieres" ist abzulehnen. Er verdreht und
verfälscht die Verschiedenheiten von Schaf, Huhn, Gans,
Esel, Pferd, Hase, Kalb, Ziege, kurz jener Wesen, die nur
dazu da sind, von mir gefressen zu werden."

Die "Arbeitssitzung der Reichsfachgruppe Hochschullehrer im
Bunde nationalsozialistischer Deutscher Juristen", die unter
dem Vorsitze von Prof. Carl Schmitt tagte, stellte den folgen-
den Lehrsatz auf: "Der Begriff des "Menschen" ist abzulehnen.
Er verdreht und verfälscht die Verschieden- heiten von
Volksgenosse, Reichsbürger, Ausländer, Jude usw."

THE TEACHING OF THE WOLF

"The term 'animal' is to be rejected. It distorts and falsifies
the differences between sheep, chicken, goose, donkey,
horse, hare, calf, goat, in short, those creatures who are
only there to be eaten by me."

The "working session of the Reich Technical Commission of
University Teachers in the League of German National
Socialist Jurists," which met under the chairmanship of Prof.
Carl Schmitt, advanced the following thesis: "The term 'man'
is to be rejected. It distorts and falsifies the differences
between national comrade, Reich citizen, foreigner, Jew,
and so on."

During the Third Reich Carl Schmitt (1888–1985) was professor of
law at Berlin University. He joined the Nazi Party in 1933 and became
its leading legal and political theorist.

DIE LEHRE DES WOLFES

Die „Arbeitssitzung der Reichsfachgruppe Hochschullehrer im Bunde nationalsozialistischer Deutscher Juristen", die unter dem Vorsitze von Prof. Carl Schmitt tagte, stellte den folgenden Lehrsatz auf: „Der Begriff des „Menschen" ist abzulehnen. Er verdreht und verfälscht die Verschiedenheiten von Volksgenosse, Reichsbürger, Ausländer, Jude usw."

„Der Begriff des »Tieres« ist abzulehnen. Er verdreht und verfälscht die Verschiedenheiten von Schaf, Huhn, Gans, Esel, Pferd, Hase, Kalb, Ziege, kurz jener Wesen, die nur dazu da sind, von mir gefressen zu werden."

Fotomontage: John Heartfield

PROGRAMM DER OL

BEILSCHWINGEN

KÖPFE ROLLEN

FECHTEN

WECHSELREITEN

MPIADE BERLIN 1936

ERWERFEN

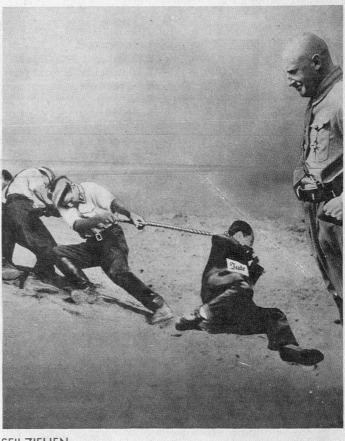

SEILZIEHEN

MPFBEUGEN

ABSCHLIESSEND GRANDIOSES SCHLACHTENFEUERWERK

PROGRAMM DER OLYMPIADE BERLIN 1936

BEILSCHWINGEN
KÖPFE ROLLEN
SPEERWERFEN
SEILZIEHEN
FECHTEN
WECHSELREITEN
RUMPFBEUGEN
ABSCHLIESSEND GRANDIOSES SCHLACHTENFEUERWERK

PROGRAM OF THE OLYMPIC GAMES BERLIN 1936

AX SWINGING
HEAD ROLLING
SPEAR THROWING
TUG-OF-WAR
FENCING
RIDING THE PROMISSORY NOTE
BODY BENDING
FINAL GRAND ARTILLERY FIREWORKS

The eleventh Olympic Games were held in Berlin in 1936. See also 22/36, 23/36.

(pages 326–27)

Alle Mann anpacken!

Everybody lend a hand!

The theme of this issue was Communist leader Georgi Dimitrov's (see 23/33, 30/33) call for an "Einheitsfront! Volksfront!" (United Front! Popular Front!).

Alle Mann anpacken!

Fotomontage: John Heartfield

ÜBERMENSCH IN NÖTEN

Auf der nächsten Tagesordnung des Völkerbundausschusses für Sanktionen steht als wichtigster Punkt: Ausdehnung der Sanktionen auf Petroleum.

SUPERMAN IN TROUBLE

The most important point on the next agenda of the League of Nations committee for sanctions: extension of petroleum sanctions.

"Zermürbender Kleinkrieg – Wendung an den Fronten in Abessinien" (Trying guerilla war – Change at the front in Abyssinia) was the lead article in this issue (pp. 786–87). See also 18/35.

In the version published in Wieland Herzfelde's *John Heartfield: Leben und Werk* (p. 199), the reference to the League of Nations was dropped and a new subtitle added, *HEILIGER ROCKEFELLER, STEH MIR BEI!* (Holy Rockefeller, stand by me!).

ÜBERMENSCH IN NÖTEN

Auf der nächsten Tagesordnung des Völkerbundausschusses für Sanktionen steht als wichtigster
Punkt: Ausdehnung der Sanktionen auf Petroleum.

Fotomontage: John Heartfield

Hurrah, die Butter ist alle!

Goering in seiner Hamburger Rede: "Erz hat stets ein Reich stark gemacht, Butter und Schmalz haben höchstens ein Volk fett gemacht".

Hurrah, the butter is finished!

Göring in his Hamburg speech: "Iron ore has always made an empire strong, butter and lard have at most made a people fat."

The motto on the wall, "Lieb Vaterland magst ruhig sein!" (Dear Fatherland you may be peaceful!) is from the patriotic song "Die Wacht am Rhein" (The watch on the Rhine), written by Max Schneckenburger. Note the Hitler portrait and the Hindenburg cushion.

Hurrah, die Butter ist alle!

Goering in seiner Hamburger Rede: „Erz hat stets ein Reich stark gemacht,
Butter und Schmalz haben höchstens ein Volk fett gemacht".

Fotomontage: John Heartfield

"O du fröhliche, o du selige, gnadenbringende Zeit"

"O joyful, o blessed, miracle-bringing time"

"O du fröhliche, o du selige, gnadenbringende Weihnachtszeit!"
(O joyful, o blessed, miracle-bringing Christmas time!) is a carol based on a Sicilian folk tune. The German text by Johannes Falk (1768–1826) dates from 1816.

„O du fröhliche, o du selige, gnadenbringende Zeit"

Fotomontage: John Heartfield

FÜHRERFAHRT INS NEUE JAHR

THE FÜHRER'S JOURNEY INTO THE NEW YEAR

For a list of montages involving Adolf Hitler, see 4/32.

FÜHRERFAHRT INS NEUE JAHR

Fotomontage: John Heartfield

Neueste Muster der Nazi-Lebensmittelindustrie 1936

Latest samples of the Nazi food industry 1936

The "samples" are "Hitlers Reden / Garantiert arisches Führerschmalz" (Hitler's speeches / guaranteed Aryan Führer lard); "Delikateß-Katzenschinken" (delicatessen cat ham); "Prima Loch-Käse" (grade A cheese with holes); "Deutsches Streckkotelett" (German stretched cutlet [note that "das Streckbett" is the rack]); "1a Fleisch im eigenen Saft" (prime meat in its own juices); "FF butteröl in tuben" (finest butter oil in tubes); "ERZ in BLAUBAND mit dem Schwan FRISCH GEKIRNT" (ore in the blue band with the swan, freshly churned). The last is a reference to Göring's "guns before butter" speech, the subject of 26/35. (Schwan in Blauband, or Swan in Blue Band, was a brand of margarine.)

Hitlers
Reden

Garantiert arisches
Führerschmalz

ERZ in BLAUBAND
mit dem Schwan
FRISCH GEKIRNT

ff Butterol
in Tuben

la
Fleisch
im eigenen
Saft

Delikateß-
Katzenschinken

Prima
Loch-Käse

Deutsches Streckkotelett

Neueste Muster der Nazi-Lebensmittelindustrie 1936

Fotomontage: John Heartfield

Uniformfassen für den Reichstag zu Worms

Da das Reich rüstet, müssen sich auch Hitlers Knappen rüsten

Für das kommende Frühjahr soll eine Sondertagung des Reichstages nach Worms a. Rh. einberufen werden. Die Wahl der Stadt Worms fiel in Erinnerung an den Reichstag 1495, auf dem Kaiser Maximilian seinen Plan einer Reichsreform verkündet hatte.   Zeitungsmeldung aus Berlin

Come get your uniforms for the Reichstag at Worms

Because the Reich arms, Hitler's pages must also arm

Early in the coming year a special meeting of the Reichstag shall be convened at Worms am Rhein. The city of Worms was chosen in memory of the Reichstag of 1495, at which Kaiser Maximilian announced his plan for a reform of the Reich.   Press report from Berlin

---

Uniformfassen is a neologism based on *Essenfassen,* which is soldiers' slang for Come and get it! *Rüsten* means both to arm or mobilize and to prepare. From left to right are Göring, Streicher, Schacht, and Goebbels (see 23/33, 11/35, 14/34, 5/33).

Uniformfassen für den Reichstag zu Worms

Für das kommende Frühjahr soll eine Berufung des Reichstages nach Worms a. Rh. erfolgen werden. Die Wahl der Stadt Worms sich in Erinnerung an den Reichstag 1495, auf dem Kaiser Maximilian seinen Plan einer Reichsform verfochten hatte. Zeitungsmeldung aus Worms.

Da das Reich rüstet, müssen sich auch Hitlers Knappen rüsten

Fotomontage: John Heartfield

4/36. **AIZ** 15, NUMBER 5, 30 JANUARY 1936, PAGE 80

**NACH DREI JAHREN
IN DER ZANGE!**

LEBENSMITTELLNOT – STEIGENDE ARBEITSLOSIGKEIT

DEVISEN- UND ROHSTOFFMANGEL

**AFTER THREE YEARS
IN THE GRIP!**

BASIC FOOD SHORTAGE – RISING UNEMPLOYMENT

LACK OF CURRENCY AND RAW MATERIALS

"Jemanden in die Zange nehmen" means to put the screws to someone.

NACH DREI JAHREN

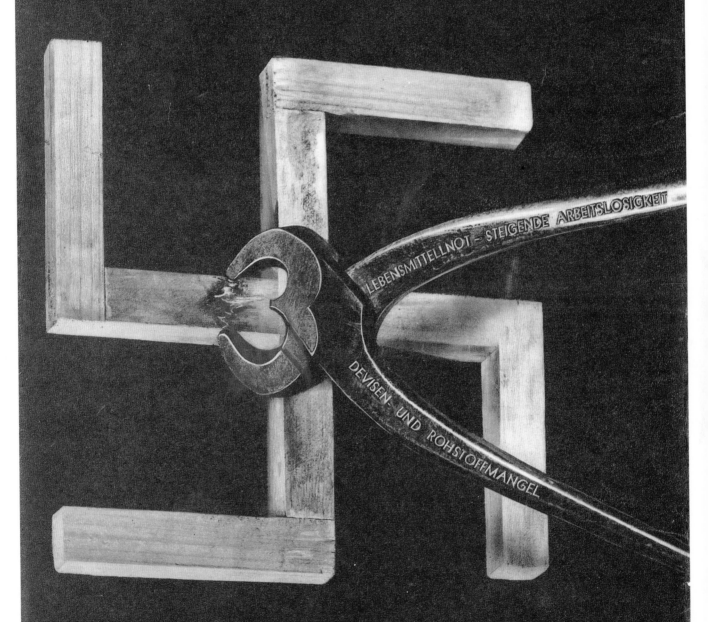

LEBENSMITTELLNOT – STEIGENDE ARBEITSLOSIGKEIT

DEVISEN- UND ROHSTOFFMANGEL

IN DER ZANGE!

Fotomontage: John Heartfield

**Zum Fall Hamsun–Ossietzky
Knut Hamsuns Kandidaten für den Friedens-
Nobelpreis**

**On the occasion of the Hamsun–Ossietzky case
Knut Hamsun's candidates for the Nobel Peace
Prize**

Carl von Ossietzky (1889–1938) was a pacifist and anti-Nazi
journalist. He was arrested and interned after the Reichstag Fire in
1933 (see 23/33). In 1935, while still under arrest, he was nominated
for the Nobel Prize. Knut Hamsun (1859–1952), a Norwegian
novelist and former Nobel Prize winner, intervened on behalf of the
Nazis. Using false documents supplied by the Gestapo, he tried to
prove that Ossietzky was a traitor. Ossietzky was awarded the prize
but was forbidden to accept it. In 1937 Hitler issued a decree which
forbade any German to accept a Nobel Prize.

      Note the credit in the top right corner: "Fotomontage:
John Heartfield. Zu den Porträts von Hitler und Göring wurden
Originalaufnahmen unverändert verwendet" (Photomontage: John
Heartfield. For the portraits of Hitler and Göring original photographs
were used unchanged.)

Zum Fall Hamsun—Ossietzky

Knut Hamsuns Kandidaten für den Friedens-Nobelpreis

An einen sterbenden italienischen Soldaten

Gefallen…
Wofür?
Den Abessiniern Kultur und Freiheit zu bringen?
Nein, zu mehren den Glanz Deiner eignen Herren!
Also, sinnlos gefallen,
ein Betrogener…?
Armer Sohn einer römischen Mutter,
Du bist nicht vergeblich gefallen:
Dein verröchelnder Atem
wird sich vereinen mit dem Deiner
sterbenden Brüder,
wird sich verdichten zum Sturm,
zum Sturm der Freiheit,
der Freiheit Italiens.

To a dying Italian soldier

Fallen…
For what?
To bring culture and liberty to the Abyssinians?
No, to increase the splendor of your own masters!
Therefore, fallen for no reason,
A betrayed one…?
Poor son of a Roman mother,
You did not fall in vain:
Your gasping breath
will unite with those of your
dying brothers,
will thicken into a storm,
into a storm of liberty,
the liberty of Italy.

For a list of other montages on the Italian invasion of Abyssinia, see
18/35.

An einen sterbenden italienischen Soldaten

Gefallen . . .
Wofür?
Den Abessiniern Kultur und Freiheit zu bringen?
Nein, zu mehren den Glanz Deiner eignen Herren!
Also, sinnlos gefallen,
ein Betrogener . . . ?
Armer Sohn einer römischen Mutter,
Du bist nicht vergeblich gefallen:
Dein verröchelnder Atem
wird sich vereinen mit dem Deiner
sterbenden Brüder,
wird sich verdichten zum Sturm,
zum Sturm der Freiheit,
der Freiheit Italiens.

Fotomontage: John Heartfield

DER SEKT IST STEUERFREI!
UND DAS IST:

DEUTSCHER SOZIALISMUS

"Die Steuer auf Schaumweine wurde aufgehoben."
Amtliche Pressemeldung aus Berlin.

THE CHAMPAGNE IS TAX FREE!
AND THAT IS:

GERMAN SOCIALISM

"The tax on sparkling wine was removed."
Official press report from Berlin.

Göring and Goebbels flank the woman in the top photograph.

DER SEKT IST STEUERFREI!
UND DAS IST:

„Die Steuer auf Schaumweine wurde aufgehoben."

DEUTSCHER SOZIALISMUS

Fotomontage: John Heartfield

Folgt dem Beispiel Spaniens!

Follow the Spanish example!

This was a special issue on the Spanish Popular Front, with a feature
article by Francisco Largo Caballero (1869–1946), leader of the
Spanish Socialist party. The montage is an adaption of 5/32, which
urged the creation of a United Front in Germany. The symbols on the
armbands represent the Communist and Social Democratic parties;
the snake decorated with swastikas is the Third Reich. Heartfield was
exhorting the German resistance to adapt the Popular Front strategy
of Spain.

Folgt dem Beispiel Spaniens!

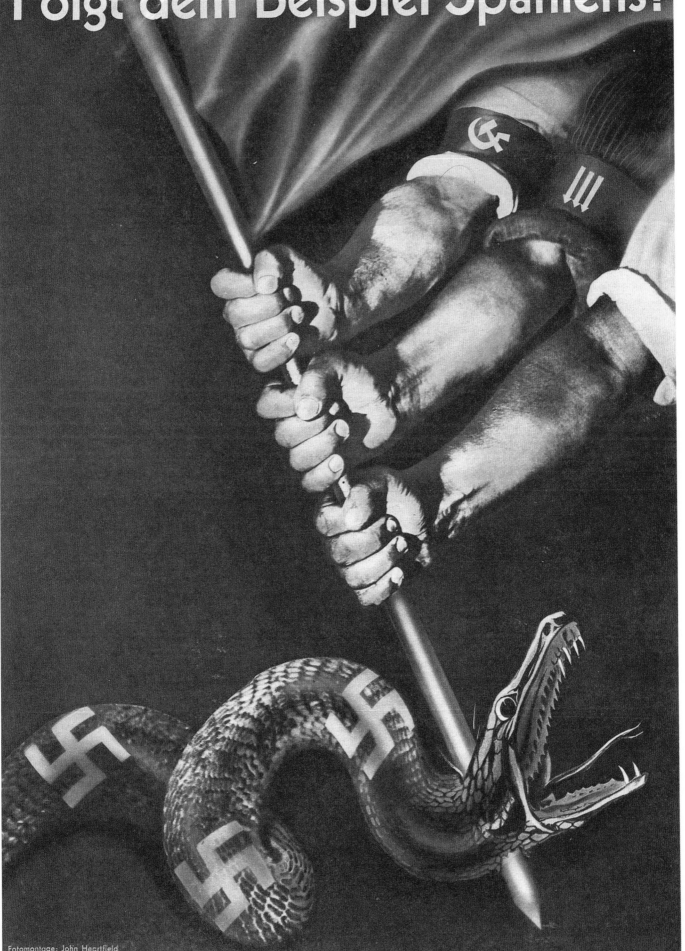

Fotomontage: John Heartfield

Hitler erzählt Märchen II

…und dann schrie der arme deutsche Michel so lange, bis
es alle Welt glaubte:
"Zu Hilfe, zu Hilfe, ich bin eingekreist!"

Hitler tells fairy tales II

…and then the poor German Michel screamed so long, that
finally the whole world believed him:
"Help, help, I'm surrounded!"

"Der deutsche Michel" – a caricature of the ordinary or average
German, or Fritz – is often depicted as a sleepyhead in a nightcap. For
the first "Hitler fairy tale," see 28/33.

Hitler erzählt Märchen

.... und dann schrie der arme deutsche Michel so lange, bis es alle Welt glaubte:

„Zu Hilfe, zu Hilfe, ich bin eingekreist!"

Fotomontage: John Heartfield

Sie richten das Volk,
solange das Volk nicht sie richtet!

Das nationalsozialistische "Volksgericht" zu Berlin hat im Richardstraßenprozeß 5 Angeklagte (3 von ihnen sind Antifaschisten, 2 Kronzeugen der Anklage) zum Tode verurteilt. In der Urteilsbegründung wird zugegeben, daß den Angeklagten eine Schuld nicht nachgewiesen werden konnte. Trotzdem fällte das Sondergericht, mit Berufung auf das "gesunde Volksempfinden", fünf Todesurteile!

They judge the people,
as long as the people do not judge them!

During the Richardstraße trial, the National Socialist "people's court" in Berlin sentenced to death 5 accused (3 of them are anti-Fascists, 2 are chief witnesses for the prosecution). In the explanation of the grounds for the sentence, it was conceded that the guilt of the accused could not be proved. Nevertheless the special court settled for five death sentences, referring to the "common sense of the people"!

A report on the case appeared in the 22 April 1936 issue of *AIZ* (15, no. 17, pp. 270–71).

Sie richten das Volk,

Das nationalsozialistische »Volksgericht« zu Berlin hat im Richardstraßenprozeß 5 Angeklagte (3 von ihnen sind Antifaschisten, 2 Kronzeugen der Anklage) zum Tode verurteilt. In der Urteilsbegründung wird
zugegeben, daß den Angeklagten eine Schuld nicht nachgewiesen
werden konnte. Trotzdem fällte das Sondergericht, mit Berufung auf
das »gesunde Volksempfinden«, fünf Todesurteile!

solange das Volk nicht sie richtet!

Fotomontage: John Heartfield

STIMME AUS DEM SUMPF

"Dreitausend Jahre konsequenter Inzucht beweisen die
Überlegenheit meiner Rasse!"

VOICE FROM THE SWAMP

"Three thousand years of consistent inbreeding prove the
superiority of my race!"

The montage was published in a special issue headlined "Juden im
III. Reich" (Jews in the Third Reich), the cover of which showed the
pillory in Breslau reserved for Jews who had broken the Nürnberg
Laws. The lead article, on the inside cover and facing Heartfield's
montage, was "RASSE: Der Mythos des Dritten Reichs" (Race: The
myth of the Third Reich). An article by Bodo Uhse about Julius
Streicher (see 11/35) began on the page following the montage.

STIMME AUS DEM SUMPF

Fotomontage: John Heartfield

„Dreitausend Jahre konsequenter Inzucht beweisen die Überlegenheit meiner Rasse!"

Das darf nicht wahr werden!

Nicht wieder darf ein als "Fetzen Papier" behandelter
Vertrag die Welt in einen Friedhof verwandeln!

It must not come true!

Never again must a treaty dealt with like a "scrap of paper"
be allowed to turn the world into a cemetery!

In a speech of 3 March 1936 Hitler denounced the Locarno Treaty of
1925, which confirmed the French-German and Belgian-German
borders and the demilitarized zone of the Rhineland. Hitler ignored
the treaty when later that month he sent troops into the Rhineland.
At the start of World War I, Reich Chancellor Bethmann Hollweg
(1856–1921) had described the Belgian treaty of neutrality as "ein
Fetzen Papier" (a scrap of paper). Heartfield also used the phrase in
36/36 and 5/37.

Das darf nicht wahr werden!

Le présent Traité, fait en un seul e...
archives de la Société des Nations, dont le ... exemplaire sera déposé ...
de remettre à chacune des Hautes Parti... Secrétaire Général sera prié ...
certifiées conformes. ...s contractantes des copies

En foi de quoi les Plénipotentiaires ...s sousnommés ont signé le
présent Traité.

Fait à Locarno le seize octobre ... mil neuf cent vingt-cinq.

Nicht wieder darf ein als „Fetzen Papier" behandelter
Vertrag die Welt in einen Friedhof verwandeln!

Fotomontage: John Heartfield

BRAUNE A-B-C-SCHÜTZEN

Das Einmaleins läßt sich auch mit Hufnägeln lehren. Für Mathematik finden sich in der Schießlehre die schönsten Anwendungsmöglichkeiten! In der Geographie kann der Weltkrieg unbeschränkt zu seinem Rechte kommen.
(Aus dem Sonderheft der "Deutschen Schule", Zeitschrift des offiziellen NS-Lehrerbundes, Berlin)

BROWN FIRST GRADERS

Multiplication can also be taught with hobnails. For mathematics, the nicest practicable applications are found at shooting practice! In geography the world war can come into its own.
(From the special issue of "German School," magazine of the official NS Federation of Teachers, Berlin)

This montage appeared in a special issue on youth. *Schütze* means marksman; an *ABC-Schütze* is someone learning the rudiments, a school beginner or a first grader.

BRAUNE A-B-C-SCHÜTZEN

Das Einmaleins läßt sich auch mit Hufnägeln lehren. Für Mathematik finden sich in der Schießlehre die schönsten Anwendungsmöglichkeiten! In der Geographie kann der Weltkrieg unbeschränkt zu seinem Rechte kommen.

Fotomontage: John Heartfield · (Aus dem Sonderheft der „Deutschen Schule", Zeitschrift des offiziellen NS-Lehrerbundes, Berlin)

Und auf Hitlers Friedensangebote folgen "alsbald" seine Friedenstauben

And his doves of peace will "immediately" ꜰ follow Hitler's overtures of peace

For a list of other montages on Hitler, see 4/32.

AIZ

Das Illustrierte Volksblatt

Erscheint wöchentlich einmal. — Preis: 1,60 Kč, 40 Gr., 1,25 Frs.,
2,20 belgische Frs., 30 Rp., 20 Pfg., 10 amer. Cts., 4 Dinar, 12 Lei.

Jahrgang XV　　　　　Nummer 15　　　　　5. April 1936

Und auf Hitlers Friedensangebote folgen »alsbald« seine Friedenstauben

Fotomontage: John Heartfield

Wenn Hitler vom Frieden spricht, denkt daran:

Der Friede sitzt mit Ernst Thälmann im Kerker. Freiheit für Thälmann – Friede für die Welt!

When Hitler speaks of peace, remember this:

Peace sits in jail with Ernst Thälmann. Freedom for Thälmann – peace for the world!

This montage appeared in a special issue celebrating German Communist Party leader Thälmann's fiftieth birthday, which he spent in prison (see also 37/34).

AIZ
Das Illustrierte Volksblatt

Wenn Hitler
vom Frieden
spricht,
denkt daran:

Der Friede sitzt mit Ernst Thälmann im Kerker.   Freiheit für Thälmann – Friede für die Welt!

Faschistische Ruhmesmale

Denkmal des Duce in Abessinien

Fascist monuments of glory

Il duce's memorial in Abyssinia

This montage became the subject of an article entitled "Der Foto-
monteur hat es vorausgeahnt!" (The photomonteur anticipated it!)
that was published in *AIZ* on 15 July 1936 (15, no. 29, p. 458), soon
after Mussolini had authorized the creation of a memorial made from
the skeletons of fallen Italian soldiers. For a list of montages on the
Italian invasion of Abyssinia, see 18/35.

Faschistische Ruhmesmale

Denkmal des Duce in Abessinien

Fotomontage: John Heartfield

**Wir lieben vereint, wir hassen vereint,
wir haben alle nur einen Feind:
Die Sowjetunion, den Frieden!**

**United we love, united we hate,
we all have but one enemy:
The Soviet Union and peace!**

Germany and Japan went on to sign a pact against the Communist
International on 25 November 1936 (see 42/36). Göring is at the left,
and at the right is General Jiro Minami, the Japanese envoy to the
puppet régime of Manchuria.

Goering

AIZ
Das Illustrierte Volksblatt

Wir lieben vereint, wir hassen vereint,
wir haben alle nur einen Feind:
Die Sowjetunion, den Frieden!

Japanischer General

Fotomontage: John Heartfield

Seht nach Spanien und Frankreich!

Wie ein Rad ins andere greift, muß eine Hand die andere greifen, damit in allen Ländern die Volksfront den Faschismus schlägt!

Look to Spain and France!

As one cog interlocks with another, one hand must grasp the other, so that in all countries the Popular Front will defeat Fascism!

This issue featured an article on the Popular Front in Spain and France (pp. 306–7).

Seht nach Spanien und Frankreich!

Wie ein Rad ins andere greift, muß eine Hand die andere greifen, damit in allen Ländern die Volksfront den Faschismus schlägt!

Fotomontage: John Heartfield

**Bevor der Krieg euch fällt, muß er fallen!
Schafft die Volksfront, die den Frieden sichert!**

**He must fall, before war fells you! Create the
Popular Front that will secure the peace!**

The flag displays the symbols of the Communists (hammer and
sickle) and the Social Democrats (three arrows). The "war machine"
has Göring's head.

Bevor der Krieg euch fällt, muß er fallen!
Schafft die Volksfront, die den Frieden sichert!

Fotomontage: John Heartfield

ANTWORT AUF EIN NAZI-PLAKAT

Wir starben für Euch!
Und Ihr wollt uns verraten?

NEIN!
*Und darum darf Hitler das Verbrechen von 1914
nicht wiederholen!*

REPLY TO A NAZI POSTER

We died for you!
And you want to betray us?

NO!
*And that is why Hitler must not be allowed to repeat the
crime of 1914!*

The Nazis had reused a 1918 poster design depicting German
frontline soldiers fearing a "stab in the back" by politicians. The
"shame" of the Treaty of Versailles was a recurrent Nazi theme.

Wir starben für Euch!
Und Ihr wollt uns verraten?

NEIN!
Und darum darf Hitler
das Verbrechen von 1914
nicht wiederholen!

Montiert: John Heartfield.

DEM UNBEKANNTEN GENOSSEN

All den namenlosen antifaschistischen Helden gewidmet, die
im Kampf für ein Deutschland des Friedens und der Freiheit
ihr Leben einsetzten!

TO THE UNKNOWN COMRADE

Dedicated to all the nameless anti-Fascist heroes who laid
down their lives in the struggle for a Germany of peace and
freedom!

The title alludes to World War I monuments dedicated to the
Unknown Soldier.

DEM
UNBEKANNTEN
GENOSSEN

All den namenlosen antifaschistischen Helden gewidmet, die im Kampf
für ein Deutschland des Friedens und der Freiheit ihr Leben einsetzten!

Fotomontage: John Heartfield

22/36. **AIZ** 15, NUMBER 26, 24 JUNE 1936, PAGE 416

Berlin ruft zur Olympiade

Antwort auf diesen Ruf: Die Olympiade-Sondernummer der AIZ nächste Woche

Berlin summons to the Olympic Games

Reply to this summons: the Olympics special issue of AIZ next week

---

For the Olympic theme, see also 23/35 and 23/36.

Berlin ruft zur Olympiade

Fotomontage: John Heartfield

Antwort auf diesen Ruf: Die Olympiade-Sondernummer der AIZ nächste Woche

23/36. **AIZ** 15, NUMBER 27, 1 JULY 1936, PAGE 432

COME AND SEE GERMANY!

Der Zweck vons Janze
"Olympiagäste, im Gleichschritt – marsch!"

COME AND SEE GERMANY!

The point of it all
"Olympic guests – forward march!"

Heartfield emphasized Goebbels's deformity by showing his clubfoot
as an animal's hoof. "Vons Janze" is Berlin dialect for "vom Ganzen"
(of it all). The montage was part of a special *AIZ* issue on the
Olympics that offered an unofficial guide to the host city and country.
A two-page map, for example, showed the locations of prisons and
concentration camps throughout Germany. See also 23/35, 22/36.

COME AND SEE GERMANY!

Der Zweck vons Janze
„Olympiagäste, im Gleichschritt — marsch!"

Fotomontage: John Heartfield

**Rettet Edgar Andrée,
den deutschen Friedenskämpfer!**

In dem Prozeß gegen den bekannten Führer der hamburger
Kriegsbeschädigten Edgar Andrée, beantragte der Staats-
anwalt die Todesstrafe und Aberkennung der bürgerlichen
Ehrenrechte.
Hamburg, Ende Juni 1936.

**Save Edgar André,
the German fighter for peace!**

In the trial against Edgar André, the well-known leader of
Hamburg's disabled veterans, the public prosecutor
requested capital punishment and deprivation of civil rights.
Hamburg, end June 1936.

Edgar André (1894–1936) was a docker and Communist activist in
Hamburg. He was arrested by Nazis in 1933 and executed in 1936.
The 22 July 1936 issue of *AIZ* has a portrait of André on its cover
and contains articles about him by Heinrich Mann and Willi Bredel
(p. 471). See also 39/36.

In dem Prozeß gegen den bekannten
Führer der hamburger Kriegsbeschä-
digten Edgar Andrée, beantragte der
Staatsanwalt die Todesstrafe und Aber-
kennung der bürgerlichen Ehrenrechte.
Hamburg, Ende Juni 1936.

Rettet Edgar Andrée,
den deutschen Friedenskämpfer!

Fotomontage: John Heartfield

GANGSTER IN GENF

"Danzig her! Dann beginnen wir den Krieg vielleicht etwas später."

"Höchste Zeit, daß mal ein Bombengeschwader die ganze Quatschbude in die Luft sprengt".
Senatspräsident Greiser vor dem Völkerbund.

GANGSTER IN GENEVA

"We want Danzig! Then perhaps we'll begin the war a bit later."

"High time a bomber squadron blew up the whole gossip club."
Senate President Greiser before the League of Nations.

Arthur Greiser (1897–1946) was a Nazi leader in Danzig. Formerly German, Danzig was made a Free City by the Treaty of Versailles to give Poland an outlet to the sea. A League of Nations commissioner, together with an elected senate, administered the city. The senate came under Nazi control in 1933, and on 1 September 1939 union with Germany was proclaimed, effectively beginning World War II.

GANGSTER IN GENF

„Höchste Zeit, daß mal ein Bombenge-
schwader die ganze Quatschbude in die
Luft sprengt".
Senatspräsident Greiser vor dem Völkerbund.

„Danzig her! Dann beginnen wir den Krieg vielleicht etwas später."

Fotomontage: John Heartfield

Normalisierung

"Diese kleine Differenz werden wir auch noch aus der Welt schaffen".

Der deutschen Kolonie in Österreich soll eine angemessene Möglichkeit zur gesellschaftlichen Betätigung gegeben werden.
Aus dem Abkommen zwischen Deutschland und Österreich über die Normalisierung der Beziehungen.

Normalization

"We'll manage to get rid of this little discrepancy yet."

The German colony in Austria is to be given a suitable opportunity for social commitment.
From the agreement between Germany and Austria about the normalization of relations.

Germany and Austria signed an agreement recognizing Austrian sovereignty on 11 July 1936 (see also 27/36). "Dieses Zeichen ist das österreichische 'Krukenkreuz'" (*sic*) (This sign is the Austrian "cross potent") explains the cross at the lower right.

Normalisierung

Fotomontage: John Heartfield

Der deutschen Kolonie in Österreich soll eine angemessene Möglichkeit zur gesellschaftlichen Betätigung gegeben werden.

Aus dem Abkommen zwischen Deutschland und Österreich über die Normalisierung der Beziehungen.

Dieses Zeichen ⊞ ist das

österreichische „Krukenkreuz"

„Diese kleine Differenz werden wir auch noch aus der Welt schaffen".

Keine Antwort ist auch eine Antwort

Und die Moral von der Geschicht:
Angle mit Fragezeichen nicht.

Anläßlich der vertragswidrigen Besetzung des Rheinlandes hat die englische Regierung der Hitlerregierung einen Fragebogen überreicht, dessen Beantwortung Aufschluß über das Verhältnis des Dritten Reichs zu Österreich geben sollte. Eine Antwort hat Hitler nicht gegeben. Statt dessen hat er den geduldigen englischen Vetter durch den Pakt von Berchtesgaden "schlagartig" überrascht.

No reply is also a reply

And the moral of the tale:
don't fish with question marks.

On the occasion of the treaty-defaulting occupation of the Rhineland, the English government submitted to Hitler's government a questionnaire, the response to which was intended to clarify the relationship of the Third Reich to Austria. Hitler gave no reply. Instead he "abruptly" surprised the patient English cousin with the Pact of Berchtesgaden.

The Dreibund (written on the dorsal fin of the fish) was the Triple Alliance (of Germany, Austria, and Italy). On the body of the fish are a swastika (Germany) and a cross potent (Austria), and its tail is made from fasces (Italy). *Schlagartig* (abruptly) can also mean with a bang.

The Pact of Berchtesgaden made official Germany's recognition of Austria's sovereignty (see 26/36).

Sorgen brauner Generale

"Verdammt, es scheint schief zu gehen – dabei haben wir das Feuerchen doch ebenso gut vorbereitet wie beim Reichstagsbrand."

Worries of brown generals

"Damn, it seems to be going wrong – yet we prepared the little blaze just as well as we did the Reichstag Fire."

This page is from a special issue on the Spanish Civil War, which had begun on 18 July 1936 with a revolt of army commanders in Spanish Morocco against the Republican government.

The worried "brown general" on the right is Göring. The Party line, faithfully registered by Heartfield, was that Göring had masterminded the Reichstag Fire, presenting it as a Communist provocation that justified strong Nazi rule (see also 23/33). Similarly, General Franco argued that his action was necessary to prevent an imminent Communist takeover of Spain. The montage suggests that the Francoists had been receiving instructions from the Nazis.

On the Spanish Civil War, see also 29/36, 30/36, 33/36, 34/36, 36/36, 40/36, 41/36, 43/36, 44/36, 3/37, 6/37, 8/37, 10/37, 17/37, 18/37, 21/37, 29/37.

Sorgen brauner Generale

„Verdammt, es scheint schief zu gehen — dabei haben wir das Feuerchen doch ebenso gut vorbereitet wie beim Reichstagsbrand."

Fotomontage: John Heartfield

Die Freiheit selbst kämpft in ihren Reihen

Zu dieser Fotomontage wurden benützt: das berühmte Bild des französischen Malers Delacroix "Die Freiheit führt das Volk an" ("Juli 1830") und eine Originalaufnahme aus Madrid, Juli 1936.

Liberty herself fights in their ranks

Used for this photomontage were: the celebrated picture of the French painter Delacroix, "Liberty Guiding the People" ("July 1830") and an original photograph from Madrid, July 1936.

This montage appeared in a special issue titled "Für Friede, Freiheit, Demokratie! Was will das Volk in Spanien und Frankreich" (For peace, freedom, democracy! What the people want in Spain and France).

The Spanish photograph shows Republican troops leaving Barcelona, not Madrid, for the Front (see Diethart Kerbs, ed., *Hans Namuth und Georg Reisner, Spanisches Tagebuch 1936* [Berlin: Dirk Nishen, 1986], p. 33). This was Heartfield's contribution to the first issue of the magazine renamed *Volks Illustrierte* (People's illustrated), a title that registered its commitment to the Popular Front.

Zu dieser Fotomontage wurden benützt: das berühmte Bild des französischen Malers Delacroix „Die Freiheit führt das Volk an" („Juli 1830") und eine Originalaufnahme aus Madrid, Juli 1936.

Die Freiheit selbst kämpft in ihren Reihen

Fotomontage: John Heartfield

"Völkische" ohne Volk

"Heil Franco! Der wird angeworben für die Eroberung von Madrid".

Londoner Zeitungsmeldung: "General Franco stößt bei seinem Plan, noch 30 000 Marokkaner gegen die Regierung zu mobilisieren, auf große Schwierigkeiten. Mehrere der bekanntesten Führer der Riffkabylen haben einen Aufruf erlassen, in dem sie ihre Stammesgenossen dringend warnen, Francos Ruf zu folgen. Der Marokkaner, so heißt es in dem Aufruf, dürfe nur gegen die Unterdrücker der Freiheit, nicht aber für eine fremde Sache kämpfen."

"National" without a nation

"Heil Franco! He will be recruited for the conquest of Madrid."

London newspaper report: "General Franco encounters great difficulties with his plan to mobilize another 30,000 Moroccans against the government. Several of the best-known leaders of the Kabyl Rif have issued an appeal in which they urgently warned their fellow tribesmen about following Franco's summons. A Moroccan, so it is commanded in the appeal, should fight only against the oppressor of liberty, and certainly not for a foreign cause."

Francisco Franco Bahamonde (1892–1975) led the revolt against the Spanish Republican government in the civil war that lasted from 1936 to 1939. When the war began he flew to Spanish Morocco to organize the participation of the Foreign Legion and Moorish troops in the insurgent army.

The adjective *völkisch* was a National Socialist invention, related to other Third Reich neologisms with racial and anti-Semitic connotations, such as *Volksgemeinschaft* (national community), *Volksgenosse* (fellow national), and *Volksgerichtshof* (people's court). See also 21/33.

„Völkische" ohne Volk

Londoner Zeitungsmeldung: „General Franco stößt bei seinem Plan, noch 30 000 Marokkaner gegen die Regierung zu mobilisieren, auf große Schwierigkeiten. Mehrere der bekanntesten Führer der Riffkabylen haben einen Aufruf erlassen, in dem sie ihre Stammesgenossen dringend warnen, Francos Ruf zu folgen. Der Marokkaner, so heißt es in dem Aufruf, dürfe nur gegen die Unterdrücker der Freiheit, nicht aber für eine fremde Sache kämpfen."

„Heil Franco! Der wird angeworben für die Eroberung von Madrid".

Fotomontage: John Heartfield

WEG FREI FÜR DEN FRIEDEN!

ZUM BRÜSSELER WELTFRIEDENSKONGRESS

Fotomontage nach einem offiziellen Plakat des französischen Schul-Ministeriums zum "Tag des Friedens" in St. Cloud, 9. VIII. 1936

MAKE WAY FOR PEACE!

ON THE OCCASION OF THE WORLD PEACE CONFERENCE, BRUSSELS

Photomontage based on an official poster of the French Ministry of Education for the "Day of Peace" in St. Cloud, 9 August 1936

Facing the montage was a report about the forthcoming conference. The snake is inscribed: *DER KRIEG* (war). In a 1955 version of the montage (see Herzfelde, *John Heartfield,* p. 240), the snake's tongue became a dollar sign and *DER KRIEG* became *ATOMKRIEG* (atomic war).

WEG FREI FÜR DEN FRIEDEN!
ZUM BRÜSSELER WELTFRIEDENSKONGRESS

Fotomontage nach einem offiziellen Plakat
des französischen Schul-Ministeriums zum
„Tag des Friedens" in St. Cloud, 9. VIII. 1936

John Heartfield

SCHATTEN ÜBER EUROPA

Zur Einführung der zweijährigen Dienstzeit im Dritten Reich

SHADOW OVER EUROPE

On the introduction of two-year military service in the Third Reich

SCHATTEN ÜBER EUROPA

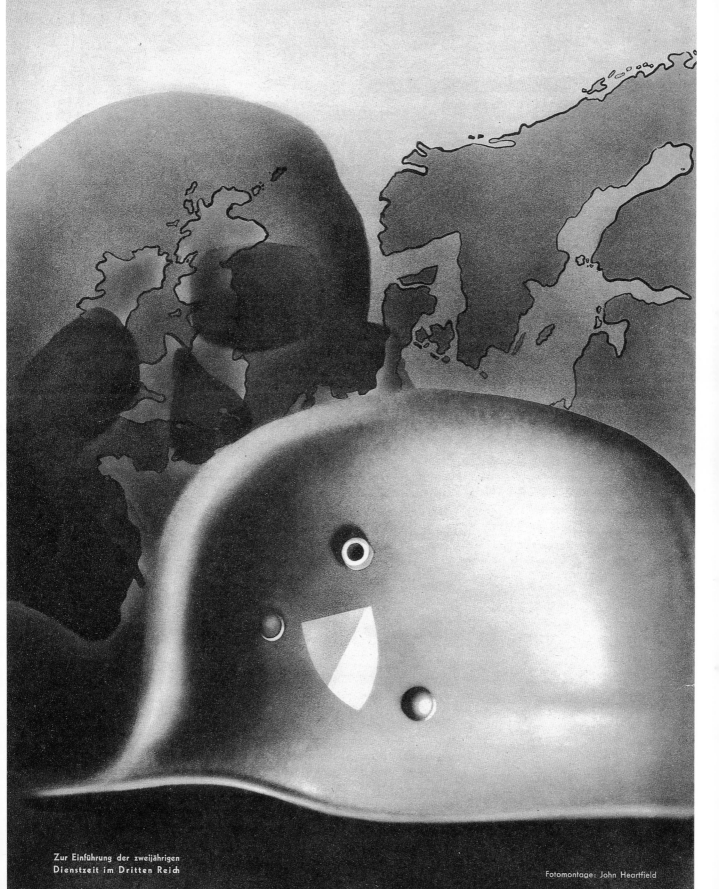

Zur Einführung der zweijährigen
Dienstzeit im Dritten Reich

Fotomontage: John Heartfield

GROSSES MONSTRE-LÜGENKABINETT

"Hereinspaziert, meine Herrschaften! Hier sehen Sie Spanien mit den Augen des unparteiischen Beobachters. Die letzten Sensationen! Nervenaufpeitschende Aufklärung! Hier können Sie das Gruseln lernen! Alles für nur einen Groschen".

GROSSER INTERNATIONALER GREUELWETTBEWERB FAVORITEN: DAILY MAIL–VÖLKISCHER BEOBACHTER, ANGRIFF BOHEMIA–ZEIT–FIGARO–ACTION FRANÇAISE

DER ERZBISCHOF VON TARRAGONA
1 mal erschossen, 3 mal verbrannt, 2 mal mit der Kathedrale in die Luft gesprengt. (Kann derzeit in CASTEL GANDOLFO interviewt werden.)

DAS TECHNISCHE WELTWUNDER
Die siebenmal endgültig abgeschnittene Wasserzufuhr von MADRID.

DIE ANARCHIE IN MADRID
Madrider Volksfront beschlagnahmt die Notgroschen eines bettelarmen monarchistischen Bankiers namens MERGUIDO im Betrage von 85,000,000 pesetas.

DER DOKUMENTEN-RAUB VON BARCELONA
Durch zynische Beschlagnahme nationalsozialistischer Geheimdokumente mischt sich spanische Volksfront in Angelegenheiten des Dritten Reichs.

Einer gewissen "großen Presse" nach Lektüre ihrer Spanienberichte in ehrfurchtsvoller Bewunderung gewidmet von John Heartfield.

GREAT MONSTER CABINET OF LIES

"Walk right up, ladies and gentlemen! Here you see Spain with the eyes of the impartial observer. The latest sensations! Rousing information! Here you can get the creeps! All for only a penny."

GREAT INTERNATIONAL HORROR COMPETITION FAVORITES: DAILY MAIL–VÖLKISCHER BEOBACHTER, ANGRIFF BOHEMIA–ZEIT–FIGARO–ACTION FRANCAISE

THE ARCHBISHOP OF TARRAGONA
1 time shot dead, 3 times burned to death, 2 times blown up with the cathedral. (Can at present be interviewed in CASTEL GANDOLFO.)

THE TECHNICAL WORLD WONDER
The water supply of MADRID, cut off for good seven times.

THE ANARCHY IN MADRID
Madrid Popular Front seizes the nest egg of desperately poor monarchist banker called MERGUIDO, a total of 85,000,000 pesetas.

THE DOCUMENTS THEFT IN BARCELONA
Through cynical seizure of National Socialist secret documents the Spanish Popular Front government interferes in the affairs of the Third Reich.

Dedicated with respectful admiration by John Heartfield to a certain "great press" after reading their Spanish reports.

The image of the carnival barker is taken from Georg Pabst's 1931 film version of Bertolt Brecht's *Die Dreigroschenoper* (The threepenny opera). The "documents theft" refers to the actions of the militia who broke into Nazi headquarters in Barcelona and discovered documentation of German ambitions in Spain. *VI* publisher Willi Münzenberg used this material for his *Nazi Conspiracy in Spain*, which was published in various languages in 1937. For Münzenberg, see 1/32.

GROSSES MONSTRE-LÜGENKABINETT

GROSSER INTERNATIONALER GREUELWETTBEWERB   FAVORITEN: DAILY MAIL-VÖLKISCHER BEOBACHTER, ANGRIFF BOHEMIA-ZEIT-FIGARO-ACTION FRANÇAISE

DER ERZBISCHOF von TARRAGONA

1 mal erschossen, 3 mal verbrannt,
2 mal mit der Kathedrale in die Luft gesprengt.
(Kann derzeit in CASTEL GANDOLFO interviewt werden.)

DAS TECHNISCHE WELTWUNDER

Die siebenmal endgültig abgeschnittene
Wasserzufuhr von MADRID.

DIE ANARCHIE IN MADRID

Madrider Volksfront beschlagnahmt die Notgroschen
eines bettelarmen monarchistischen Bankiers namens
MERGUIDO im Betrage von 85,000.000 Pesetas.

DER DOKUMENTEN-RAUB von BARCELONA

Durch zynische Beschlagnahme
nationalsozialistischer Geheimdokumente mischt sich spanische
Volksfront in Angelegenheiten
des Dritten Reichs.

„Hereinspaziert, meine Herrschaften! Hier sehen Sie Spanien mit den Augen des
unparteiischen Beobachters. Die letzten Sensationen! Nervenaufpeitschende Aufklärung! Hier können Sie das Gruseln lernen! Alles für nur einen Groschen".

Einer gewissen „großen Presse" nach Lektüre ihrer Spanienberichte in ehrfurchtsvoller Bewunderung gewidmet von John Heartfield.

Franco-Geographie

Lissabon ist die Hauptstadt, Marokko das Herz Spaniens. Dessau, der Sitz der Junkers-Flugzeugwerke, liegt in Andalusien. Burgos ist ein Vorort von Nürnberg.

"Seine oft recht verworrenen und stets mit unvorstellbar saftigen Kraftworten gespickten täglichen Rundfunkreden am Sender von Sevilla pflegt der General Llano mit dem Satz zu schließen: "So, und jetzt gehe ich saufen!", wie denn überhaupt neben dem Blut der spanische Südwein das beliebteste Getränk dieses wackeren Generals bildet."
Aus einer Pariser Zeitungsmeldung

Franco Geography

Lisbon is the capital city, Morocco the heart of Spain. Dessau, the site of the Junkers airplane factory, is situated in Andalusia. Burgos is a suburb of Nürnberg.

"General Llano usually closes his daily radio speeches from the radio station of Seville, which are often rather confused and always peppered with unimaginably juicy swear words, with the sentence: 'Well, and now I'm going out to booze!' For after all, next to blood, Spanish sweet wine is the favorite drink of this valiant general."
From a Parisian newspaper report

Portugal (capital city, Lisbon) and Germany (Dessau and Nürnberg) supported Franco, and his uprising began in Spanish Morocco. Francoist headquarters were in the Spanish town of Burgos.

On the wall hangs a framed photograph of the Reichstag Fire (see 23/33), which according to the Communists was an inspiration for the Francoists. See also 28/36.

Franco-Geographie

„Seine oft recht verworrenen und stets mit unvorstellbar saftigen Kraftworten gespickten täglichen Rundfunkreden am Sender von Sevilla pflegt der General Llano mit dem Satz zu schließen: »So, und jetzt gehe ich saufen!«, wie denn überhaupt neben dem Blut der spanische Südwein das beliebteste Getränk dieses wackeren Generals bildet.'
Aus einer Pariser Zeitungsmeldung

Lissabon ist die Hauptstadt, Marokko das Herz Spaniens. Dessau, der Sitz der Junkers-Flugzeugwerke, liegt in Andalusien. Burgos ist ein Vorort von Nürnberg.

Fotomontage: John Heartfield

Wieder einmal in der Welt voran...

Rapport eines braunen Alchimisten: "Mein Führer, es ist mir gelungen, Fleischkarten in einen Extrakt zu verwandlen, der an Nährkraft das beste Mastfleisch übertrifft."

Once again first in the world...

Report of a brown alchemist: "My Führer, I have succeeded in changing meat-ration cards into an extract that surpasses the best beef in nutritional value."

Brotkarte is a bread-ration card. "FLEISCHKARTE / SORTE: ZWEITER VIERJAHRESPLAN" means meat-ration card / type: second Four Year Plan. On the top shelf is a funnel labeled "NÜRNBERGER TRICHTER" (Nürnberg funnel). "Jemandem etwas mit dem Nürnberger Trichter beibringen" (literally, to teach someone something with the Nürnberg funnel) means to drum something into somebody. Heartfield was alluding to the Nürnberg rallies and the anti-Jewish Nürnberg Laws, which were announced at the 1935 rally.

Wieder einmal in der Welt voran...

Rapport eines braunen Alchimisten: „Mein Führer, es ist mir gelungen, Fleischkarten in einen Extrakt zu verwandeln, der an Nährkraft das beste Mastfleisch übertrifft."

Fotomontage: John Heartfield

**1914 Belgien, 1936 Spanien
Neutralität? Ein Fetzen Papier!**

**1914 Belgium, 1936 Spain
Neutrality? A scrap of paper!**

The pilot's armband says: "GESCHWADER FIESELER" (Fieseler
squadron). Gerhard Fieseler was a German airplane manufacturer.
For "Ein Fetzen Papier" (a scrap of paper), see 12/36.

Heartfield was comparing Fascist intervention in Spain in
1936 with Germany's invasion of neutral Belgium at the start of
World War I.

1914 Belgien, 1936 Spanien

Neutralität? Ein Fetzen Papier!

Fotomontage: John Heartfield

Beefsteaks raus! Nieder mit den Schnitzeln!

Beefsteaks und Schnitzel will nur der marxistische Untermensch. Der Arier hält sich an den nordischen Wal.

"Noch immer treiben sich in Deutschland allzuviele ausländische Filets, Beefsteaks und Rumpsteaks herum." Hannoverscher Kurier.

"Fleischnahrung mindert die Fruchtbarkeit der Frauen." Deutsche Mediz. Wochenschrift.

"Die Sendung der deutschen Kochkunst geht dahin, die an die Scholle gebundenen Gerichte wieder auf die Speisekarte zu bringen."
Reichsköcheführer Leitz.

"Unter Beteiligung von Vertretern des Reichsernährungs-ministers, der Partei- und Reichsbehörden fand ein Walfischprobeessen statt, bei dem es sich erwies, daß Walfischfleisch durchaus genießbar ist."
Mitteilungen des Reichsnährstandes.

Ich bin ein fremdstämmiges Beefsteak.
Ich habe deutsche Magen geschändet.

Beefsteaks out! Down with cutlets!

Only the Marxist subhuman wants beefsteaks and cutlets. The Aryan sticks to the Nordic whale.

"Still all too many alien filet steaks, beefsteaks and rump steaks are knocking about in Germany."
Hannoverscher Kurier.

"A diet of meat reduces the fertility of women."
Deutsche Mediz. Wochenschrift.

"The mission of the German art of cookery is to bring indigenous country dishes back onto the menu."
Reichsköcheführer Leitz.

"With the participation of representatives of the Reich food minister, Party and Reich authorities, a tasting of whale took place, at which it was proved that the meat of the whale is quite edible."
Reports of the Reich food trade.

I am an alien beefsteak.
I have violated German stomachs.

Nazi German contrasted *volksstämmig* (rooted in the people) with *fremdstämmig* (alien). *Volksstamm* conventionally means tribe. *Schänden* (to violate) in National Socialist terminology described any sexual relationship involving an Aryan and a Jew (see 11/35). The montage probably also alludes to the "Beefsteak Nazi," a term of abuse used to describe Communists and Socialists who switched to the NSDAP for opportunistic reasons. A "Beefsteak Nazi" was brown on the outside, red on the inside.

A report on Nazi protests about this montage was published in the 27 October 1937 issue of *VI* (no. 43).

Beefsteaks raus! Nieder mit den Schnitzeln!

„Noch immer treiben sich in Deutschland allzuviele ausländische Filets, Beefsteaks und Rumpsteaks herum."
Hannoverscher Kurier.

„Fleischnahrung mindert die Fruchtbarkeit der Frauen."
Deutsche Mediz. Wochenschrift.

„Die Sendung der deutschen Kochkunst geht dahin, die an die Scholle gebundenen Gerichte wieder auf die Speisekarte zu bringen."
Reichsköcheführer Leitz.

„Unter Beteiligung von Vertretern des Reichsernährungsministers, der Partei- und Reichsbehörden fand ein Walfischprobeessen statt, bei dem es sich erwies, daß Walfischfleisch durchaus genießbar ist."
Mitteilungen des Reichsnährstandes.

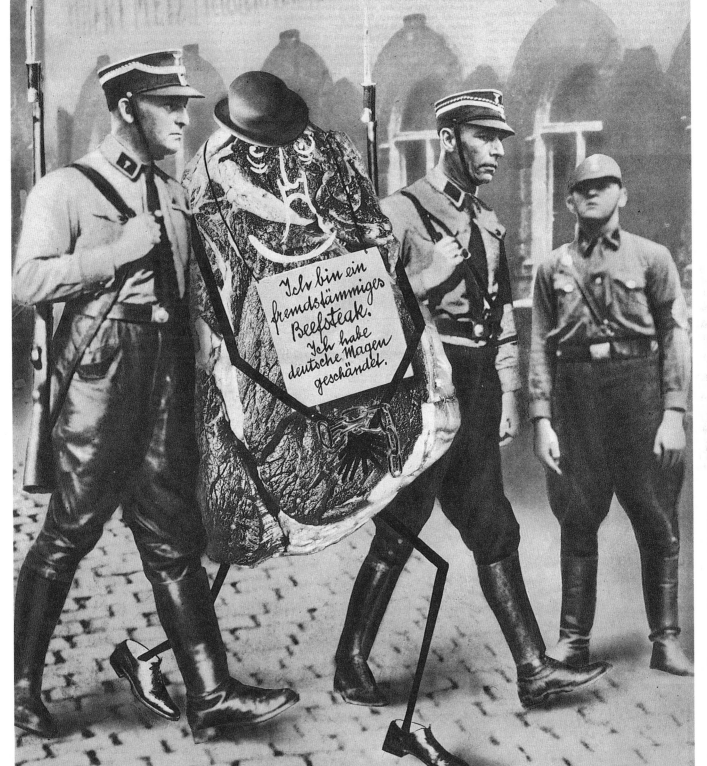

Ich bin ein fremdstämmiges Beefsteak. Ich habe deutsche Magen geschändet.

Beefsteaks und Schnitzel will nur der marxistische Untermensch.
Der Arier hält sich an den nordischen Wal.

Fotomontage: John Heartfield

Hunger ist der beste Koch

"Der Mann hat sich unpatriotisch ernährt, er hat erst 7 Pfund abgenommen."

"Ich selbst esse schon seit längerer Zeit keine Butter mehr und habe um 20 Pfund abgenommen."
Aus der Rede, mit der Göring seine Tätigkeit als Vierjahrplandiktator einleitete.

Hunger is the best cook

"The man has fed himself unpatriotically, he has only lost 7 pounds so far."

"I myself have not been eating butter for a long time and have lost about 20 pounds."
From the speech in which Göring introduced his function as dictator of the Four Year Plan.

The title is a German proverb. The Four Year Plan, run by Göring and designed to achieve national self-sufficiency, was proclaimed on 9 September 1936. "Vierjahrplan-Waage" are, literally, Four Year Plan scales; "Reichs-Abmagerungsdienst" is the Reich Slimming Service.

Hunger ist der beste Koch

„Ich selbst esse schon seit längerer Zeit keine
Butter mehr und habe um 20 Pfund abgenommen."
Aus der Rede, mit der Göring seine Tätigkeit als Vier-
jahrplandiktator einleitete.

Vierjahrplan-Waage

10 Pf D

Reichs...

„Der Mann hat sich unpatriotisch ernährt, er hat erst 7 Pfund abgenommen."

Fotomontage: John Heartfield

EDGAR ANDRÉ

Sollten Sie trotzdem das Unmögliche möglich machen und
einen Kämpfer zum Richtblock bringen, so bin ich bereit,
diesen schweren Gang zu gehen; denn ich will keine Gnade.

Als Kämpfer habe ich gelebt und als Kämpfer werde ich
sterben!
Aus Edgar Andrés letzter Rede vor dem Sondergericht

Dem deutschen Helden Edgar André, der sein Leben auf
dem Richtblock ließ für die Freiheit seines Volkes und den
Frieden der Welt

EDGAR ANDRÉ

Should you nevertheless make the impossible possible and
bring a fighter to the executioner's block, I am ready to go
this difficult way; for I want no mercy.

As a fighter have I lived and as a fighter will I die!
From Edgar André's last speech before the special court

To the German hero Edgar André, who sacrificed his life on
the executioner's block for the freedom of his people and
world peace

Edgar André was a Communist activist (see also 24/36).

Dem deutschen Helden Edgar André, der sein
Leben auf dem Richtblock ließ für die Freiheit
seines Volkes und den Frieden der Welt

EDGAR
ANDRÉ

Sollten Sie trotzdem

das Unmögliche möglich machen

und einen Kämpfer zum Richtblock bringen,

so bin ich bereit, diesen schweren Gang zu gehen;

denn ich will keine Gnade.

Als Kämpfer habe ich gelebt und als Kämpfer werde ich sterben!

Fotomontage: John Heartfield

Aus Edgar Andrés letzter Rede vor dem Sondergericht

MADRID 1936

¡NO PASARAN! ¡PASAREMOS!
Sie kommen nicht durch! Wir kommen durch!

MADRID 1936

THEY SHALL NOT PASS! WE SHALL PASS!
They shall not pass! We shall pass!

This was the back cover of a special issue on Spain that included
(pp. 228–29) an article entitled "Madrid, die heroische Stadt"
(Madrid, the heroic city).

At the start of November 1936 the insurgents threatened
Madrid. By the end of the month there was a stalemate. See also 29/37.

MADRID 1936

¡NO PASARAN! PASAREMOS!
Sie kommen nicht durch! Wir kommen durch!

Fremdenlegionäre fern vom Schuß

Nichts liegt ferner uns als Lüge, aber Franco ist unser Held,
ihm erfinden wir seine Siege, denn dazu sind wir bestellt.

Vor 3 Wochen, am 8. und 9. November, meldete eine
hochlöbliche Weltpresse die Einnahme Madrids. Der Berliner
"Angriff" leitete die Meldung mit den Worten ein: "Seit
Wochen hoffen wir Zeitungsmänner auf den Fall Madrids!"
Und wenn sie nicht gestorben sind, so hoffen sie noch heute…

Foreign legionnaires far from the shooting

Nothing lies further from us than lies, but Franco is our hero,
we invent his victories for him, because that is what we've
been asked to do.

Three weeks ago, on 8 and 9 November, a venerated world
press reported the taking of Madrid. The Berlin "Angriff"
introduced the report with the words: "For weeks we
newspapermen have been hoping for the fall of Madrid!"
And unless they are dead, they are still hoping today…

The title links the pro-Franco world press and the foreign
legionnaires recruited by Franco in Spanish Morocco. Heartfield
adapted the colloquial saying "Weit vom Schuß sein" (literally, to be
far from the shooting), meaning to be miles away from the action.
The final sentence – "Und wenn sie nicht gestorben sind, so hoffen
sie noch heute…" – is an adaption of a traditional ending for fairy
tales: "Und wenn sie nicht gestorben sind, so leben sie noch heute"
(And unless they are dead, they are still living today).

Fremdenlegionäre fern vom Schuß

Vor 3 Wochen, am 8. und 9. November, meldete eine hochlöbliche Weltpresse die Einnahme Madrids. Der Berliner »Angriff« leitete die Meldung mit den Worten ein: „Seit Wochen hoffen wir Zeitungsmänner auf den Fall Madrids!" Und wenn sie nicht gestorben sind, so hoffen sie noch heute...

Nichts liegt ferner uns als Lüge,
aber Franco ist unser Held,
ihm erfinden wir seine Siege,
denn dazu sind wir bestellt.

Fotomontage: John Heartfield

Der Sinn des Paktes Berlin–Tokio

"Abgemacht. Wer nicht mit uns ist, ist Kommunist."

The meaning of the Berlin–Tokyo pact

"Settled. Whoever is not with us is a Communist."

The pact between Germany and Japan against the Communist
International was signed on 25 November 1936. See also 17/36.

Der Sinn des Paktes Berlin—Tokio

„Abgemacht. Wer nicht mit uns ist, ist Kommunist."

Fotomontage: John Heartfield

Die Mütter an ihre Söhne in Francos Diensten

Ich habe dich unter den Palmen Marokkos getragen…
Ich habe dich in Hamburg zur Schule geschickt…
Ich habe dich, mein Kind, in Rom ans Herz gedrückt…

Und jetzt?
Ihr sprecht fremde Zungen,
Könnt einander nicht fragen,
Wozu man euch gedungen,
Auf wen man euch hetzt.
So lasst uns Mütter es euch sagen:

Wir grämen uns um euch, ihr Jungen.
Nein, wir haben euch nicht zu Mördern erzogen.
Ihr lasst euch missbrauchen. Ihr seid betrogen!
Die Feinde, gegen die man euch schickt,
Sind Feinde der Not, die auch uns bedrückt,
Sind Feinde des Kriegs, der die Welt bedroht.
Man heisst euch, die Freiheit in Spanien erschlagen,
Auf dass wir weiter die Knechtschaft ertragen.
Ihr wagt euer Leben. Wagt mehr! Wagt zu denken!
Weigert euch, eure Brüder zu henken!
Fluch eurem Gehorsam, eurem falschen Mut!
Wisst ihr denn nicht, was ihr tut?!
An euren Waffen klebt unser Blut…

Wieland Herzfelde.

The mothers to their sons in the service of Franco

I bore you under the palm trees of Morocco…
I sent you to school in Hamburg…
I hugged you, my child, in Rome…

And now?
You speak in foreign tongues,
Cannot ask one another,
For what you were hired,
Whom you are hounding.
So permit us mothers to tell you:

We grieve for you, young ones.
No, we did not raise you to murder.
You are allowing yourselves to be abused. You have been betrayed!
The enemies against whom you have been sent
Are enemies of the poverty that also troubles us,
Are enemies of the war that threatens the world.
You are ordered to kill liberty in Spain,
So that we continue to endure slavery.
You risk your lives. Risk more! Dare to think!
Refuse to execute your brothers!
Damned be your obedience, your false courage!
Don't you know what you are doing?!
Our blood sticks to your weapons…

Wieland Herzfelde.

The first verse alludes to three areas that were providing military support to Franco: Spanish Morocco, Nazi Germany, and Fascist Italy.

Die Mütter an ihre Söhne in Francos Diensten

Ich habe dich unter den Palmen Marokkos getragen...
Ich habe dich in Hamburg zur Schule geschickt...
Ich habe dich, mein Kind, in Rom ans Herz gedrückt...

Und jetzt?
Ihr sprecht fremde Zungen,
Könnt einander nicht fragen,
Wozu man euch gedungen,
Auf wen man euch hetzt.
So lasst uns Mütter es euch sagen:

Wir grämen uns um euch, ihr Jungen.
Nein, wir haben euch nicht zu Mördern erzogen.
Ihr lasst euch missbrauchen. Ihr seid betrogen!
Die Feinde, gegen die man euch schickt,
Sind Feinde der Not, die auch uns bedrückt,
Sind Feinde des Kriegs, der die Welt bedroht.
Man heisst euch, die Freiheit in Spanien erschlagen,
Auf dass wir weiter die Knechtschaft ertragen.
Ihr wagt euer Leben. Wagt mehr! Wagt zu denken!
Weigert euch, eure Brüder zu henken!
Fluch eurem Gehorsam, eurem falschen Mut!
Wisst ihr denn nicht, was ihr tut?!
An euren Waffen klebt unser Blut...

Wieland Herzfelde

Fotomontage: John Heartfield

44/36. **VI** 1, NUMBER 20, 30 DECEMBER 1936, PAGE 305

Noch immer kein "Friede auf Erden"

Heute Spanien.... Morgen die Welt?
Es darf nicht sein. Schließt die Reihn!
Reicht euch die Hände. Macht dem Frevel ein Ende!

Still no "Peace on Earth"

Today Spain.... Tomorrow the world?
It must not be. Close ranks!
Join hands. End the outrage!

For a list of montages on the Spanish Civil War, see 28/36.

VI

DIE VOLKS-ILLUSTRIERTE

JAHRGANG 1936 ● NR. 2?
30. DEZEMBER

Noch immer kein „Friede auf Erden"

Heute Spanien .... Morgen die Welt?
Es darf nicht sein. Schließt die Reihn!
Reicht euch die Hände. Macht dem Frevel ein Ende!

Fotomontage: John Heartfield

So muss es kommen!

Die deutsche Schmach zerstört vom Zorn des Volkes.

1937 wird das Jahr der deutschen Volksfront sein

It is bound to happen this way!

The German disgrace destroyed by the anger of the people.

1937 will be the year of the German Popular Front

For the Nazis, the Treaty of Versailles was always "die deutsche Schmach" (the German disgrace). *Konzentrationslager* is a concentration camp.

This montage appeared in the special issue "Die Hölle Dachau" (The hell of Dachau).

So muss es kommen!

Die deutsche Schmach zerstört vom Zorn des Volkes.

1937 wird das Jahr der deutschen Volksfront sein

Fotomontage: John Heartfield

Ein Millionär möchte den Ersatz-"Sozialismus" retten

Deterding:
"Nazis, haltet durch! Ich bringe für einen halben Tag Lebensmittel"

Der Ölkönig Henry Deterding will dem Deutschen Reich mit Lebensmitteln im Werte von 10 Millionen holländischen Gulden zur Linderung der Ernährungsschwierigkeiten zu Hilfe kommen.

A millionaire would like to save the ersatz "Socialism"

Deterding:
"Nazis, don't give up! I am bringing half a day's provisions"

The oil king Henry Deterding wants to come to the aid of the German Reich with provisions worth 10 million Dutch guilders for alleviating food crises.

Henry Deterding (1865–1939) was a Dutch oil magnate with Nazi sympathies (see also 5/33). Heartfield was suggesting that the "Ersatz-'Sozialismus'" of National Socialism was as fake as the "Ersatz-Kaffee" that had been introduced to further economic autarky.

Ein Millionär möchte den Ersatz-„Sozialismus" retten

Der Ölkönig Henry Deterding will dem Deutschen Reich mit Lebensmitteln im Werte von 10 Millionen holländischen Gulden zur Linderung der Ernährungsschwierigkeiten zu Hilfe kommen.

Deterding:

„Nazis, haltet durch! Ich bringe für einen halben Tag Lebensmittel"

Fotomontage: John Heartfield

Blut für Eisen

Absender: SS Leibstandarte München
Empfänger: Franco u. Co.

Ladung: Eisenerz
Bestimmungsort: *Essen, Krupp*
Absender: >Mines del Rif<
Span. Marokko

Blood for iron

Sender: SS bodyguard Munich
Recipient: Franco & Co.

Freight: Iron ore
Destination: *Essen, Krupp*
Sender: >Rif mines<
Span. Morocco

The title alludes to Bismarck's famous "blood and iron" speech of 1886 (see 10/34). The montage implies that the Third Reich's policy toward Spain was in fact aimed at satisfying the demand for raw materials for the Nazi armaments program: German military aid in exchange for Spanish iron ore.

Absender:
SS Leibstandarte München
Empfänger:
Franco u. Co.

Ladung:
Eisenerz
Bestimmungsort:
Essen, Krupp
Absender:
»Minas del Rif«
Span. Marokko

Blut für Eisen

Fotomontage: John Heartfield

Ist es auch Wahnsinn, hat es doch Methode

"Besichtigung? Nein, meine Herren! Kommt gar nicht in Frage. Ich kann nicht zulassen, daß es keine Sowjetflugplätze in der Tschechoslowakei gibt. Wir brauchen sie, um das Volk aufzuklären. Man muß endlich begreifen:
der Augenschein ist eine jüdisch-materialistische Erfindung".

Der Propagandaapparat des III. Reichs verbreitet systematisch das Märchen von angeblichen Sowjetflugplätzen in der CSR. Die tschechoslowakische Regierung hat nun den deutschen und den englischen Militär-Attaché eingeladen, sich durch Augenschein vom wahren Sachverhalt zu überzeugen. Der Engländer nahm sofort an. Der deutsche Militärattaché lehnte auf Weisung von Berlin die Einladung zum Besuch aller Flugplätze "aus begreiflichen Gründen" ab.

Though this be madness, yet there is method in't

"Inspection? No, gentlemen! That's out of the question. I cannot concede that there are no Soviet airfields in Czechoslovakia. We need them to enlighten the people. We must finally realize:
the inspection is a Jewish-materialist invention."

The propaganda machine of the Third Reich systematically spreads the fairy tale of alleged Soviet airfields in Czechoslovakia. The Czechoslovakian government has now invited the German and English military attachés to see the truth with their own eyes. The Englishman accepted immediately. The German military attaché, on orders from Berlin, refused the invitation to visit all airfields "for understandable reasons."

The headline is a quote from *Hamlet* (Act 2, Scene 2). Goebbels, the human megaphone, announces: "Bolschewistische Flugplätze bei Prag / Tschechisches Paddelboot rammt deutsche Hochseeflotte" (Bolshevik airfields in Prague / Czech paddleboat rams German battle fleet).

An article in this issue of *VI* (p. 78) and one published 27 January 1937 (no. 4, p. 52) considered Nazi threats to Czechoslovakia and drew parallels with Spain.

Ist es auch Wahnsinn, hat es doch Methode

Der Propagandaapparat des III. Reichs verbreitet systematisch das Märchen von angeblichen Sowjetflugplätzen in der ČSR. Die tschechoslowakische Regierung hat nun den deutschen und den englischen Militär-Attaché eingeladen, sich durch Augenschein vom wahren Sachverhalt zu überzeugen. Der Engländer nahm sofort an. Der deutsche Militärattaché lehnte auf Weisung von Berlin die Einladung zum Besuch aller Flugplätze „aus begreiflichen Gründen" ab.

Bolschewistische Flugplätze bei Prag

Tschechisches Paddelboot rammt deutsche Hochseeflotte

„Besichtigung? Nein, meine Herren! Kommt gar nicht in Frage. Ich kann nicht zulassen, daß es keine Sowjetflugplätze in der Tschechoslowakei gibt. Wir brauchen sie, um das Volk aufzuklären. Man muß endlich begreifen: der Augenschein ist eine jüdisch-materialistische Erfindung".

Fotomontage: John Heartfield

Kriegsgeld 1917/1937

Und da spricht man noch von einer Katastrophe, wenn ein
Fetzen Papiers abgewertet wird.
Aus Hitlers Rede am 30.1.1937.

Beitrag der "VI" für die von Hitler angekündigte Ausstellung
der Wunder des ersten Vierjahrplans

War money 1917/1937

And they still talk about a catastrophe, when a scrap of
paper is being devalued.
From Hitler's speech on 1/30/1937.

"VI"'s contribution to the exhibition, heralded by Hitler, of
the miracles of the first Four Year Plan

On the "scrap of paper," see 12/36. Heartfield was comparing the
contemporary situation with the multiple currencies that existed in
1917.

Kriegsgeld 1917/1937

Und da spricht man noch von einer Katastrophe, wenn ein Fetzen Papiers abgewertet wird.

Aus Hitlers Rede am 30. I. 1937.

Register-Mark
Kredit-Sperrmark
Effekten-Sperrmark
Auswanderer-Sperrmark
Noten-Sperrmark
Tilgungs-Sperrmark
Sperr-Mark
Reise-Mark
Silber-Mark

Beitrag der „VJ" für die von Hitler angekündigte Ausstellung der Wunder des ersten Vierjahrplans

Fotomontage: John Heartfield

Durch Einheit zum Sieg

Es fiel Brachet, ein Sozialist. / Es fiel Hans Beimler,
Kommunist. / Es fiel Joža Majek, ein junger Christ. / Es fiel
Durutti, ein Anarchist.

Wofür sind sie gefallen?

I. Er war Student und Journalist.
    Jung-Belgiens bester Mann.
    Den Weg zur Einheit, ohne List,
    Ging Pierre Brachet voran.

II. Metallarbeit war sein Beruf.
    Das Dritte Reich sein Feld,
    Wo illegale Kader schuf
    Hans Beimler, deutscher Held.

III. Er teilte in der Slowakei
     Mit Bauern Brot und Wein.
     Für seine christliche Partei
     Trat Joža Majek ein.

IV. Sein Leben: Kampf und Rebellion!
    Verfolgt, vom Tod bedroht.
    Trug Kataloniens stolzer Sohn
    Durutti jede Not.

Vier Männer. Ungleich Weg und Ziel.
Verschieden Land und Wort.
Doch als man Spanien überfiel,
War aller Zwiespalt fort.

Für Frieden auf Erden, für Freiheit und Recht,
Gingen als Brüder sie ins Gefecht,
Ein Beispiel der Einheit uns Allen:
Der Anarchist, der junge Christ, der Kommunist, der
Sozialist.

Dafür sind sie gefallen!

Wieland Herzfelde

Through unity to victory

Brachet, a Socialist, died in action. / Hans Beimler, a
Communist, died in action. / Joža Majek, a Young Christian,
died in action. / Durutti, an anarchist, died in action.

For what did they die?

I. He was a student and journalist.
    Young Belgium's best man.
    Sincerely, Pierre Brachet
    Showed the way to unity.

II. Metalwork was his profession.
    The Third Reich his field of operation
    Where he created illegal cadres
    Hans Beimler, German hero.

III. In Slovakia he shared
     Bread and wine with peasants.
     Joža Majek committed himself
     To his Christian Party.

IV. His life: struggle and rebellion!
    Persecuted, threatened with death.
    Catalonia's proud son
    Durutti bore each misery.

Four men. Different outlooks.
Different country and language.
Yet as Spain was invaded,
All discord was gone.

For peace on earth, for freedom and justice,
They went into combat as brothers,
An example of unity to us all:
The Anarchist, the Young Christian, the Communist, the
Socialist.

For that they died!

Wieland Herzfelde

The Heartfield-Herzfelde montage is a celebration of the International
Brigade, Communists and leftist sympathizers from many countries
who went to fight in Spain on the Republican side. It appeared in a
special issue called "Das Gesicht des Republikanischen Spanien"
(The face of Republican Spain).

Durch Einheit zum Sieg

Es fiel Brachet,   Es fiel Hans Beimler,   Es fiel Joža Majek,   Es fiel Dürütti,
ein Sozialist.   Kommunist.   ein junger Christ.   ein Anarchist.

Wofür sind sie gefallen?

I. Er war Student und Journalist.   II. Metallarbeit war sein Beruf.
    Jung-Belgiens bester Mann.   Das Dritte Reich sein Feld,
    Den Weg zur Einheit, ohne List,   Wo illegale Kader schuf
    Ging Pierre Brachet voran.   Hans Beimler, deutscher Held.

III. Er leibte in der Slowakei   IV. Sein Leben: Kampf und Rebellion!
     Mit Bauern Brot und Wein.   Verfolgt, vom Tod bedroht.
     Für seine christliche Partei   Trug Kataloniens stolzer Sohn
     Trat Joža Majek ein.   Dürütti jede Not.

Vier Männer. Ungleich Weg und Ziel   Für Frieden auf Erden, für Freiheit und Recht,
Verschieden Land und Wort.   Gingen als Brüder sie ins Gefecht,
Doch als man Spanien überfiel,   Ein Beispiel der Einheit uns Allen:
War aller Zwiespalt fort.   Der Anarchist, der junge Christ, der Kommunist, der Sozialist.

Dafür sind sie gefallen!

Fotomontage: John Heartfield   Wieland Herzfelde.

Bild ohne Worte...

aber nur einstweilen, denn unsere Leser sollen diesmal den Text dazu finden. Wir werden den Einsender des besten Textes – es kann eine einfache Titelzeile sein, aber auch ein Gedicht oder eine kleine Fabel – durch einen Buchpreis auszeichnen.

Picture without words...

but only temporarily, for this time our readers shall find the text to go with it. The sender of the best text – it could be simply a title or a poem or little fable – will be rewarded with a book prize.

A selection from the 711 entries *VI* received appeared in the 26 May issue (no. 21, p. 337). On the links between the arms manufacturer Krupp and Nazism, see also 2/34.

Bild ohne Worte...

aber nur einstweilen, denn unsere Leser sollen diesmal den Text dazu finden. Wir werden den Einsender
des besten Textes - es kann eine einfache Titelzeile
sein, aber auch ein Gedicht oder eine kleine Fabel -
durch einen Buchpreis auszeichnen.

KRUPP

Fotomontage: John Heartfield

Deutscher Mütter Los

"Was hat sie denn verbrochen?"
"Sie trägt Trauer, weil ihr Sohn im Krieg gegen Spanien gefallen ist".

"Den Angehörigen der in Spanien gefallenen deutschen Soldaten wird mitgeteilt, daß ihr Sohn oder Bruder "im Manöver tödlich verunglückt" ist. Sie erhalten gleichzeitig strengste Weisung, über den Fall nicht zu sprechen. Das Tragen von Trauerkleidung wird ihnen verboten, und es sind Fälle bekannt, in denen Mütter wegen Übertretung dieses Verbots verhaftet wurden." Meldungen englischer Berichterstatter aus Berlin.

The fate of German mothers

"What is her offense?"
"She is wearing black, because her son fell in the war against Spain."

"The families of German soldiers killed in Spain are notified that their son or brother had 'a fatal accident during maneuvers.' At the same time they are given the strictest orders not to talk about the case. They are forbidden to wear mourning, and there are known cases of mothers being arrested for violating this rule." English journalists' reports from Berlin.

Deutscher Mütter Los

"Den Angehörigen der in Spanien gefallenen deutschen Soldaten wird mitgeteilt, daß ihr Sohn oder Bruder »im Manöver tödlich verunglückt« ist. Sie erhalten gleichzeitig strengste Weisung, über den Fall nicht zu sprechen. Das Tragen von Trauerkleidung wird ihnen verboten, und es sind Fälle bekannt, in denen Mütter wegen Übertretung dieses Verbots verhaftet wurden." Meldungen englischer Berichterstatter aus Berlin.

„Was hat sie denn verbrochen?"
„Sie trägt Trauer, weil ihr Sohn im Krieg gegen Spanien gefallen ist".

Fotomontage: John Heartfield

In der Sackgasse

"Aus Butter Kanonen machen, das ging…aber jetzt möcht'
ich wissen: wie macht man aus Kanonen wieder Butter?"

At a dead end

"Making guns from butter, that worked…but now I'd like
to know: how do you change guns back into butter?"

This is another reference to Göring's "guns before butter" speech,
which is satirized in 26/35.

In der Sackgasse

„Aus Butter Kanonen machen, das ging... aber jetzt möcht'
ich wissen: wie macht man aus Kanonen wieder Butter?"

Fotomontage: John Heartfield

Unterhaltung im Grab

Das Schwarzhemd: "Wieso kommst denn du hierher in die spanische Erde, Kamerad?"
Das Braunhemd: "Durch die Nichteinmischung."
Das Schwarzhemd: "Ich auch."

Conversation in the grave

The Blackshirt: "How did you end up here in the Spanish earth, comrade?"
The Brownshirt: "Through nonintervention."
The Blackshirt: "Me too."

An article titled "Die faschistische Einmischung in Spanien – eine Kriegserklärung an Europa" (The Fascist intervention in Spain – a declaration of war against Europe) appeared in *VI* two weeks later (no. 14 [7 April 1937], pp. 210–11).

Unterhaltung im Grab

Das Schwarzhemd: „Wieso kommst denn du hierher
in die spanische Erde, Kamerad?"
Das Braunhemd: „Durch die Nichteinmischung."
Das Schwarzhemd: „Ich auch."

Fotomontage: John Heartfield

11/37. **VI** 1937, NUMBER 15, 14 APRIL, PAGE 237

Die Saat des Todes

Wo dieser Sämann geht durchs Land,
Erntet er Hunger, Krieg und Brand.

The seeds of death

Where this sower walks through the country,
He reaps hunger, war and fire.

Die Saat des Todes

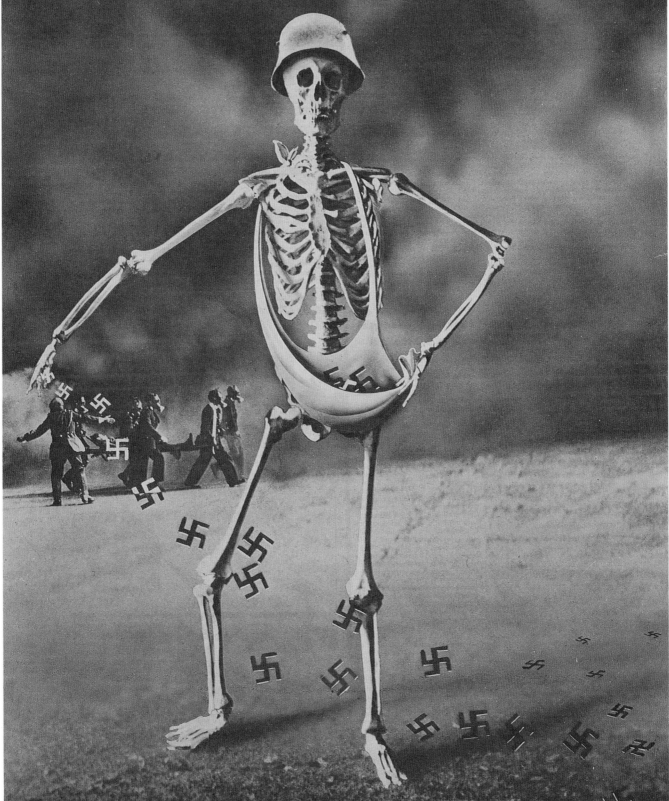

Wo dieser Sämann geht durchs Land,
Erntet er Hunger, Krieg und Brand.

Fotomontage: John Heartfield

Die Stimme der Freiheit in deutscher Nacht – auf Welle 29,8

Gewidmet dem "Schwarzsender", der Abend für Abend "trotz Gestapo" den Kampf für Frieden, Freiheit und Demokratie führt.

The voice of freedom in the German night – on wavelength 29.8

Dedicated to the "underground radio station," which night after night, "despite the Gestapo," leads the struggle for peace, freedom and democracy.

Facing the montage was a one-page article, "Der Sender auf Welle 29,8" (The radio station on wavelength 29.8).

Gewidmet dem »Schwarzsender«, der Abend für Abend „trotz Gestapo" den Kampf für Frieden, Freiheit und Demokratie führt.

Die Stimme der Freiheit in deutscher Nacht – auf Welle 29,8

Fotomontage: John Heartfield

Der Gipfel ihrer Wirtschaftsweisheit

"Noch nie, solange die Erde besteht, ist so viel Blech geredet und gesammelt worden."

Die Fahne hoch,
die Butter ist verschwunden…

The summit of their economic wisdom

"Never before, as long as the earth has existed, has so much rubbish been talked and collected."

Raise the flag,
the butter has disappeared…

Gipfel here means not only summit but also limit, as in "Das ist der Gipfel!" (That's the limit!). *Blech* is sheet metal or tinplate. *Blech reden* means to talk nonsense; a *Blechdose* is a tin can. As an economy measure, tin cans were collected for industrial recycling. Heartfield also made use of the double meaning in 4/32, *Adolf der Übermensch: Schluckt Gold und redet Blech* (Adolf the Superman: Swallows gold and spouts rubbish).

"Die Fahne hoch" (Raise the flag) evokes the "Horst-Wessel-Lied," the Nazi Party anthem (see 2/34): "Die Fahne hoch! Die Reihen fest geschlossen!" (Raise the flag! Close ranks!).

Der Gipfel
ihrer
Wirtschaftsweisheit

Die Fahne hoch, die Butter ist verschwunden...

„Noch nie, solange die Erde besteht, ist so viel Blech geredet und gesammelt worden."

Fotomontage: John Heartfield

"Liberté, Liberté chérie, combat avec tes défenseurs!"

"Freiheit, geliebte Freiheit, kämpfe mit deinen Verteidigern!"
Aus der "Marseillaise"

Dem Volk von Frankreich gewidmet

"Liberty, beloved liberty, fight with your defenders!"

"Liberty, beloved liberty, fight with your defenders!"
From the "Marseillaise"

Dedicated to the people of France

The French national anthem, the "Marseillaise," written in 1792, was the hymn of the French Revolution. This was a special May Day issue. Facing the montage was a selection of pictures and reports from Popular Front France.

„Liberté, Liberté chérie, combat avec tes défenseurs!"

FRONT POPULAIRE

1er mai 1937

Dem Volk von Frankreich gewidmet

Fotomontage: John Heartfield

„Freiheit, geliebte Freiheit, kämpfe mit deinen Verteidigern!"

Aus der „Marseillaise"

Der friedfertige Raubfisch

"Ich verabscheue die kollektive Sicherheit! Ich lade die kleinen Fische einzeln ein, zweiseitige Verträge mit mir abzuschließen".

The peaceful fish of prey

"I abhor collective security! I invite the little fishes to conclude individual bilateral pacts with me."

This montage was illustrated in a report in the Nazi organ *Völkischer Beobachter* on 14 October 1937 (no. 287, p. 8) as an example of the anti-German art being openly exhibited in Prague. The hybrid clearly has Göring's stomach.

Der friedfertige Raubfisch

„Ich verabscheue die kollektive Sicherheit! Ich lade die kleinen Fische einzeln ein, zweiseitige Verträge mit mir abzuschließen".

Fotomontage: John Heartfield

DIE URSACHE

Autarkie

Das verunglückte Luftschiff "Hindenburg" war zwecks Devisenersparnis mit dem hochexplosiven Wasserstoffgas gefüllt, statt mit dem nichtbrennenden Heliumgas, weil der "Vierjahrplan" infolge der riesigen Rüstungsausgaben die Autarkie (Selbstgenügsamkeit und Abschließung von der Weltwirtschaft) auf allen anderen Gebieten durchführen muß.

THE CAUSE

Autarky

To save foreign currency, the perished airship "Hindenburg" was filled with highly explosive hydrogen gas instead of nonflammable helium gas. This was because the "Four Year Plan," on account of the gigantic armaments expenses, must exercise autarky (self-sufficiency and isolation from the world economy) in all other areas.

DIE URSACHE

Autarkie

Das verunglückte Luftschiff »Hindenburg« war zwecks Deviseneinsparnis mit dem hochexplosiven Wasserstoffgas gefüllt, statt mit dem nichtbrennenden Heliumgas, weil der „Vierjahrplan" infolge der riesigen Rüstungsausgaben die Autarkie (Selbstgenügsamkeit und Abschließung von der Weltwirtschaft) auf allen anderen Gebieten durchführen muß.

Fotomontage: John Heartfield

Baskenland

Zur "Woche der Internationalen Solidarität mit Spanien 24.–30. Mai"

Das Oberhaupt des baskischen Landes, Präsident Aguirre, Führer der katholischen Nationalpartei, erhielt von dem berliner Botschafter Chiles Porto Seguro ein Telegramm, in dem er ersucht wurde, die zwei vom baskischen Kriegsgericht wegen Bombardierung offener Städte und Teilnahme an einer hochverräterischen Rebellion zum Tode verurteilten Nazi-flieger Kienzle und Schulz zu begnadigen. Darauf sandte Aguirre folgendes Antworttelegramm: "Ich verstehe das Interesse und die menschlichen Beweggründe Ew. Exzellenz, kann aber nicht umhin, unserem Erstaunen über das Still-schweigen Ausdruck zu verleihen, das angesichts des unmen-schlichen Bombardements Guernicas zur Schau getragen wurde. Bei diesem und anderen Bombardements wurden in Durango 2000 Zivilisten, in Bilbao, Amorebieta und Eibar 600 Frauen und Kinder getötet…"
Meldung der "Times", London

Basque country

On the occasion of the "Week of International Solidarity with Spain 24–30 May"

The head of the Basque country, President Aguirre, leader of the Catholic National Party, received a telegram from Chile's ambassador in Berlin, Porto Seguro, in which he had requested amnesty for the two Nazi pilots, Kienzle and Schulz, sentenced to death by a Basque war tribunal for bombarding unprotected cities and participating in a treasonable rebellion. Aguirre sent the following telegram in reply: "I understand the interest and the humanitarian motives of Your Excellency, but cannot refrain from expressing our astonishment at the silence concerning the inhumane bombardment of Guernica. As a result of this and other bombardments, 2,000 civilians in Durango and 600 women and children in Bilbao, Amorebieta and Eibar were killed…"
Report in the "Times," London

Guernica, the ancient capital of the Basques, was bombed by German planes on 27 April 1937.

Baskenland

Das Oberhaupt des baskischen Landes, Präsident Aguirre, Führer der katholischen Nationalpartei, erhielt von dem berliner Botschafter Chiles Porto Seguro ein Telegramm, in dem er ersucht wurde, die zwei vom baskischen Kriegsgericht wegen Bombardierung offener Städte und Teilnahme an einer hochverräterischen Rebellion zum Tode verurteilten Naziflieger Kienzle und Schulz zu begnadigen. Darauf sandte Aguirre folgendes Antworttelegramm: »Ich verstehe das Interesse und die menschlichen Beweggründe Ew. Exzellenz, kann aber nicht umhin, unserem Erstaunen über das Stillschweigen Ausdruck zu verleihen, das angesichts des unmenschlichen Bombardements Guernicas zur Schau getragen wurde. **Bei diesem und anderen Bombardements wurden in Durango 2000 Zivilisten, in Bilbao, Amorebieta und Eibar 600 Frauen und Kinder getötet...«**
Meldung der »Times«, London

Fotomontage: John Heartfield

Den katholischen Opfern des Faschismus zum Gedenken! Allen katholischen Männern und Frauen zur Mahnung!

In Durango getötet durch faschistische Flieger: 12 Nonnen, 2 Priester. – In Durango zerstört durch dieselben Flieger: Kloster der Augustinerinnen, Jesuitenkirche, Kirche Santa Maria. – In Eibar getötet durch Junkersbomber: 112 katholische Männer, Frauen, Kinder und Geistliche. – In Amorebieta und Bilbao getötet durch Junkers- und Heinkelbomber: 480 katholische Männer, Frauen, Kinder und Geistliche. – In Guernica getötet durch national-sozialistische Flieger Francos: 2000 Zivilpersonen, darunter die Mehrzahl Frauen und Kinder sowie mehrere Nonnen und Priester, alles katholische Basken. – In Guernica zerstört durch die gleichen Flieger: alle Kirchen bis auf eine einzige. – In Amorebieta zerstört durch Heinkelbomber: das abseits liegende, deutlich gekennzeichnete Augustinerkloster. – In Madrid zerstört seit Beginn der Belagerung: sieben Kirchen; beschädigt: fast alle. – In Almería zerstört durch die Schiffsgeschütze der deutschen Flotte: die Kathedrale, die Kirche des Heiligen Sebastian und das Hospiz. – [repeated]

Christus Marmorstatue von Balthasar Permoser (1651–1732)

In memory of the Catholic victims of Fascism! A warning to all Catholic men and women!

In Durango killed by Fascist pilots: 12 nuns, 2 priests. – In Durango destroyed by the same pilots: Augustinian monastery, Jesuit church, church of Santa Maria. – In Eibar killed by Junkers bombers: 112 Catholic men, women, children and clerics. – In Amorebieta and Bilbao killed by Junkers and Heinkel bombers: 480 Catholic men, women, children and clerics. – In Guernica killed by Franco's National Socialist pilots: 2,000 civilians, the majority women and children, as well as several nuns and priests, all Catholic Basques. – In Guernica destroyed by the same pilots: all churches except one. – In Amorebieta destroyed by Heinkel bombers: the out-of-the-way and clearly identifiable Augustinian monastery. – In Madrid destroyed since the beginning of the siege: seven churches; damaged: almost all. – In Almería destroyed by the naval guns of the German fleet: the cathedral, the church of Saint Sebastian and the hospice. – [repeated]

Marble statue of Christ by Balthasar Permoser (1651–1732)

In Durango getötet durch faschistische Flieger: 12 Nonnen, 2 Priester. — In Durango zerstört durch dieselben Flieger: Kloster der Augustinerinnen, Jesuitenkirche, Kirche Santa Maria. — In Eibar getötet durch Junkersbomber: 112 katholische Männer, Frauen, Kinder und Geistliche. — In Amorebieta und Bilbao getötet durch Junkers- und Heinkelbomber: 480 katholische Männer, Frauen, Kinder und Geistliche. — In Guernica getötet durch nationalsozialistische Flieger Francos: 2000 Zivilpersonen, darunter die Mehrzahl Frauen und Kinder sowie mehrere Nonnen und Priester, alles katholische Basken. — In Guernica zerstört durch die gleichen Flieger: alle Kirchen bis auf eine einzige. — In Amorebieta zerstört durch Heinkelbomber: das abseits liegende, deutlich gekennzeichnete Augustinerkloster. — In Madrid zerstört seit Beginn der Belagerung: sieben Kirchen; beschädigt: fast alle. — In Almería zerstört durch die Schiffsgeschütze der deutschen Flotte: die Kathedrale, die Kirche des Heiligen Sebastian und das Hospiz. — In Durango getötet durch faschistische Flieger: 12 Nonnen, 2 Priester. — In Durango zerstört durch dieselben Flieger: Kloster der Augustinerinnen, Jesuitenkirche, Kirche Santa Maria. — In Eibar getötet durch Junkersbomber: 112 katholische Männer, Frauen, Kinder und Geistliche. — In Amorebieta und Bilbao getötet durch Junkers- und Heinkelbomber: 480 katholische Männer, Frauen, Kinder und Geistliche. — In Guernica getötet durch nationalsozialistische Flieger Francos: 2000 Zivilpersonen, darunter die Mehrzahl Frauen und Kinder sowie mehrere Nonnen und Priester, alles katholische Basken. — In Guernica zerstört durch die gleichen Flieger: alle Kirchen bis auf eine einzige. — In Amorebieta zerstört durch Heinkelbomber: das abseits liegende, deutlich gekennzeichnete Augustinerkloster. — In Madrid zerstört seit Beginn der Belagerung; sieben Kirchen; beschädigt: fast alle. — In Almería zerstört durch die Schiffsgeschütze der deutschen Flotte: die Kathedrale, die Kirche des Heiligen Sebastian und das Hospiz. — In Durango getötet durch faschistische Flieger: 12 Nonnen, 2 Priester. — In Durango zerstört durch dieselben Flieger: Kloster der Augustinerinnen, Jesuitenkirche, Kirche Santa Maria. — In Eibar getötet durch Junkersbomber: 112 katholische Männer, Frauen, Kinder und Geistliche. — In Amorebieta und Bilbao getötet durch Junkers- und Heinkelbomber: 480 katholische Männer, Frauen, Kinder und Geistliche. — In Guernica getötet durch nationalsozialistische Flieger Francos: 2000 Zivilpersonen, darunter die Mehrzahl Frauen und Kinder sowie mehrere Nonnen und Priester, alles katholische Basken. — In Guernica zerstört durch die gleichen Flieger: alle Kirchen bis auf eine einzige. — In Amorebieta zerstört durch Heinkelbomber: das abseits liegende, deutlich gekennzeichnete Augustinerkloster. In Madrid zerstört seit Beginn der Belagerung: sieben Kirchen; beschädigt: fast alle. — In Almería die Schiffsgeschütze der deutschen Flotte: die k Heiligen S In Dura Flie

Den katholischen Opfern des Faschismus zum Gedenken!
Allen katholischen Männern und Frauen zur Mahnung!

Christus-Marmorstatue von Balthasar Permoser (1651-1732)   Fotomontage: John Heartfield

Briefmarken sprechen

Nicht nur Knaben interessieren sich leidenschaftlich für Briefmarken, auch viele Erwachsene sind Markensammler, Markenliebhaber. Doch nicht von philatelistischen Dingen soll hier die Rede sein, sondern von anderem.

Die Briefmarke ist – neben ihrem eigentlichen Zweck – längst nicht nur Sammler-Objekt, sondern auch Propaganda-Werkzeug.

Die Staaten benutzen die bunten Bilderchen, die durch Millionen Hände gehen, zur Propaganda von Ideen und Dingen, die ihnen wichtig erscheinen.

So wird die Briefmarke zum Zeugnis für Gesinnungen und Absichten: für friedliche und für unfriedliche, menschenfreundliche und menschenfeindliche.

Wer die Marken auf dieser Seite aufmerksam betrachtet, dem halten sie einen kleinen, aber sehr lehrreichen Vortrag über Sozialismus, Volksfront, Demokratie und Frieden auf der einen – über Kriegsvorbereitung, Menschenvernichtung, Faschismus auf der andern Seite.

Es ist vor allem die Jugend, die das Markensammeln betreibt – und die Erwachsenen sollten nicht verfehlen, den Marken in den Alben ihrer Söhne die Zunge zu lösen, auf daß sie zu sprechen beginnen: gegen Faschismus und Krieg und für den Frieden.

Postage stamps speak

It is not only boys who are passionately interested in postage stamps; many adults are also stamp collectors, stamp lovers. But we are talking here not about philatelic matters, but about other things.

The postage stamp – apart from its actual purpose – has long been not just a collector's item but also a propaganda tool. Governments use the pretty little pictures, which pass through millions of hands, to propagandize ideas and things they deem important.

Stamps thus become evidence of attitudes and aims: peaceful and unpeaceful, humane and inhumane.

Whoever carefully examines the stamps on this page will get a brief yet very instructive lecture on socialism, the Popular Front, democracy and peace on the one hand – about preparation for war, the extermination of people, Fascism on the other.

Above all it is the young who pursue stamp collecting – and adults should not fail to loosen the tongues of the stamps in their sons' albums, so that they begin to speak: against Fascism and war and for peace.

The inscription at the bottom reads: "Zusammengestellt von John Heartfield" (Compiled by John Heartfield). The stamps in the left column are from the Spanish and French Republics, Switzerland, the Netherlands, and Czechoslovakia; those in the center are from the Soviet Union; and those in the right column are from Fascist Germany and Italy.

Briefmarken sprechen

Nicht nur Knaben interessieren sich leidenschaftlich für Briefmarken, auch viele Erwachsene sind Markensammler, Markenliebhaber. Doch nicht von philatelistischen Dingen soll hier die Rede sein, sondern von anderem.

Die Briefmarke ist — neben ihrem eigentlichen Zweck — längst nicht nur Sammler-Objekt, sondern auch Propaganda-Werkzeug.

Die Staaten benutzen die bunten Bilderchen, die durch Millionen Hände gehen, zur Propaganda von Ideen und Dingen, die ihnen wichtig erscheinen.

So wird die Briefmarke zum Zeugnis für Gesinnungen und Absichten: für friedliche und für unfriedliche, menschenfreundliche und menschenfeindliche.

Wer die Marken auf dieser Seite aufmerksam betrachtet, dem halten sie einen kleinen, aber sehr lehrreichen Vortrag über Sozialismus, Volksfront, Demokratie und Frieden auf der einen — über Kriegsvorbereitung, Menschenvernichtung, Faschismus auf der andern Seite.

Es ist vor allem die Jugend, die das Markensammeln betreibt — und die Erwachsenen sollten nicht verfehlen, den Marken in den Alben ihrer Söhne die Zunge zu lösen, auf daß sie zu sprechen beginnen: gegen Faschismus und Krieg und für den Frieden.

Marken der spanischen Republik

Der Maler Velasquez   Spielende Kinder

Marken der französischen Volksfront-Regierung

Huldigung für den Frieden   Die Freiheitshymne

Jaurès, der große Friedenskämpfer

Der Dichter der Marseillaise

Der Dichter Victor Hugo

Pierre Corneille, der Dichter des spanischen Heldendramas „Le Cid"

Der Forscher Pasteur

„Für die arbeitslosen Geistesarbeiter"   „Für die Kinder der Arbeitslosen"

Der Humanist Erasmus von Rotterdam   Der Maler Rembrandt

Familienbild von Josef Mánes   „Wiegenlied", Relief von Sucharda

Marken der Sowjetunion

Das Grab Karl Marx'   Friedrich Engels   Solidaritäts-Marke

Der Dichter Puschkin   Kalinin, Staatsoberhaupt der RSFSR   Maxim Gorki

Fünf Anti-Kriegs-Marken

Kollektivwirtschaft

Arktis-Forschung   Befreiung der Nationen

Bau der Turk-Sib-Bahn

Marken des III. Reichs

Stahlhelme .. Stahlhelme .. Prachtbauten für Kriegszwecke

Marken des »Imperio fascista«

Zusammengestellt von John Heartfield

Der wahre Torpedo gegen den Frieden

HETZE GEGEN DIE SOWJETUNION
ERFUNDENER ANGRIFF AUF KREUZER LEIPZIG
BOMBARDIERUNG VON ALMERÍA
ZERSTÖRUNG VON GUERNICA
FALL WEIGEL – HETZE GEGEN DIE TSCHECHOSLOWAKEI
GRIFF NACH MAROKKO – HETZE GEGEN FRANKREICH

The real torpedo against peace

BAITING THE SOVIET UNION
FABRICATED ATTACK AGAINST THE CRUISER LEIPZIG
BOMBARDMENT OF ALMERÍA
DESTRUCTION OF GUERNICA
WEIGEL CASE – BAITING CZECHOSLOVAKIA
GRAB FOR MOROCCO – BAITING FRANCE

Nazi hostility toward the Soviet Union was a recurring theme in Heartfield's montages. See, for example, 35/34, 6/35, 8/35, 14/35, 16/35, 17/35.

On the page facing this montage was a complementary article, "Der Friede wird torpediert" (Peace is torpedoed), about the alleged attack by a Spanish Republican submarine on the German cruiser *Leipzig*. The Spanish towns of Almería and Guernica were victims of German attacks (see 17/37, 18/37). Bruno Weigel was a Reich German who was arrested in Czechoslovakia on espionage charges. The Nazi press and radio capitalized on his claim to have been tortured by Czechoslovak police (see also 23/37). That the Nazis were encouraging unrest in French Morocco was viewed by *VI* as a sign of the renewal of German colonial ambitions in Africa.

Der wahre Torpedo gegen den Frieden

Fotomontage: John Heartfield

Seit einem Jahr kämpft Spanien für die Freiheit und den Frieden!

For a year Spain has been struggling for liberty and peace!

This issue's theme was the Spanish Civil War, which had begun on 18 July 1936. For a list of other montages on the subject, see 28/36.

VI

DIE VOLKS-ILLUSTRIERTE

JAHRGANG 1937 • NR. 30 • 28. JUL

Fotomontage: John Heartfield

Seit einem Jahr kämpft Spanien für die Freiheit und den Frieden!

TOD DEM KRIEGSPOLYPEN!
Erst wenn wir ihn vernichtet haben,
"dann scheint die Sonn' ohn' Unterlass"

DEATH TO THE OCTOPUS OF WAR!
Only when we have destroyed him
"will the sun always shine"

The last line is from the Communist anthem, the "Internationale" (1871). The lead article in this issue, "August 1914 – August 1937," on the twenty-third anniversary of the outbreak of the First World War, saw Japanese intervention in northern China and German and Italian intervention in Spain as dangers to world peace.

TOD DEM KRIEGSPOLYPEN!
Erst wenn wir ihn vernichtet haben,
„dann scheint die Sonn' ohn' Unterlass"

Fotomontage: John Heartfield

Großer internationaler Lügenwettbewerb
unter dem Protektorat von Dr. Josef Goebbels

"Nur immer feste blasen, meine Herren! Wenn sie auch platzen, es bleibt doch immer etwas hängen."

Great international lies competition
under the protectorate of Dr. Joseph Goebbels

"Just keep on blowing hard, gentlemen! Even if they burst, something always sticks."

"Stickgas aus der Reichslügenküche" translates literally as nitrogen gas from the Reich lies factory. Each figure represents a newspaper: *Prager Montagsblatt, Völkischer Beobachter, Angriff, Prager Tagblatt, Le Matin,* and so on. "Geheimniße" (secrets) is written on the inflatable duck. The inscriptions on the balloons read: "Miaja seines Kommandos enthoben" (Miaja relieved of his command); "Krilenko verhaftet" (Krylenko under arrest); "Blücher abgesetzt" (Blücher dismissed); "Attentat auf Woroschilow" (Attempt on Voroshilov's life); "Dimitroff in Ungnade gefallen" (Dimitrov fallen out of favor); and "Fall Weigel" (The Weigel Case).

General Miaja (1878–1958) organized the Republican defense of Madrid. Nicolai Krylenko (1885–1938) commanded the Bolshevik forces in 1917–18 and later served as Lenin's private secretary and as people's commissar for justice (1931–36); he is believed to have been a victim of the Stalinist purges in 1938. General Vasily Blücher (1889–1936), whose original surname was Gurov and who used the pseudonym Galen, also fought in the Russian revolution and later served in the Far East; he was dismissed and disappeared in 1938. Kliment Voroshilov (1881–1969), people's commissar for defense from 1925 to 1940, survived the purges and eventually succeeded Stalin as president of the Presidium (1953–57). Georgi Dimitrov (see 23/33, 30/33), head of the Communist International from 1934 to 1943, also survived the purges. For the Weigel case, see 20/37.

Certainly some of the stories from the Soviet Union had a basis in fact.

Großer internationaler Lügenwettbewerb

unter dem Protektorat von Dr. Josef Goebbels

„Nur immer feste blasen, meine Herren! Wenn sie auch platzen, es bleibt doch immer etwas hängen."

Fotomontage: John Heartfield

Ob Nazimann, ob Samurai, es ist dieselbe Melodei.

"Wir führen keinen Krieg, wir säubern nur China von den Chinesen."

Whether Nazi, or Samurai, it is the same tune.

"We are not conducting a war, we are only clearing China of the Chinese."

In this context, *säubern* means to clean or clear and also to purge. The lead article in this issue was called "Mittelmeer und Fernost – die großen Gefahrenherde" (Mediterranean and Far East – the great trouble spots).

Ob Nazimann, ob Samurai, es ist dieselbe Melodei.

„Wir führen keinen Krieg, wir säubern nur China von den Chinesen."

Fotomontage: John Heartfield

Windstärke 1917

"Macht euch bereit, macht euch bereit, jetzt segeln wir in die GROSSE ZEIT!"

"Ich scheue mich nicht davor, die Brotkarte einzuführen. Ob das populär ist oder nicht, darauf pfeife ich." General Göring in Stuttgart.

Gale Force 1917

"Get ready, get ready, now we are sailing into GREAT TIMES!"

"I am not afraid of introducing bread-ration cards. Whether it's popular or not, I don't give a damn." General Göring in Stuttgart.

Food rationing had been introduced in Germany once before, in 1917.

Windstärke 1917

»Ich scheue mich nicht davor, die Brotkarte einzuführen.
Ob das populär ist oder nicht, darauf pfeife ich.«
General Göring in Stuttgart.

386103
Fettkarte
1/2 Pfd. 932070
1/2 Pfd. Brotka
50 Gramm Brot   50 Gramm Brot
50 Gramm Brot   50 Gramm Brot
406100
783 0   608400
Brotkarte
50 Gramm Brot   50 Gramm Brot   73064 Brotkarte
50 Gramm Brot   50 Gramm Brot   50 Gramm Brot   50 Gramm Brot
50 Gramm Brot   50 Gramm Brot

„Macht euch bereit, macht euch bereit, jetzt segeln wir in die GROSSE ZEIT!"

Fotomontage: John Heartfield

Mahnung

Heute noch seht ihr im Film den Krieg in anderen Ländern.
Doch wisset: wenn ihr nicht einig euch wehrt, mordet er
morgen auch euch!

Warning

Today you still see the war in other countries on film.
But know this: if you don't unite to defend yourselves,
tomorrow it will kill you too!

The montage appeared in a special issue on the war in China. In the
updated version, dated 1967 and signed "Heartfield / Herzfelde," that
was published in *John Heartfield, 1891–1968: Photomontages*
(1969), the words "in anderen Ländern" in the subtitle have become
"im fernen Vietnam" (in far-off Vietnam).

Mahnung

Heute noch seht ihr im Film den Krieg in anderen Ländern.
Doch wisset: wenn ihr nicht einig euch wehrt, mordet er morgen auch euch!

Fotomontage: John Heartfield

SCHACH DEN FRIEDENSSTÖRERN!

"Wenn die Sintflut hereinbricht, gibt es für niemand
Neutralität oder Entkommen...Die 90 Prozent, die in
Frieden, gesetzlichen Verhältnissen und Einvernehmen leben
wollen, müssen einen Weg finden, um ihrem Willen gegen
die 10 Prozent Friedensstörer Geltung zu verschaffen."
Roosevelt

"Der Friede ist unteilbar...Es kommt nicht auf die
Universalität an, sondern auf den Zusammenschluß der
Friedenskräfte gegen den Angreifer."   Litwinow

CHECK TO THE DISTURBERS OF THE PEACE!

"When the deluge engulfs us, there will be neutrality or
escape for no one...The 90 percent who want to live in
peace, as law-abiding citizens, must find a way to force
their will on the 10 percent who disturb the peace."
Roosevelt

"Peace is indivisible...It depends not upon universal
agreement, but upon the alliance of the powers of peace
against the attacker."   Litvinov

Franklin Delano Roosevelt (1882–1945) was president of the United
States from 1933 to 1945. Maksim Litvinov (1876–1951), a Soviet
politician and diplomat, led his country into the League of Nations in
1934 and championed collective security, especially against Nazi
Germany.

"Wenn die Sintflut hereinbricht, gibt es für niemand Neutralität oder Entkommen ... Die 90 Prozent, die in Frieden, gesetzlichen Verhältnissen und Einvernehmen leben wollen, müssen einen Weg finden, um ihrem Willen gegen die 10 Prozent Friedensstörer Geltung zu verschaffen."
Roosevelt

"Der Friede ist unteilbar ... Es kommt nicht auf die Universalität an, sondern auf den Zusammenschluß der Friedenskräfte gegen den Angreifer."
Litwinow

SCHACH DEN FRIEDENSSTÖRERN!

Fotomontage: John Heartfield

XX JAHRE SOWJETUNION

XX YEARS OF THE SOVIET UNION

This special issue commemorated the USSR's twentieth anniversary. The montage incorporates Vera Muchina's monument from the Soviet Pavilion at the International Exhibition in Paris in 1937.

EIN JAHR VERTEIDIGUNG DER SPANISCHEN HAUPTSTADT

Madrid! Madrid!
Die Welt, die Recht und Freiheit liebt, ist stolz auf deinen Namen.

Zu dieser Fotomontage wurden benutzt: ein Bild des seit einem Jahr der Beschießung trotzenden Telegrafengebäudes in Madrid und eine Aufnahme des "Denkmals der ersten Madrider Milizen" in Valencia.

A YEAR OF DEFENDING THE SPANISH CAPITAL

Madrid! Madrid!
The world that loves justice and liberty is proud of your name.

Used for this photomontage were a picture of the telegraph building in Madrid that has been braving a year of bombardment and a photograph of the "Monument of the First Madrid Militia" in Valencia.

On the siege of Madrid, see also 40/36.

EIN JAHR
VERTEIDIGUNG
DER SPANISCHEN
HAUPTSTADT

Zu dieser Fotomontage wurden benutzt: ein Bild des seit einem Jahr der Beschießung trotzenden Telegrafengebäudes in Madrid und eine Aufnahme des »Denkmals der ersten Madrider Milizen« in Valencia.

Madrid! Madrid!
Die Welt, die Recht und Freiheit liebt, ist stolz auf deinen Namen.

Fotomontage: John Heartfield

Stamm und Rembte zum Gedächtnis

Sie sind ermordet worden, doch sie leben weiter, solang es
Deutsche gibt, die ihre Helden ehren.

Am 4. November fielen die Köpfe von Robert Stamm und
Adolf Rembte unter dem Beil, weil sie für ihr deutsches Volk
Frieden und Freiheit wollten.

In memory of Stamm and Rembte

They have been murdered, yet they live on, so long as there
are Germans who honor their heroes.

On 4 November the heads of Robert Stamm and Adolf
Rembte fell under the ax, because they wanted peace and
liberty for their German people.

Both Stamm and Rembte were sentenced to death for trying to
rebuild trade unions in Germany. For a report on their case, see *VI*,
30 June 1937 (no. 26, p. 407).

Stamm und Rembte zum Gedächtnis

Robert Stamm

Adolf Rembte

Sie sind ermordet worden, doch sie leben weiter, solang es Deutsche gibt, die ihre Helden ehren.

Am 4. November fielen die Köpfe von Robert Stamm und Adolf Rembte unter dem Beil, weil sie für ihr deutsches Volk Frieden und Freiheit wollten.

Montiert: John Heartfield.

So würde Tell in unseren Tagen handeln

Unser ist durch tausendjährigen Besitz
Der Boden – und der fremde Herrenknecht
Soll kommen dürfen und uns Ketten schmieden
Und Schmach antun auf unsrer eignen Erde?
Ist keine Hilfe gegen solche Drang?

Nein, eine Grenze hat Tyrannenmacht:
Wenn der Gedrückte nirgends Recht kann finden,
Wenn unerträglich wird die Last – greift er
Hinauf getrosten Mutes in den Himmel
Und holt herunter seine ew'gen Rechte.

Schiller, Wilhelm Tell, 2. Aufzug, 2. Auftritt.

Zur Montage wurde das Bild des großen Schweizer Malers
Ferdinand Hodler "Der Holzfäller" benutzt. Auf der Stange
der Geßlerhut, Modell 1937

This is how Tell would act in our day

This settlement
Has been our own a thousand years! And shall
The vassals of a foreign lord enchain us?
Insult us in our home? Are we resourceless?

No! I say no! For tyranny has bounds.
When justice is denied and burdens grow
Intolerable, then misery may reach
Courageously to heaven! And bring down
Eternal right that hangs immutable.

Schiller, Wilhelm Tell, Scene 2, Act 2.

The picture "The Woodcutter" by the great Swiss painter
Ferdinand Hodler was used for the montage. On the post,
the Geßler hat, 1937 model

On 31 March 1937 (no. 13, pp. 207–8) the magazine had published
an article called "'Nein, eine Grenze hat Tyrannenmacht…' Tell Spiele
in der Schweizerbergen" ("No, tyranny has bounds…"Tell play in the
Swiss mountains). It reported a revival of the open-air performance
of Schiller's drama and drew parallels between the play's portrayal of
oppression and resistance in the Middle Ages and the present
situation in Germany. Governor Geßler's hat played a key role in the
drama: greeting it was a form of deference, and when Tell refused,
his punishment was to shoot an apple from his son's head.

This was a special issue on Switzerland, with an emphasis
on the resistance of Swiss democrats against their Fascist
neighbors. The quote from Schiller, "Tyranny has bounds," is also
used in 47/34. The translation here is from Friedrich von Schiller,
Wilhelm Tell, translated by John Prudhoe (Manchester: Manchester
University Press, 1970), p. 46.

So würde Tell in unseren Tagen handeln

Unser ist durch tausendjährigen Besitz
Der Boden — und der fremde Herrenknecht
Soll kommen dürfen und uns Ketten schmieden
Und Schmach antun auf unsrer eignen Erde?
Ist keine Hilfe gegen solchen Drang?

Nein, eine Grenze hat Tyrannenmacht:
Wenn der Gedrückte nirgends Recht kann finden,
Wenn unerträglich wird die Last — greift er
Hinauf getrosten Mutes in den Himmel
Und holt herunter seine ew'gen Rechte.

Schiller, Wilhelm Tell, 2. Aufzug, 2. Auftritt.

Fotomontage: John Heartfield
Zur Montage wurde das Bild des großen
Schweizer Malers Ferdinand Hodler »Der
Holzfäller« benutzt. Auf der Stange der
Geßlerhut, Modell 1937

GEWERKSCHAFTSEINHEIT
schützt den Frieden der Welt

Bei den Verhandlungen zwischen dem "Internationalen Gewerkschaftsbund" und dem "Zentralrat der Sowjetgewerkschaften" wurden die Grundbedingungen für den Beitritt der Sowjetgewerkschaften zum "Internationalen Gewerkschaftsbund" vereinbart. Nach Bestätigung der Vereinbarung durch die beiden großen Organisationen wird der Zusammenschluß verwirklicht werden. Der Internationale Gewerkschaftsbund wird dann – da auch die amerikanischen Gewerkschaften den Beitritt beschlossen haben – 40 Millionen Mitglieder zählen!

UNITY OF TRADE UNIONS
protects world peace

During the negotiations between the "International League of Trade Unions" and the "Central Council of the Soviet Trade Unions" the basic conditions for the Soviet unions' joining the "International League of Trade Unions" were agreed upon. After ratification of the agreement by both large organizations, the alliance will become a reality. The International League of Trade Unions will then – as the American trade unions have also decided to join – number 40 million members!

Bei den Verhandlungen zwischen dem „Internationalen Gewerkschaftsbund" und dem „Zentralrat der Sowjetgewerkschaften" wurden die Grundbedingungen für den Beitritt der Sowjetgewerkschaften zum „Internationalen Gewerkschaftsbund" vereinbart. Nach Bestätigung der Vereinbarung durch die beiden großen Organisationen wird der Zusammenschluß verwirklicht werden. Der internationale Gewerkschaftsbund wird dann — da auch die amerikanischen Gewerkschaften den Beitritt beschlossen haben — 40 Millionen Mitglieder zählen!

GEWERKSCHAFTSEINHEIT
schützt den Frieden der Welt

Fotomontage: John Heartfield

Cagoulards der Börse

Laut Meldung der sehr gut informierten dänischen Zeitung "Politiken" hat der französische Innenminister die Beweise in die Hand bekommen, daß zwei hervorragende Mitglieder des "Comitée de forges" (der mächtigen Zentrale der französischen Schwerindustrie) an der Cagoulards-Verschwörung leitend beteiligt waren. Aus denselben Kreisen werden auch die Angriffe auf den Franc dirigiert, um das Land in Panik und Unruhe zu halten.

Cagoulards of the stock exchange

According to the announcement of the very well informed Danish newspaper "Politiken," the French minister of the interior has evidence in hand that two distinguished members of the "Comité de forges" (the powerful head-quarters of French heavy industry) were prominently involved in the Cagoulard plot. Attacks on the franc are being directed from the same circles to keep the country in a state of panic and unrest.

This issue devoted its cover and main feature to the Cagoulards, which *VI* described as a secret Fascist organization with connections in big business. The Cagoulards were held responsible for a series of bomb attacks in Paris in 1937. According to *VI*, the attacks were intended to create the conditions for a Franco-style putsch.

Cagoulards der Börse

Laut Meldung der sehr gut informierten dänischen Zeitung »Politiken« hat der französische Innenminister die Beweise in die Hand bekommen, daß zwei hervorragende Mitglieder des »Comitée de forges« (der mächtigen Zentrale der französischen Schwerindustrie) an der Cagoulards-Verschwörung leitend beteiligt waren. Aus denselben Kreisen werden auch die Angriffe auf den Franc dirigiert, um das Land in Panik und Unruhe zu halten.

Fotomontage: John Heartfield

Illustration zu Grimms Märchen von der Katze und der Maus.

Es war einmal eine Katze und eine Maus; die beschlossen, fürderhin in eitel Freundschaft zu leben. Sie hatten als gemeinsamen Vorrat ein Töpfchen mit Schmalz angeschafft und hinter einem Haus verborgen. Eines Tages gelüstete es die Katze nach dem Schmalz und sie sagte: "Liebes Mäuslein, du mußt allein das Haus hüten, ich bin zu einer Kindstaufe eingeladen." Sie schlich zum Vorrat hin und schleckte die oberste Schmalzschicht ab. Als sie zurückkehrte, fragte die Maus: "Wie heißt das Kind?" – "Hautab," antwortete die Katze. Das Mäuslein entsetzte sich darob, doch ließ es sich nichts anmerken. Bald darauf mußte die Katze abermals zu einer Kindstaufe. Diesmal schleckte sie den Schmalztopf halb aus. "Wie heißt das Kind?" fragte die Maus wieder. "Halbaus", antwortete die Katze. Das Mäuslein entsetzte sich aber es ließ alles beim alten bewenden. Die Katze gelüstete es aber auch noch nach dem Rest und sie nahm wieder einmal Urlaub unter dem Vorwand, daß sie ein drittesmal Pate stehen müsse. Diesmal leckte sie den Topf ganz aus. Als das Mäuslein sie wieder nach dem Namen des Kindes fragte, erwiderte sie: "Ganzaus!" – "O weh, was sind das für schreckliche Namen! Mir wird ganz angst und bange!" jammerte das Mäuslein. Da fuhr die Katze sie an: "Unterschreib mir einen Schein, daß ich auch mit dir Ganzaus machen kann, oder... ich freß dich, mein liebes Mäuslein!" Und wenn es nicht gestorben wär, so lebte es noch heute. Und wer's nicht glaubt, der zahlt einen harten Taler.

Illustration to Grimm's fairy tale about the cat and the mouse.

Once upon a time there were a cat and a mouse; they decided from that time on to live in pure friendship. As a joint provision they had bought a jar of lard and hid it behind a house. One day the cat craved the lard, and he said: "Dear little mouse, you must guard the house alone. I am invited to a christening." He sneaked up to the supply and licked off the top layer of lard. When he came back, the mouse asked: "What is the child called?" – "Skinoff," replied the cat. The little mouse was shocked at that, yet showed no reaction. Soon after, the cat again had to go to a christening. This time he licked the lard jar half empty. "What is the child called?" asked the mouse again. "Halfempty," replied the cat. The little mouse was shocked, but left it at that. But the cat also craved the rest, and he took a holiday again, with the excuse that he must be a godparent for the third time. This time he licked the jar clean. When the little mouse asked again about the name of the child, he replied, "Allgone!" – "Oh my, what terrible names these are! I am becoming quite anxious and afraid!" wailed the little mouse. Then the cat snapped: "Sign a document for me saying that I can also make you Allgone, otherwise... I'll devour you, my dear little mouse!" And if he had not died, he would still be alive today. And whoever does not believe it will pay a high price.

Union between Austria and Germany was banned by the Treaty of Versailles but became a major issue as soon as Hitler, himself born in Austria, rose to power. German troops finally crossed the Austrian border on 12 March 1938. In a referendum held in Austria on 10 April, over 99 percent of the voters supported union.

The cat represents Germany, the mouse Austria. In the background is a screech owl, in German folklore the bird of death that informs people that they have not long to live.

Illustration zu Grimms
Märchen von der Katze und der Maus.

Es war einmal eine Katze und eine Maus; die beschlossen, fürderhin in eitel Freundschaft zu leben. Sie hatten als gemeinsamen Vorrat ein Töpfchen mit Schmalz angeschafft und hinter
einem Haus verborgen. Eines Tages gelüstete es die Katze
nach dem Schmalz und sie sagte: „Liebes Mäuslein, du mußt
allein das Haus hüten, ich bin zu einer Kindtaufe eingeladen."
Sie schlich zum Vorrat hin und schleckte die oberste Schmalzschicht ab. Als sie zurückkehrte, fragte die Maus: „Wie heißt
das Kind?" — „Hautab," antwortete die Katze. Das Mäuslein
entsetzte sich darob, doch ließ es sich nichts anmerken. Bald
darauf mußte die Katze abermals zu einer Kindtaufe. Diesmal
schleckte sie den Schmalztopf halb aus. „Wie heißt das Kind?"
fragte die Maus wieder. „Halbaus", antwortete die Katze. Das
Mäuslein entsetzte sich, aber es ließ alles beim alten bewenden.
Die Katze gelüstete es aber auch noch nach dem Rest und sie nahm
wieder einmal Urlaub unter dem Vorwand, daß sie ein drittesmal Pate stehen müsse. Diesmal leckte sie den Topf ganz aus.
Als das Mäuslein sie wieder nach dem Namen des Kindes
fragte, erwiderte sie: „Ganzaus!" — „O weh, was sind das für
schreckliche Namen! Mir wird ganz angst und bange!" jammerte das Mäuslein. Da fuhr die Katze sie an: „Unterschreib
mir einen Schein, daß ich auch mit dir Ganzaus machen kann,
oder... ich freß dich, mein liebes Mäuslein!" Und wenn es
nicht gestorben wär, so lebte es noch heute. Und wer's nicht
glaubt, der zahlt einen harten Taler.

Auf der Wacht für den Schutz der Heimat und den Frieden der Welt!

On guard for the protection of the homeland and the peace of the world!

This montage was part of a special issue on the twentieth anniversary of the Red Army.

Auf der Wacht für den
Schutz der Heimat
und den
Frieden der Welt!

Fotomontage: John Heartfield

Die Geschichte von Meister Grau und Vetter Pferd

Kopenhagens größte Zeitung "Politiken" berichtet, daß der Führer der "NS-Bewegung" in Dänisch Nordschleswig, Graf Sehested, erklärte: "Wer nicht auf die Stimme des Blutes hört, dem wird sie eingebläut!"

Meister Grau: "Es wird umgebrochen, ausgebrochen, aufgebrochen, angebrochen. Ich gebe dir fünf Minuten Frist…"
Vetter Pferd: "Was soll ich tun? Wie kann ich mich retten?"
Meister Grau: "Folge der Stimme deines Blutes, schwöre, daß du fortan ein Grautier bist!"
Vetter Pferd: "Bei allen Eseln, ich schwöre es!"
Meister Grau: "Und nun laß uns gemeinsam singen: "Und wollt ihr nicht willig I-A schrei'n, so schlagen wir andere Wege ein!…"

Stimme aus dem Hintergrund: "BANGE MACHEN GILT NICHT!"

The story of Master Gray and Cousin Horse

Copenhagen's largest newspaper, "Politiken," reports that the leader of the "National Socialist movement" in Danish North Schleswig, Count Sehested, declared: "Whoever does not listen to the voice of blood will get it hammered into his head."

Master Gray: "Everything is being broken down, broken out, broken up, broken open. I give you five minutes to think about it…"
Cousin Horse: "What should I do? How can I save myself?"
Master Gray: "Follow the voice of your blood. Swear that from now on you are an ass!"
Cousin Horse: "In the name of all jackasses, I swear it!"
Master Gray: "And now let us sing together: 'And if you don't want to scream Eee Aww, we will use different methods!…'"

Voice from the background: "INTIMIDATION ISN'T ON!"

In German fables the donkey is Master Gray. *Grautier* (donkey or ass) means literally gray animal or gray beast. Master Gray's final statement is a rewording of the colloquial saying "Und willst du nicht mein Bruder sein, so schlag' ich dir den Schädel ein" (And if you don't want to be my brother, I'll crack your skull).

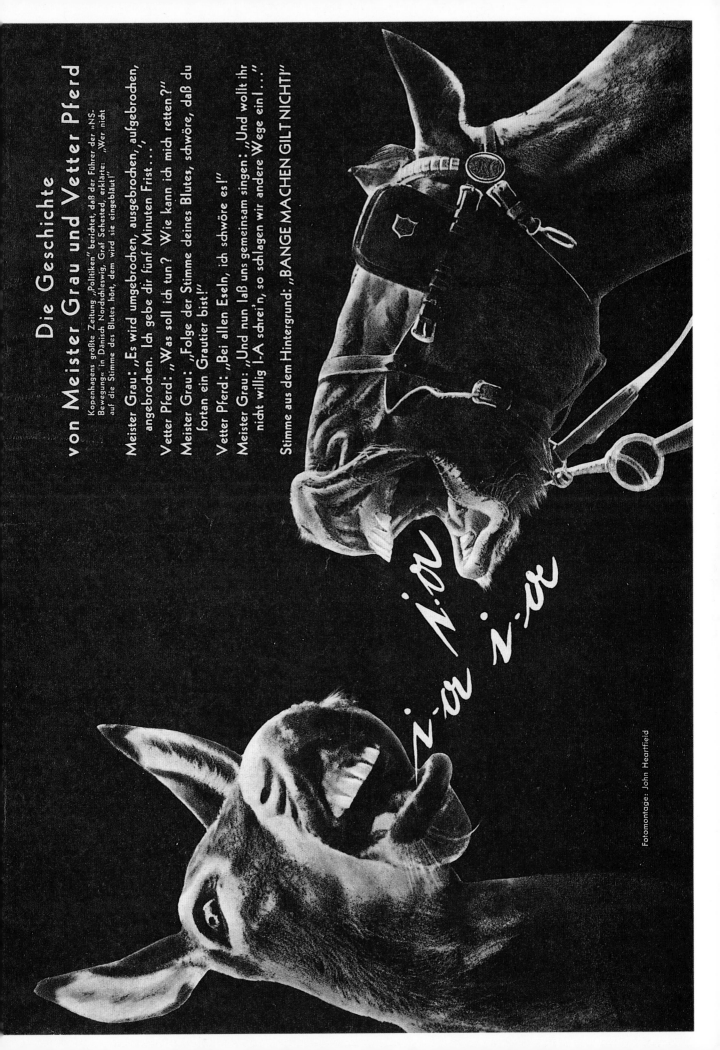

Die Geschichte
von Meister Grau und Vetter Pferd

Kopenhagens größte Zeitung „Politiken" berichtet, daß der Führer der „NS-
Bewegung" in Dänisch Nordschleswig, Graf Schested, erklärte: „Wer nicht
auf die Stimme des Blutes hört, dem wird sie eingebläut!"

Meister Grau: „Es wird umgebrochen, ausgebrochen, aufgebrochen,
angebrochen. Ich gebe dir fünf Minuten Frist..."

Vetter Pferd: „Was soll ich tun? Wie kann ich mich retten?"

Meister Grau: „Folge der Stimme deines Blutes, schwöre, daß du
fortan ein Grautier bist!"

Vetter Pferd: „Bei allen Eseln, ich schwöre es!"

Meister Grau: „Und nun laß uns gemeinsam singen: „Und wollt ihr
nicht willig I-A schrei'n, so schlagen wir andere Wege ein!..."

Stimme aus dem Hintergrund: „BANGE MACHEN GILT NICHT!"

Fotomontage: John Heartfield

5/38. **VI** 1938, NUMBER 18, 4 MAY

China, der Riese, erwacht – wehe dem Eindringling!

China, the giant, awakes – woe to the invader!

China's occupation by Japan is being compared to Gulliver's capture by the Lilliputians in Jonathan Swift's *Gulliver's Travels* (1726).

China, der Riese, erwacht – wehe dem Eindringling!

Fotomontage · John Heartfield

Ihr Kampf...

und wer trägt die Kosten?

In den Palästen haben sie immer noch sich gefunden...

In den Hütten immer noch nationale Zwietracht gesät!

Auf dem Prager "Graben" stehen einander tschechische und deutsche Banken gegenüber. Die Fenster haben die tschechischen und deutschen Bankgewaltigen und Großaktionäre einander noch niemals eingeschlagen. Im Gegenteil, die Herren Mühlig und Richter von der SdP sitzen friedlich mit den tschechischen Robětins, Preis und anderen in den Verwaltungsräten zusammen.

Their fight...

and who bears the costs?

In the palaces they have always accommodated each other...

It is in the huts that they have always sown national discord!

On the "Graben" in Prague, Czech and German banks face one another. The Czech and German bank managers and major shareholders have never smashed each others' windows. On the contrary, Messrs. Mühlig and Richter of the SdP sit peacefully with the Czechs Robětins, Preis and others on the board of management.

This was part of a special issue titled "Schützt die Sudeten, ihre Freiheit, ihren Frieden!" (Protect the Sudetens, their liberty, their peace!). Konrad Henlein, leader of the SdP (Sudeten German Party), called for autonomy for Sudeten Germans on 24 April 1938. See 14/38 and also 7/38, 11/38, 12/38, 15/38.

Ihr Kampf...

und wer trägt die Kosten?

Auf dem Prager „Graben" stehen einander tschechische und deutsche Banken gegenüber. Die Fenster haben die tschechischen und deutschen Bankgewaltigen und Großaktionäre einander noch niemals eingeschlagen. Im Gegenteil, die Herren Mühlig und Richter von der SdP sitzen friedlich mit den tschechischen Robětins, Preis und anderen in den Verwaltungsräten zusammen.

In den Palästen haben sie immer noch sich gefunden...

In den Hütten immer noch nationale Zwietracht gesät!

Der Fuchs und der Igel.
Eine Tierfabel nach Lafontaine

Es sprach der Fuchs zum Igel klein:
"Vertrau mir, zieh die Stacheln ein,
Nie hätt ich dich gebissen!
Du störst den Frieden ohne Not,
Ich fühle mich direkt bedroht,
Ich wollt' dich ja nur – küssen!"

The fox and the hedgehog.
An animal fable after La Fontaine

Said the fox to the little hedgehog:
"Trust me, pull in the quills.
I would never have bitten you!
You disturb the peace needlessly.
I feel downright threatened.
I only wanted to – kiss you!"

The fox represents Germany, the hedgehog Czechoslovakia.

Der Fuchs und der Igel.

Eine Tierfabel nach Lafontaine

Es sprach der Fuchs zum Igel klein:
„Vertrau mir, zieh die Stacheln ein,
Nie hätt ich dich gebissen!
Du störst den Frieden ohne Not,
Ich fühle mich direkt bedroht,
Ich wollt' dich ja nur – küssen!"

Fotomontage: John Heartfield

Das ist das Heil, das sie bringen!

"In der Zeitschrift "Archiv für Biologie und Rassenforschung", Berlin, ist ein Artikel unter dem Titel "Nutzen, welchen das Luftbombardement vom Standpunkt der rassischen Selektion und der Sozialhygiene bringt" erschienen. In dem Artikel heißt es u. a.: "Am meisten leiden unter Luftbombardements die stark bewohnten Teile der Städte. Da diese Gegenden zumeist vom Lumpenproletariat bewohnt sind, wird die Gesellschaft dadurch von diesen Elementen befreit. Schwere Bomben mit einem Gewicht von einer Tonne bringen nicht nur den Tod, sondern rufen auch sehr oft Irrsinn hervor. Menschen mit schwachen Nerven können derartige Erschütterungen nicht aushalten. Das gibt uns die Möglichkeit, Neurastheniker zu konstatieren. Dann bleibt nur noch übrig, solche Menschen zu sterilisieren. Dadurch wird die Reinheit der Rasse gesichert.""
(Prager Abendzeitung, Nr. 118)

Tokio. (United Press.) Ein Sprecher der japanischen Marine, Vizeadmiral Noda, erklärte, daß die Marine mit den bisherigen Erfolgen des Bombardements auf Kanton sehr zufrieden sei. Die Bombardements würden fortgesetzt werden.

That is the salvation they bring!

"In the journal 'Archive for Biology and Race Research,' Berlin, is an article entitled 'The gain of aerial bombing seen from the standpoint of racial selection and social hygiene.' The article says, among other things: 'It is mainly the heavily populated parts of the towns that suffer from aerial bombardments. As it is mainly the lumpenproletariat who live in these areas, society will thus be liberated from these elements. Heavy bombs with a weight of a ton not only bring death but very often also cause insanity. People with weak nerves cannot bear such shocks. That offers us an opportunity to identify neurasthenics. Then all that is left to do is to sterilize such people. Thereby the purity of the race will be secured.'" (Prager Abendzeitung, No.118)

Tokyo. (United Press.) A spokesman for the Japanese navy, Vice-Admiral Noda, announced that the navy is most content with the success so far of the bombardments of Canton. The bombardments are to be continued.

Heil, as in the Nazi greeting "Heil Hitler!" (Long live Hitler!), means well-being, but in a religious context it means salvation. *Ewige Heil*, for example, is eternal salvation; *heilig* is holy.

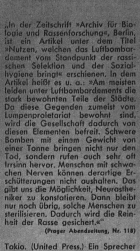

„In der Zeitschrift »Archiv für Biologie und Rassenforschung«, Berlin, ist ein Artikel unter dem Titel »Nutzen, welchen das Luftbombardement vom Standpunkt der rassischen Selektion und der Sozialhygiene bringt« erschienen. In dem Artikel heißt es u. a.: »Am meisten leiden unter Luftbombardements die stark bewohnten Teile der Städte. Da diese Gegenden zumeist vom Lumpenproletariat bewohnt sind, wird die Gesellschaft dadurch von diesen Elementen befreit. Schwere Bomben mit einem Gewicht von einer Tonne bringen nicht nur den Tod, sondern rufen auch sehr oft Irrsinn hervor. Menschen mit schwachen Nerven können derartige Erschütterungen nicht aushalten. Das gibt uns die Möglichkeit, Neurastheniker zu konstatieren. Dann bleibt nur noch übrig, solche Menschen zu sterilisieren. Dadurch wird die Reinheit der Rasse gesichert.«"
(Prager Abendzeitung, Nr. 118)

Tokio. (United Press.) Ein Sprecher der japanischen Marine, Vizeadmiral Noda, erklärte, daß die Marine mit den bisherigen Erfolgen des Bombardements auf Kanton sehr zufrieden sei. Die Bombardements würden fortgesetzt werden.

Das ist das Heil, das sie bringen!

Fotomontage: John Heartfield

Brauner Künstlertraum

Selbstgespräch im Traum: "Franco und Beethoven, wie schaff' ich dies bloß? Am besten mach' ich wohl einen Kentauren, halb Tier, halb Mensch."

"Der Berliner Bildhauer Georg Kolbe erhielt den ehrenhaften Auftrag, ein Denkmal des Generalissimus Franco zu schaffen. Gleichzeitig wurde er mit der Herstellung eines Beethovendenkmals für die Stadt Frankfurt am Main betraut."
Berliner Zeitungsmeldung

Brown artist's dream

Conversation with himself in a dream: "Franco and Beethoven, just how do I do it? The best thing, I suppose, would be to make a centaur, half beast, half human."

"The Berlin sculptor Georg Kolbe received the honorable commission to create a monument to General Franco. At the same time he was entrusted with the production of a Beethoven monument for the city of Frankfurt am Main."
Berlin newspaper report

Georg Kolbe (1877–1947) was a German sculptor who evolved a monumental style that won Nazi approval. His studio was frequently visited by guided tours led by the Nazi cultural organization known as Kraft durch Freude (Strength Through Joy).

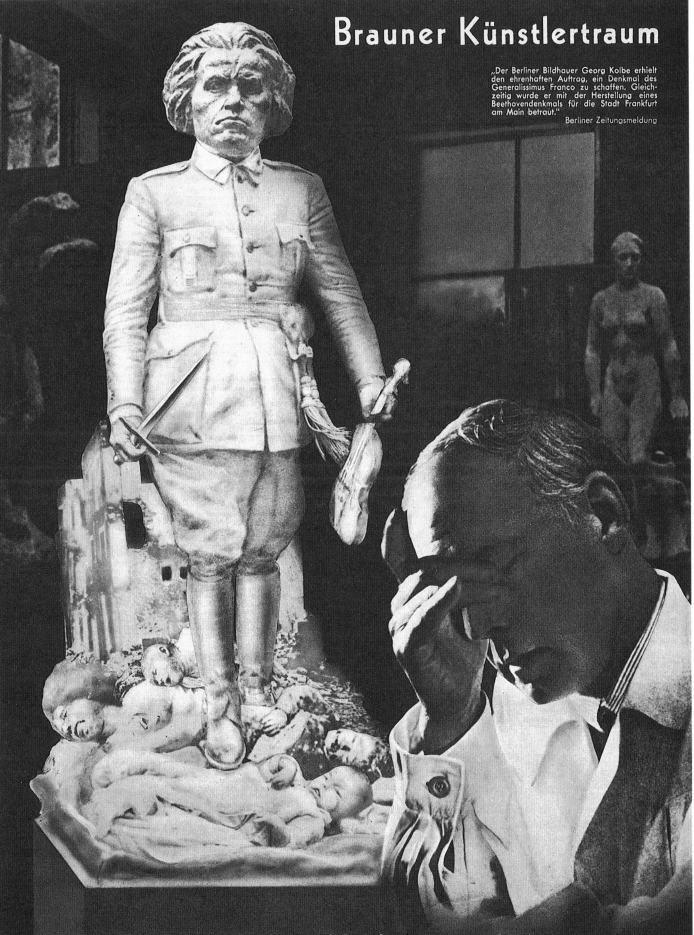

Brauner Künstlertraum

„Der Berliner Bildhauer Georg Kolbe erhielt den ehrenhaften Auftrag, ein Denkmal des Generalissimus Franco zu schaffen. Gleichzeitig wurde er mit der Herstellung eines Beethovendenkmals für die Stadt Frankfurt am Main betraut."

Berliner Zeitungsmeldung

Selbstgespräch im Traum: „Franco und Beethoven, wie schaff' ich dies bloß? Am besten mach' ich wohl einen Kentauren, halb Tier, halb Mensch."

Montiert: John Heartfield.

**Im Westen wie im Osten
Steht sie auf Posten,
Die stärkste Armee der Welt!**

Kein Ablenkungsmanöver, keine Drohung vermag die
Tatsache aus der Welt zu schaffen, daß die Sowjetunion
jeden Angriff auf ihr Land oder die verbündeten Länder mit
vernichtendem Gegenschlag beantworten würde. Und das ist
heute eine der größten Waffen des Friedens.

TSCHANG-KUFENG

**In the West as in the East
It stands ready,
The strongest army in the world!**

No diversionary tactic, no threat can do away with the fact
that the Soviet Union would respond to each attack on its
land or its allies with devastating retaliation. And that today
is one of the greatest weapons of peace.

CHANG-KU FENG

The issue the montage appeared in included an article entitled
"Japans falsche Rechnung – Die Schüsse von Tschang-Kufeng und
ihr Echo" (Japan's false calculation – the shots of Chang-ku Feng
and their echo). According to *VI*, the incident at Chang-ku Feng, a hill
on the frontier of the Soviet Union, Korea, and China, was a
Japanese provocation aimed at luring the Soviet Union into war.

Im Westen wie im Osten
Steht sie auf Posten,
Die stärkste Armee der Welt!

Kein Ablenkungsmanöver, keine Drohung vermag die Tatsache aus der Welt zu schaffen, daß die Sowjetunion jeden Angriff auf ihr Land oder die verbündeten Länder mit vernichtendem Gegenschlag beantworten würde. Und das ist heute eine der größten Waffen des Friedens.

TSCHANG-KUFENG

Kein Fraß für Krebse!

Es war einmal ein großer Krebs,
Der kannt' nur ein Verlangen:
Er wollt' erbeuten, was er sah;
Wozu hat man denn Zangen?

Ein paarmal geht die Sache gut,
Dann greift man nach der falschen Beute
Und wandert selber in den Topf
Und kriegt den Rotlauf, liebe Leute.

Der Regierungsrat und Reichtagsabgeordnete Hans Krebs
(ein sudetendeutscher Emigrant, der in Berlin nicht nur zum
Staatsbeamten und Abgeordneten, sondern auch zum
Gauleiter ohne Gaubezeichnung gemacht wurde!) erklärte
unserem Korrespondenten: "Die sudetendeutsche Frage kann
so lange nicht als gelöst betrachtet werden, als die
Sudetendeutschen einem Staat angehören, der ein Bündnis
mit der Sowjetunion besitzt. "Daily Telegraph".

Das Eingeständnis des Herrn Krebs muß man sich merken.
Es zeigt, daß es der Henleinpartei und Berlin nicht um die
nationalen Rechte der Sudetendeutschen geht, sondern um
die Durchsetzung imperialistischer Machtbestrebungen, die
Europa nicht dulden darf. "Daily Horald"

No food for crabs!

Once upon a time there was a big crab
Who knew only one desire:
He wanted to capture what he saw;
Why else does one have pincers?

A couple of times things go well,
Then he attacks the wrong prey
And wanders into the pot himself
And gets Saint Anthony's fire, dear people.

Government Minister and Member of Parliament Hans Krebs
(a Sudeten German emigrant who in Berlin had not only
been made a civil servant and a member of parliament but
also an area commander without a designated area!)
announced to our correspondent: "The Sudeten German
question cannot be considered settled as long as the Sudeten
Germans belong to a state that has an alliance with the
Soviet Union." "Daily Telegraph."

One would do well to heed Mr. Krebs's admission. It shows
that the Henlein Party and Berlin are concerned not with the
national rights of the Sudeten Germans, but rather with
carrying out imperialistic power ploys, which Europe must
not tolerate. "Daily Herald."

The surname of the Sudeten German politician Krebs means crab.
Rotlauf is erysipelas, or Saint Anthony's fire, a febrile disease that
causes intense inflammation of the skin. For Konrad Henlein, see 14/38.

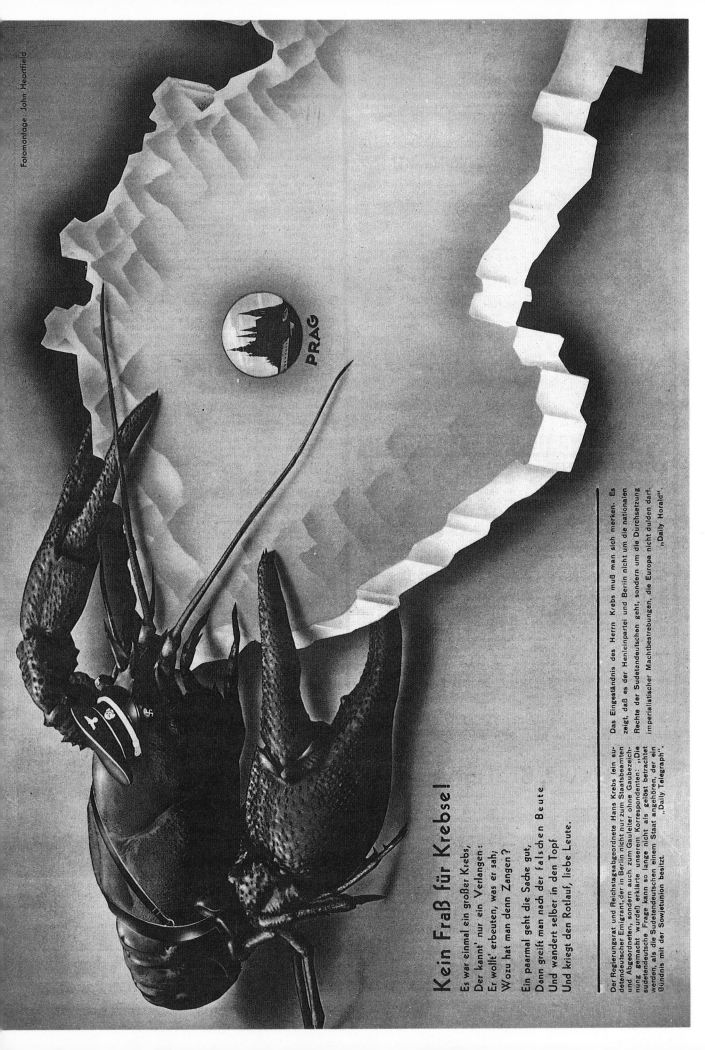

PRAG

Kein Fraß für Krebse!

Es war einmal ein großer Krebs,
Der kannt' nur ein Verlangen:
Er wollt' erbeuten, was er sah;
Wozu hat man denn Zangen?

Ein paarmal geht die Sache gut,
Dann greift man nach der falschen Beute
Und wandert selber in den Topf
Und kriegt den Rotlauf, liebe Leute.

Der Regierungsrat und Reichstagsabgeordnete Hans Krebs (ein sudetendeutscher Emigrant, der in Berlin nicht nur zum Staatsbeamten
und Abgeordneten, sondern auch zum Gauleiter ohne Gaubezeichnung gemacht wurde) erklärte unserem Korrespondenten: „Die
sudetendeutsche Frage kann so lange nicht als gelöst betrachtet
werden, als die Sudetendeutschen einem Staat angehören, der ein
Bündnis mit der Sowjetunion besitzt.   „Daily Telegraph".

Das Eingeständnis des Herrn Krebs muß man sich merken. Es
zeigt, daß es der Henleinpartei und Berlin nicht um die nationalen
Rechte der Sudetendeutschen geht, sondern um die Durchsetzung
imperialistischer Machtbestrebungen, die Europa nicht dulden darf.
                                                     „Daily Horald".

KRIEG

Sudetendeutsche, euch trifft es zuerst!

WAR

Sudeten Germans, it will hit you first!

"Euch trifft es zuerst!" could mean either it will hit you first or it will affect you first. The lead article in this issue was "In den Sudeten – der Fieberzone Europas" (In the Sudeten – Europe's potential trouble spot).

KRIEG

Sudetendeutsche, euch trifft es zuerst!

Fotomontage: John Heartfield

Einig und furchtlos!

Wie diese zwei im Soldatenrock und im Arbeitskittel, so ist heute die ganze große demokratische Bevölkerungsmehrheit der Tschechoslowakei einig und entschlossen in dem "unerschütterlichen Glauben an ihren Staat, an seine Gesundheit, seine Kraft, seine Widerstandsfähigkeit, an seine glänzende Armee und an den unbeugsamen Geist und die Ergebenheit seiner Bevölkerung". Präsident Dr. Beneš in seiner Rundfunkrede vom 10.9.1938

Wenn die Tschechoslowakei angegriffen wird ...
"...so werden wir unsere Bündnispflicht sofort und bis aufs i-Tüfelchen erfüllen," erklärte Litwinow erst in diesen Tagen wieder. (Auf dem Bild: Maschinengewehrschütze der Roten Armee.)

Wenn die Tschechoslowakei angegriffen wird ...
"...so wird Frankreich marschieren, das steht fest," eröffnete der Oberbefehlshaber der französischen Luftflotte, General Vuillemin, seinem deutschen Kollegen Goering. (Auf dem Bild: In der Maginotlinie.)

Wenn die Tschechoslowakei angegriffen wird ...
"...würde ein Weltkrieg entstehen, aus dem sich England nicht heraushalten könnte," versicherte namens der britischen Regierung Lord Simon. (Auf dem Bild: Luftschutzübung der englischen Grenadiere.)

United and fearless!

Just like these two men clad in a soldier's uniform and in a worker's clothing, united and determined, so the great democratic Czech majority is today, in their "unshakable confidence in their State, in its health, its strength, its ability to resist, its formidable army, and the steadfast spirit and dedication of its population." President Dr. Beneš in his radio speech of 10 September 1938

If Czechoslovakia is to be attacked ...
"...we shall instantly and to the very last detail live up to our commitment to the alliance," repeated Litvinov only recently. (The picture: A machine gunner of the Red Army.)

If Czechoslovakia is to be attacked ...
"...France shall be marching, that much is certain," announced Vuillemin, commander-in-chief of the French Air Fleet, to his colleague Göring. (The picture: At the Maginot line.)

If Czechoslovakia is to be attacked ...
"...a world war would be the result, and England could not keep out of it," stated Lord Simon on behalf of the British government. (The picture: Air-raid drill of English grenadiers.)

On the Soviet diplomat Maksim Litvinov, see 27/37. Sir John Allsebrook Simon (1816–1904), a British politician who led the Liberal National Party in the 1930s, favored rapprochement between Great Britain and Nazi Germany. Edvard Beneš (1884–1948) had been the Czech representative at the Versailles peace conference in 1919–20. He served as president of Czechoslovakia from 1935 to 1938, when he resigned after the Germans occupied Sudetenland. In exile from 1938 to 1945, he was president of the Czechoslovak government in England from 1940 to 1945. In 1945 he returned to govern from Prague, but in 1948 he resigned as president rather than sign the new Communist constitution.

VI

DIE VOLKS-ILLUSTRIERTE

1938 ● NR. 38 ● 21. SEPT.

Preis: 1.60 Kč; 40 Gr.; 1.60 Hrs.; 30 Rp.;
10 amer. cts.; 4 Dinar; 12 Lei; 0.35 Schw.
Oere. — Erscheint wöchentlich. — Kon-
trollpostamt Praha 14.

Wenn die Tschechoslowakei angegriffen wird...
„...so werden wir unsere Bündnispflicht, sofort und bis aufs i-Tüpfel-
chen erfüllen," erklärte Litwinow erst
in diesen Tagen wieder. (Auf dem
Bild: Maschinengewehrschütze der
Roten Armee.)

Wenn die Tschechoslowakei angegriffen wird...
„...so wird Frankreich marschieren,
das steht fest," eröffnete der Oberbefehlshaber der französischen Luftflotte, General Vuillemin, seinem
deutschen Kollegen Goering. (Auf
dem Bild: In der Maginotlinie.)

Wenn die Tschechoslowakei angegriffen wird...
„...würde ein Weltkrieg entstehen,
aus dem sich England nicht heraushalten könnte," versicherte namens
der britischen Regierung Lord Simon.
(Auf dem Bild: Luftschutzübung der
englischen Grenadiere.)

Einig und furchtlos!

Wie diese zwei im Soldatenrock und im Arbeitskittel, so ist heute die ganze große demokratische Bevölkerungsmehrheit der Tschechoslowakei einig und entschlossen in dem

**„unerschütterlichen Glauben an ihren Staat, an seine Gesundheit,
seine Kraft, seine Widerstandsfähigkeit, an seine glänzende Armee
und an den unbeugsamen Geist und die Ergebenheit seiner Bevölkerung".** Präsident Dr. Beneš in seiner Rundfunkrede vom 10. 9. 1938

HEIMGEFUNDEN!

Jeder Hahn kräht auf dem Mist, der ihm angemessen ist.

RADIOLÜGEN–
MISTHAUFEN

BACK HOME!

Every cock crows on the dung that is appropriate for him.

RADIO LIES–
DUNGHILLS

Konrad Henlein (1898–1945), whom Heartfield has portrayed as a cock, founded the Sudeten German Heimatfront (Home Front) in 1933 to replace the banned Nazi Party. In 1935 it became the Sudetendeutsche Partei (Sudeten German Party or SdP). It demanded autonomy for Sudeten Germans within the Czechoslovak state. Henlein secretly met Hitler after the annexation of Austria to evolve a strategy for the German occupation of Czechoslovakia.

The title is meant to convey several senses of *Heim* (home). *Heimfinden* is to find one's way home. The Nazi phrase "heim ins Reich holen" (literally, to fetch home into the Reich) was used to express the German desire to annex areas like Austria or Sudetenland that have German-speaking inhabitants. The subtitle alludes to the colloquial saying "Wenn der Hahn kräht auf dem Mist, ändert sich's Wetter oder's bleibt wie's ist" (When the cock crows on the dung, the weather changes or stays as it is).

HEIMGEFUNDEN!

RADIO WIEN

RADIOLÜGEN-
MISTHAUFEN

Jeder Hahn kräht auf dem Mist,
der ihm angemessen ist.

Fotomontage: John Heartfield

Das gigantischeste Lügenmaul aller Zeiten

Aber die Zähne sind faul: Demonstrationen in Hamburg, Berlin, München und Wien.

The most gigantic liar of all time

But the teeth are decayed: demonstrations in Hamburg, Berlin, Munich and Vienna.

In a speech he made on 26 September 1938 Hitler declared that Sudetenland was Germany's last territorial claim in Europe. Germany acquired Sudetenland as a result of the Munich Agreement of 29 September 1938. *Lügenmaul* (literally, lying trap) is a colloquial word for liar.

Shortly before this issue appeared, *VI* was ordered by the Czechoslovak government to cease publishing Heartfield's montages or face censorship. This montage is obliterated through overprinting, but the text is still partly visible, and Hitler's mouth and mustache are still identifiable.

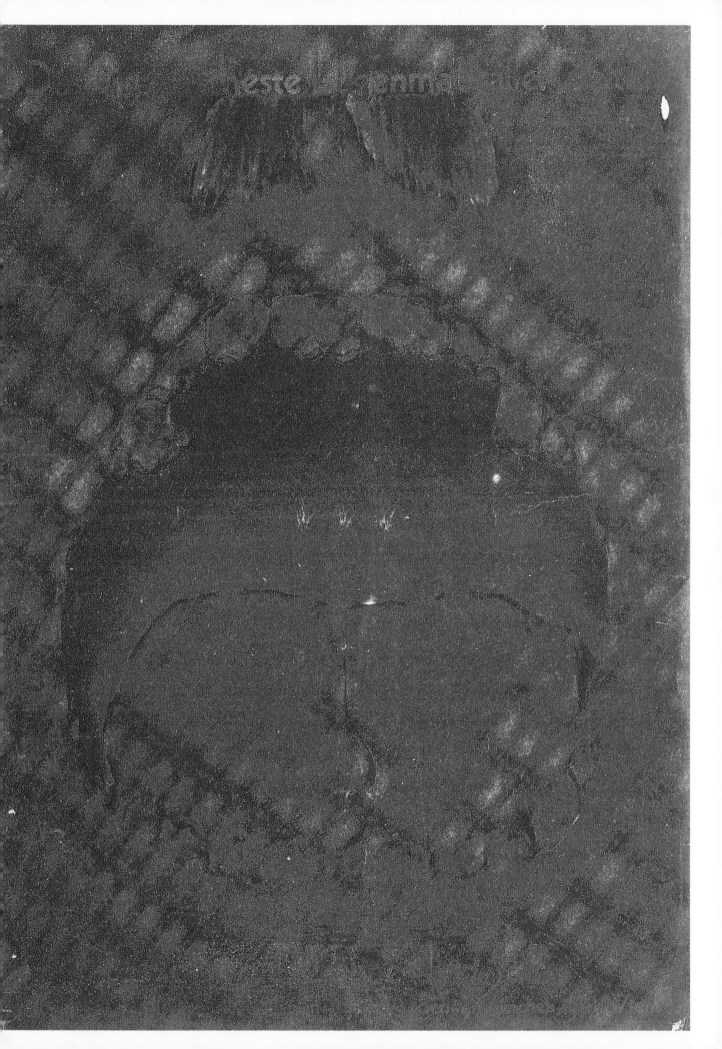

BIBLIOGRAPHY

ARCHIVES

Bauhaus-Archiv, Museum für Gestaltung, Berlin.

Bertolt Brecht Archiv, Berlin.

Bibliothèque Marxiste de Paris, Paris.

Bibliothèque Nationale, Paris.

Getty Center for the History of Art and the Humanities, Santa Monica.

Institut für Geschichte der Arbeiterbewegung, Berlin. (Formerly, Institut des Marxismus-Leninismus.)

John Heartfield Archiv, Akademie der Künste zu Berlin.

Marco Pinkus Collection, Instituto Valenciano de Arte Moderno/Centre Julio Gonzalez, Valencia.

Museum of Fine Arts, Houston.

National Art Library, Victoria and Albert Museum, London.

Staatsbibliothek Preussischer Kulturbesitz, Berlin.

Wieland Herzfelde Archiv, Akademie der Künste zu Berlin.

Wiener Library, London.

BOOKS, PERIODICALS, AND ARTICLES BY AND ABOUT HEARTFIELD

Adkins, Helen. "Der Sträfling: Monteur John Heartfield." In *John Heartfield* (1991), pp. 256–65.

Aragon, Louis. "John Heartfield et la beauté révolutionnaire." *Commune*, no. 20 (May 1935), pp. 985–91. English translation by Fabrice Ziolkowski in Phillips, *Photography in the Modern Era*, pp. 60–67.

Berger, John. "The Political Uses of Photomontage" (1969). In Berger, *The Look of Things*, pp. 183–89. Harmondsworth: Penguin, 1972.

Durus [Alfred Kemény]. "John Heartfield und die satirische Photomontage" (1934). In Farner, *John Heartfield*, pp. 17–28.

Farner, Konrad, ed. *John Heartfield: Photomontagen zur Zeitgeschichte*. Zürich: Schriftenreihe der Vereinigung *Volk und Kultur*, 1945.

Gaßner, Hubertus. "Heartfields Moskauer Lehrzeit, 1931–1932." In *John Heartfield* (1991), pp. 300–337.

Heartfield, John. *Krieg im Frieden: Fotomontagen zur Zeit 1930–1938*. Essay by Wieland Herzfelde. Munich: Carl Hanser Verlag, 1972.

_____. *Photomontages of the Nazi Period*. Translation by Nancy Reynolds of *Krieg im Frieden*. Essay by Wieland Herzfelde translated by Eva Bergoffen. New York and London: Universe and Gordon Fraser, 1977.

Heartfield, John, and Kurt Tucholsky. *Deutschland, Deutschland über alles*. Berlin: Neuer Deutscher Verlag, 1929. English translation, Amherst: University of Massachusetts Press, 1972.

Herzfelde, Wieland. *John Heartfield: Leben und Werk*. Dresden: VEB Verlag der Kunst, 1962. New editions 1971, 1976, and 1986. Unless otherwise noted, all citations refer to the 1976 edition.

Hölterhoff, Manuela. "Heartfield's Contempt." *Artforum* 15, no. 3 (November 1976), pp. 58–65.

John Heartfield. Exhibition catalogue. Cologne: DuMont Buchverlag, 1991.

John Heartfield, 1891–1968: Photomontages. Exhibition catalogue. Berlin: Deutsche Akademie der Künste; London: Arts Council of Great Britain, 1969.

Klingender, Francis. "Diskussion mit John Heartfield über Dadaismus und Surrealismus." Manuscript, London, 1944. Reprinted in März, *John Heartfield*, pp. 48–64.

Lavin, Maud. "Heartfield in Context." *Art in America* 73 (February 1985), pp. 85–92.

März, Roland, ed. *John Heartfield: Der Schnitt entlang der Zeit*. Dresden: VEB Verlag der Kunst, 1981.

Patzwall, Elizabeth. "Zur Rekonstruktion des Heartfield-Raums der Werkbundausstellung von 1929." In *John Heartfield* (1991), pp. 294–99.

Pommeranz-Liedtke, Gerhard, ed. *John Heartfield und die Kunst der Fotomontage*. Exhibition catalogue. Berlin: Deutsche Akademie der Künste zu Berlin, 1957.

Reiss, Wolf [János Reismann]. "Als ich mit John Heartfield zusammenarbeitete" (1934). Reprinted in März, *John Heartfield*, pp. 188–91.

Siepmann, Eckhard. *Montage: John Heartfield vom Club Dada zur Arbeiter-Illustrierten Zeitung; Dokumente–Analysen–Berichte*. Berlin: Elefanten Press, 1977.

Stanic, Milovan. "John Heartfield (1891–1968): Portrait d'un artiste engagé." In *Paris-Berlin: Rapports et contrastes France-Allemagne 1900–1933,* pp. 420–27. Exhibition catalogue. Paris: Centre Georges Pompidou, 1978.

Töteberg, Michael. *John Heartfield in Selbstzeugnissen und Bilddokumenten.* Hamburg: Rowohlt, 1978.

Tretjakov, Sergei. "Johnny" (1936). German translation in Mierau, *Sergej Tretjakow* (1972), pp. 302–19, and Mierau, *Sergej Tretjakow* (1985), pp. 137–52.

Tretjakov, Sergei, and Solomon Telingater. *John Heartfield* (in Russian). Moscow: Ogis, 1936. German translation in März, *John Heartfield*, pp. 291–315.

Uhse, Bodo. "John Heartfield und seine Fotomontagen." In Pommeranz-Liedtke, *John Heartfield und die Kunst der Fotomontage*, pp. 7–20. Reprinted in März, *John Heartfield*, pp. 443–52.

RELATED BOOKS AND ARTICLES

Ades, Dawn. *Photomontage.* London: Thames and Hudson; New York: Pantheon, 1976. New edition 1986.

Alice Lex-Nerlinger/Oskar Nerlinger. Exhibition catalogue. Berlin: Neue Gesellschaft für Bildende Kunst, 1975.

Aragon, Louis. *Pour un réalisme socialiste.* Paris: Denoël et Steele, 1935.

_____. Untitled essay. In Fauchereau, *Querelle du réalisme* (1936), pp. 55–68. English translation by James Johnson Sweeney in Phillips, *Photography in the Modern Era,* pp. 68–77.

_____. *Les Collages.* Paris: Hermann, 1965.

Art & Pub: Art & Publicité, 1890–1990. Exhibition catalogue. Paris: Centre Georges Pompidou, 1990.

Ästhetik und Kommunikation, no. 10 (January 1973). Special issue on *AIZ* and Worker Photography.

Bakhtin, Mikhail. *Rabelais and His World.* Translated by Helene Iswolsky. Bloomington: Indiana University Press, 1984.

Bathrick, David. "Affirmative and Negative Culture: The Avant-garde Under 'Actually Existing Socialism'—the Case of the GDR." *Social Research* 47, no. 1 (Spring 1980), pp. 166–87.

Beetham, David. *Marxists in Face of Fascism: Writings by Marxists on Fascism from the Inter-War Period.* Manchester: Manchester University Press, 1983.

Benjamin, Walter. *Understanding Brecht.* Translated by Anna Bostock. London: NLB, 1973.

Bloch, Ernst, et al. *Aesthetics and Politics.* London: NLB, 1977.

Buchloh, Benjamin. "From Faktura to Factography." *October,* no. 30 (Fall 1984), pp. 83–119.

Buck-Morss, Susan. *The Dialectics of Seeing: Walter Benjamin and the Arcades Project.* Cambridge, Mass., and London: MIT Press, 1989.

Büthe, Joachim, et al., eds. *Der Arbeiter-Fotograf: Dokumente und Beiträge zur Arbeiterfotografie, 1926–1932.* Cologne: Prometheus Verlag, 1977.

Creative Camera, no. 197/198 (May/June 1981). Special issue on Worker Photography.

Droste, Magdalena. *Herbert Bayer: Das künstlerische Werk, 1918–1938.* Exhibition catalogue. Berlin: Bauhaus-Archiv, 1982.

Durus [Alfred Kemény]. "Fotomontage, Fotogramm." *Der Arbeiter-Fotograf* 5, no. 7 (1931), pp. 166–68. English translation by Joel Agee in Phillips, *Photography in the Modern Era,* pp. 182–85.

_____. "Fotomontage als Waffe im Klassenkampf." *Der Arbeiter-Fotograf* 6, no. 3 (1932), pp. 55–57. English translation by Joel Agee in Phillips, *Photography in the Modern Era,* pp. 204–6.

_____. "Photomontage und Buchgraphik: Zur 3. Ausstellung des Bundes revolutionärer Künstler." *Die Rote Fahne,* no. 17 (1932). Reprinted in März, *John Heartfield*, pp. 178–79.

Eskildsen, Ute, and Jan-Christopher Horak, eds. *Film und Foto der zwanziger Jahre.* Exhibition catalogue. Stuttgart: Württembergischer Kunstverein, 1979.

Evans, David, and Sylvia Gohl. *Photomontage: A Political Weapon.* London: Gordon Fraser, 1986.

Fauchereau, Serge, ed. *La querelle du réalisme.* Reprint of 1936 edition with a new introduction. Paris: Diagonales, 1987.

Film and Foto. Exhibition catalogue. Stuttgart: Deutsches Werkbund, 1929. Reprint, New York: Arno Press, 1979.

Fotomontage. Exhibition catalogue by Cesar Domela-Nieuwenhuis, Gustav Klucis, et al. Berlin: Kunst-gewerbemuseum, 1931.

Fowkes, Ben. *Communism in Germany Under the Weimar Republic.* London: Macmillan, 1984.

Friedrich, Ernst. *Krieg dem Kriege! Guerre à la guerre! War Against War! Oorlog aan den Oorlog!* Berlin: "Freie Jugend," 1924.

Gaßner, Hubertus, and Eckhart Gillen, eds. *Zwischen Revolutionskunst und Sozialistischem Realismus: Dokumente und Kommentare, Kunstdebatten in der Sowjetunion von 1917 bis 1934.* Cologne: DuMont Buchverlag, 1979.

Gaßner, Hubertus, and Roland Nachtigäller, eds. *Gustav Klucis.* Stuttgart: Verlag Gerd Hatje, 1991.

Gombrich, Ernst H. "The Cartoonist's Armoury" (1963). In Gombrich, *Meditations on a Hobby Horse and Other Essays on the Theory of Art,* pp. 127–42. London: Phaidon, 1963.

Gombrich, Ernst H., and E. Kris. *Caricature.* Harmondsworth: Penguin, 1940.

Gross, Babette. *Willi Münzenberg: A Political Biography.* Translated by Marian Jackson. [East Lansing]: Michigan State University Press, 1974.

Hausmann, Raoul. "Fotomontage." *a bis z*, no. 16 (May 1931), pp. 61–62. English translation by Joel Agee in Phillips, *Photography in the Modern Era*, pp. 178–81.

Herzfelde, Wieland. *Der Malik-Verlag, 1916–1947*. Exhibition catalogue. Berlin: Deutsche Akademie der Künste zu Berlin, 1966.

Höllering, Franz. "Fotomontage." *Der Arbeiter-Fotograf 2*, no. 8 (1928), pp. 3–4. English translation by Joel Agee in Phillips, *Photography in the Modern Era*, pp. 128–31.

Jürgens-Kirchhoff, Annegret. *Technik und Tendenz der Montage in der bildenden Kunst des 20. Jahrhunderts*. Gießen: Anabas Verlag, 1978.

Klein, Wolfgang. *Commune: Revue pour la défense de la culture, 1933–1939*. Paris: Editions du CNRS, 1988.

Leclanche-Boulé, Claude. *Typographies et photomontages constructivistes en U.R.S.S.* Paris: Editions Papyrus, 1984.

Lemoine, Serge. "Merz, Futura, DIN et cicéro." In *Art & Pub*, pp. 238–69.

Lewis, Helena. *The Politics of Surrealism*. New York: Paragon House, 1988.

Lissitzky-Küppers, Sophie. *El Lissitzky: Life–Letters–Texts*. London: Thames and Hudson, 1968.

Lodder, Christina. *Russian Constructivism*. New Haven and London: Yale University Press, 1983.

Lunn, Eugene. *Marxism and Modernism: An Historical Study of Lukács, Brecht, Benjamin, and Adorno*. Berkeley and Los Angeles: University of California Press, 1982.

Lusk, Irene-Charlotte. *Montagen ins Blaue: Laszlo Moholy-Nagy, Fotomontagen und -collagen, 1922–1943*. Gießen: Anabas Verlag, 1980.

Mellor, David, ed. *Germany, the New Photography, 1927–33: Documents and Essays*. London: Arts Council of Great Britain, 1978.

Mierau, Fritz, ed. *Sergej Tretjakow: Lyrik, Dramatik, Prosa*. Leipzig: Verlag Philipp Reclam, 1972.

_____. *Erfindung und Korrektur: Tretjakows Ästhetik der Operativität*. Berlin: Akademie-Verlag, 1976.

_____, ed. *Sergej Tretjakow: Gesichter der Avantgarde*. Berlin and Weimar: Aufbau Verlag, 1985.

Moholy-Nagy. Stuttgart: Verlag Gerd Hatje, 1991.

Neumann, Eckhard. "De l'enseignement du Bauhaus au métier de graphiste." In *Art & Pub*, pp. 304–19.

Palmier, Jean-Michel. *Weimar en exil: Le destin de l'émigration intellectuelle allemande antinazie en Europe et aux Etats-Unis*. 2 vols. Paris: Payot, 1988.

Phillips, Christopher, ed. *Photography in the Modern Era: European Documents and Critical Writings, 1913–1940*. New York: Metropolitan Museum of Art, 1989.

Photomontages: Photographic expérimentale de l'entre-deux-guerres. Paris: Centre National de la Photographie, 1987.

Rasch, Heinz, and Bodo Rasch. *Gefesselter Blick*. Exhibition catalogue. Stuttgart: Wissenschaftlicher Verlag, Dr. Zaugg & Co., 1930.

Revolution und Realismus: Revolutionäre Kunst in Deutschland, 1917 bis 1933. Exhibition catalogue, Berlin: Staatliche Museen zu Berlin, 1978.

Ring neuer Werbegestalter: Amsterdamer Ausstellung von 1931. Exhibition catalogue. Wiesbaden: Landesmuseum, 1990.

Robin, Régine. *Le réalisme socialiste: Une ésthetique impossible*. Paris: Payot, 1986.

Schmied, Wieland, and Ute Eskildsen. *Neue Sachlichkeit and German Realism of the Twenties*. Exhibition catalogue. London: Arts Council of Great Britain, 1978.

Stallybrass, Peter, and Allon White. *The Politics and Poetics of Transgression*. London: Methuen, 1986.

Tschichold, Jan. *Die neue Typographie*. Berlin: Bildungsverband der deutschen Buchdrucker, 1928.

Wem gehört die Welt: Kunst und Gesellschaft in der Weimarer Republik. Exhibition catalogue by Jürgen Kleindienst. Berlin: Neue Gesellschaft für Bildende Kunst, 1977.

Wescher, Herta. *Die Geschichte der Collage*. Cologne: DuMont Buchverlag, 1968.

Willett, John. *The New Sobriety: Art and Politics in the Weimar Period, 1917–33*. London: Thames and Hudson, 1978.

Willmann, Heinz. *Geschichte der Arbeiter-Illustrierten Zeitung, 1921–1938*. Berlin: Dietz Verlag, 1974.

Wilson, Sarah. "La beauté révolutionnaire? Réalisme socialiste and French Painting, 1935–1954." *Oxford Art Journal 3*, no. 2 (1980), pp. 61–69.